indonesia

1972

No. 13 (April)

© Cornell Modern Indonesia Project, 1972

Note from the Editors

The Editors for the April 1972 issue of Indonesia are Anthony Reid, James Siegel, and Linda Weinstein. The Associate Editor is Peggy Lush.

Prospective contributors should submit their manuscripts in a typewritten, double-spaced format with footnotes and other stylistic conventions in accordance with the University of Chicago Handbook of Style. A short statement of the author's institutional affiliation and status should be included with the original manuscript as these will be needed for the "List of Contributors" in case of eventual publication. Please address all correspondence to: Indonesia, Cornell Modern Indonesia Project, 102 West Avenue, Ithaca, New York 14850.

The charge for a one year's subscription is $8.00 and the price for a single issue, $4.50.

HABIB ABDOE'RRAHMAN ALZAHIR.

Table of Contents

On the Importance of Autobiography (Anthony Reid)	1
Tuanku Iman Bondjol (1772-1864) (Christine Dobbin)	5
Habib Abdur-Rahman az-Zahir (1833-1896) (Anthony Reid)	37
Arung Singkang (1700-1765): How the Victory of Wadjo' Began (J. Noorduyn)	61
Dipanagara (1787?-1855) (Ann Kumar)	69
Mahmud, Sultan of Riau and Lingga (1823-1864) (Virginia Matheson)	119
The Post-Revolutionary Transformation of the Indonesian Army: Part II (Ruth McVey)	147
Divisions and Power in the Indonesian National Party, 1965-1966 (Angus McIntyre)	183
In Memoriam: Harry J. Benda (George McT. Kahin)	211

ON THE IMPORTANCE OF AUTOBIOGRAPHY

Anthony Reid

Foreign scholars have generally been reluctant to acknowledge the importance of personalities in Indonesian history. Even if no modern scholar would claim like Crawfurd to see "hardly an individual, of such prominent fortune or endowment, as to rank with the great men of other countries,"[1] the great figures which undoubtedly do punctuate the course of Indonesian history have seldom been allowed to occupy the center of the stage. For traditional colonial historians they appeared as problems for Dutch policy makers--fascinating perhaps, but essentially troublesome deviants from the broader themes. Modern social science, which has established the priorities for postwar scholarship on Indonesia, has been concerned with defining the broad patterns and categories of Indonesian society and culture rather than with exploring the individual mentality. The few serious biographical studies which have begun to appear center on figures from either the remote[2] or the immediate past,[3] and this fact emphasizes how little we know of the way in which Indonesians of the intervening centuries looked out on their world.

If there is an exception to this neglect, it is in the area of Dutch historical romance. In the 1850's and 1860's there was a fashion for novels centered on such colorful rebels as Dipanagara, Sentot, and Surapati.[4] Works of the same genre have appeared in this century,

---

1. John Crawfurd, History of the Indian Archipelago (Edinburgh: Archibald Constable, 1820), II, p. 287.

2. Notably H. J. de Graff's two monographs, De Regering van Panembahan Sénapati Ingalaga (Verhandelingen van het Koninklijk Instituut, XIII [The Hague: Martinus Nijhoff, 1954]), and De Regering van Sultan Agung, Vorst van Mataram 1613-1645 en die van zijn Voorganger Panembahan Séda-ing-Krapjak 1601-1613, (Verhandelingen van het Koninklijk Instituut, XXIII [The Hague: Martinus Nijhoff, 1958]); and Denys Lombard, Le Sultanat d'Atjéh au temps d'Iskandar Muda, 1607-1636 (Paris: Ecole Francaise d'Extreme-Orient, 1967). All of these, however, are more directly interested in the structure of the state than in the personality of the ruler.

3. Notably the biographies of Sukarno by Bernhard Dahm, Sukarno and the Struggle for Indonesian Independence (Ithaca: Cornell University Press, 1969) and John Legge, Sukarno (Melbourne: Penguin, 1972).

4. R. Nieuwenhuys, "De Houding van de Nederlanders in Indonesia zoals deze weerspiegeld wordt in de toenmalige letterkunde," Bijdragen en Mededelingen betreffende de Geschiedenis der Nederlanden, LXXXVI, Part 1 (1971), p. 66.

of which one of the most faithful to fact is Mrs. Szekely-Lulofs' historical novel about the Atjehnese heroine Tjut Njak Dien.[5] But as Rob Nieuwenhuys has recently pointed out,[6] this literature was in many ways the product of a European-centered vision, casting its subjects in the mold of contemporary western romantic convention.

It might be argued in defense that biography is the most difficult type of history for the foreigner to attempt; that the sympathy or identification with great men, through which most of us first establish some feeling for our own history, involves too great a danger of distortion if attempted across a wide cultural divide.

If caution of this type has indeed inhibited potential biographers, it renders more urgent the need for translations of Indonesian autobiographies or close contemporary biographies. Indonesians have been as conscious as any other people of the importance of great men in shaping their destiny. Some of the most important works of traditional Javanese, Malay, and South Celebes literature are devoted to the glorification of individual rulers or military leaders. The nationalist concern to commemorate *pahlawan nasional* in the names of streets, universities, and army units, and through a series of laudatory biographies, attests to the same sense of the power of great men. They have the power to lead, to inspire, perhaps even power over nature itself.

Many prominent Indonesians have left some sort of autobiographical record. Some twentieth-century examples, such as the memoirs or letters of Kartini, Pangeran Achmad Djajadiningrat, Tan Malaka, Sjahrir, and Hamka, are fortunately well known and relatively accessible. For earlier periods, as the five examples below show, the difficulties confronting the historian wishing to use such material are considerably greater. In the first place, the problems of translation are forbidding. As far as is known, Dr. Noorduyn's chronicle of Arung Singkang is the first Buginese text to be translated into English. Similarly, there are simply too few scholars capable of tackling texts like the Javanese of the *Babad Dipanagara* or the Malay of the *Tuhfat al-Nafis*.

Moreover, the combination of political leader and writer is a very rare one prior to 1900. Most of the memoirs translated below, therefore, are to some extent second hand. Dipanagara's alone may have been written by himself, if not by a *pudjangga* (court poet) of his entourage. Imam Bondjol's and Habib Abdur-Rahman's memoirs have both been filtered through a Dutch intermediary. The other two are not autobiographies but biographical sketches by compatriots and contemporaries, who knew Arung Singkang and Sultan Mahmud respectively, although they did not share all their objectives. In each case the narrative is undoubtedly affected by the hand which penned it. In particular, Imam Bondjol and Habib Abdur-Rahman might have interpreted their actions differently had they been addressing their Indonesian followers rather than their Dutch conquerors. These difficulties do not diminish the interest of the texts, but they must be borne in mind.

---

5. M. H. Szekely-Lulofs, <u>Tjoet Nja Dinh</u> (Amsterdam, 1948).

6. Nieuwenhuys, "De Houding van de Nederlanders."

Although scattered across one and a half centuries and five distinct cultural regions, the pieces which follow have been selected with an eye to a common theme. Their heroes each offered a serious challenge to the rising power of the Dutch, using traditional weapons of warfare and circuitous diplomacy. Four of them engaged in major wars against the Dutch, all of which were ultimately unsuccessful. The challenge of the fifth, Sultan Mahmud of Lingga, was limited by his essential powerlessness to a stubborn refusal to cooperate. Of common interest in each translation, therefore, is the way in which the author explains the process leading up to the eventual act of defiance. Were the Dutch perceived as an alien force of a different and oppressive kind, or as simply another Indonesian power to be combated by traditional means? How did the leaders interpret and explain to their followers the militant course on which they embarked?

One of the most striking points to emerge is the almost total absence of appeals to freedom or liberation from alien rule in any absolute sense. In each case, our heroes appear to see themselves driven into hostilities against the Dutch or their allies by forces beyond their control--the persistent crassness or bad faith of the Dutch in matters of detail; the obligation to defend their own injured honor; the impatience of their followers; or the inexorable demands of cosmic forces. The earliest of these figures, Arung Singkang, is, significantly, the most "modern" in this sense; only he is portrayed with anything like a positive mission of liberation. His biographer shows more optimism than the other writers not only because he is writing before the eventual defeat of Wadjo', but also because the jealously guarded autonomy of the eighteenth-century Buginese states gave immediate relevance to the notion of freedom, which no broader authority, European or Indonesian, had been able to erode.

The greatest merit or these five accounts, however, and the reason for translating them here, is that they allow Indonesians to speak from the center of the historical stage. How faithfully they record the real motives of their heroes is something that can never be known with certainty. Nevertheless, they provide the indispensable starting point for evaluating some of the great events in Indonesian history from the perspective of the participants involved. They force us to accept them as real people with real responsibilities and real decisions to make.

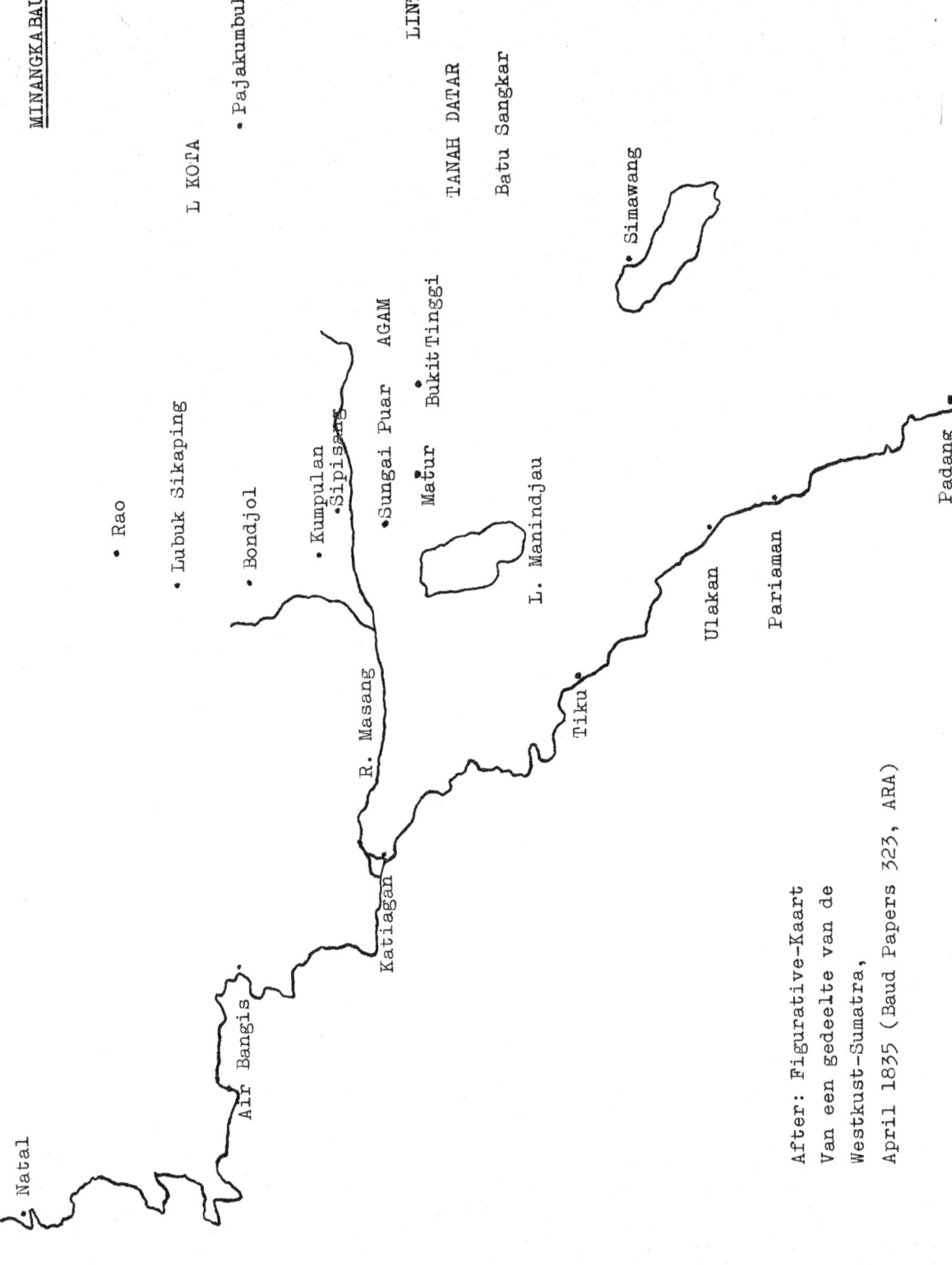

TUANKU IMAM BONDJOL (1772-1864)

Christine Dobbin

The memoirs of Imam Bondjol reproduced here are largely confined to the period of the Dutch military campaigns in the Minangkabau interior from 1821 to 1837, and more particularly to the campaign against his own *negeri* (the Minangkabau village unit),[1] Bondjol. He devotes only a few paragraphs to the founding of Bondjol and, although the negeri was envisaged as a bulwark of the Islamic faith, he makes little mention of his own devotion to that faith or of the civil war which broke out in Minangkabau in the early nineteenth century between the *orang putih* and the *orang hitam*, known generally as the Padri War.[2] Similarly, although he paints a picture of Bondjol as a center of active trade, he makes no mention of the important part played by the Bondjollers in trying to wrest control of Minangkabau trade from the hands of foreigners, both by removing the latter from their dominating position on the west coast, and encouraging market towns in the interior to become centers for goods coming from Penang and later Singapore by way of the east coast.

Islam and Minangkabau

Imam Bondjol was before all else a devout Muslim. We known little of the conversion of Minangkabau to Islam, but it seems likely that it took place during the period of Atjehnese domination of the coast in the late sixteenth and early seventeenth centuries.[3] In the early seventeenth century a preacher of the Sufi Naksjabandijah *tarikat*

---

1. For a discussion see L. C. Westenenk, De Minangkabausche Nagari (3rd edition; Weltevreden: Boekhandel Visser & Co., 1918).

2. The derivation of the term Padri has often been disputed, but it seems most likely that the word was originally *pidari* and meant a man from Pedir (Pidiĕ), referring to pilgrims who had returned from Mecca by way of Atjeh; see Ph. S. van Ronkel, "Inlandsche getuigenissen aangaande den Padri-oorlog," De Indische Gids, XXXVII, No. 2 (1915), p. 1103. The terms *orang putih* and *orang hitam* derive from the color of clothing. The Padri were distinguished by their white robes, while black or dark blue clothing was the mark of a *penghulu* or head of a Minangkabau clan.

3. It is possible that missionaries also came from the east coast; see B. Schrieke, Indonesian Sociological Studies (2nd edition; The Hague: W. van Hoeve, 1966), I, p. 52. Hamka, Sedjarah Islam di Sumatera (2nd edition; Medan: Pustaka Nasional, 1950), p. 11, states that Islam entered Minangkabau by two routes; from Malacca by way of the east coast rivers Siak and Kampar, and by way of Atjeh and the west coast. There is evidence of isolated conversions even earlier; see A. Cortesão, ed., The Suma Oriental of Tomé Pires (London: The Hakluyt Society, 1944), I, pp. 160-161.

(mystical order) visited Pariaman from Atjeh and lived for a time in two of the three *luhak*[4] of Minangkabau--Agam and Lima Puluh Kota.[5] Later in the seventeenth century we know of four leading Minangkabau *tuanku*[6] (religious teachers) who taught grammar, Islamic law, syntax, and exegesis respectively.[7] Whether or not they were Naksjabandijah followers, they came under the influence of the Sjattarijah tarikat when it was planted at Ulakan by Burhanuddin, a pupil of the famed Atjehnese mystic Abdurrauf. The pupils of Burhanuddin gained considerable influence for the Sjattarijah in the Minangkabau *darat*,[8] where its original center was Pemansiangan in Agam.[9] The leading tuanku of the late eighteenth century had all studied at Ulakan, which was regarded as the chief source of religious authority in the country.[10]

However, one of the most brilliant of them, later known as Tuanku Nan Tua or Tuanku Kota Tua[11] of Empat Angkat, a district in Agam, seems to have come under Naksjabandijah influences on returning to the darat.[12] The Naksjabandijah tarikat was regarded as being closer to the *sunna*[13] and was more acceptable than the Sjattarijah to the Shafi'i school of law.[14] There seems to have arisen around Tuanku

---

4. The term luhak refers to the heartlands of Minangkabau. The third luhak is Tanah Datar.

5. Ph. S. van Ronkel, "Een Maleisch Getuigenis over den Weg des Islams in Sumatra," Bijdragen tot de Taal-, Land- en Volkenkunde, LXXV (1919), pp. 369 and 374.

6. Tuanku is one of the highest titles accorded religious teachers; the generality of religious are known as malim.

7. Ph. S. van Ronkel, "Het Heiligdom te Oelakan," Tijdschrift voor Indische Taal-, Land- en Volkenkunde, LVI (1914), p. 294, ftn. 15.

8. The darat comprises Minangkabau proper, as opposed to the rantau, the acquired territories, which included the west coast.

9. Van Ronkel, "Het Heiligdom," pp. 281-309; H. A. Steijn Parvé, "De Secte der Padaries (Padries) in de Bovenlanden van Sumatra, Tijdschrift voor Indische Taal-, Land- en Volkenkunde, III (1855), pp. 264-265.

10. D. D. Madjolelo and A. Marzoeki, Tuanku Imam Bondjol Perintis Djalan ke Kemerdekaan (Djakarta and Amsterdam: Penerbit Djambatan, 1951), pp. 40-41.

11. Well-known teachers were generally known by their place of residence.

12. Hamka, Ajahku. Riwajat Hidup Dr. H. Abd. Karim Amrullah dan Perdjuangan Kaum Agama di Sumatera (3rd edition; Djakarta: Penerbit Djajamurni, 1967), pp. 23-26.

13. The sunna refers to the tradition and customs of the Prophet accepted as proper conduct to be followed.

14. Hamka, Ajahku, p. 23.

Nan Tua a center for the study of *fikh*,[15] that all embracing Islamic jurisprudence which comprises laws regulating not only religious observances but all aspects of social life. This center was at odds with the authority of Ulakan.[16] Tuanku Nan Tua himself, however, seems to have been mystically inclined and spent long hours in meditation.[17] Nevertheless he had a thorough knowledge of the Koran, and he was concerned to indicate to his pupils, especially those he saw destined for more worldly concerns, the failure of Minangkabau society to follow the precepts of Islam and the general dissolution of morals. He taught them the necessity of change in society, but the means he recommended were gentleness and persuasion.[18] Tuanku Nan Tua's pupils were known for the zeal with which they desired reform in Minangkabau. Among them was Imam Bondjol, known in his youth successively as Mohammad Sjahab, Peto Sjarif, and Malim Besar.[19] He had been born in 1772 in the *kampung* Tandjung Bunga in the valley of Alahan Pandjang, just north of Agam and was, according to Dutch sources, "of low birth."[20]

The position of the *malim* in Minangkabau society at the time of Imam Bondjol's birth was not one of influence. In so far as Minangkabau society was governed at all, it was administered by its *penghulu*, the hereditary heads of the *suku* or clans.[21] Administration at the negeri level in the darat was carried on by the *penghulu suku* in the *rapat* or assembly. A token obligation to consult Islamic law was recognized, but in general matters in the *rapat penghulu* were decided by *adat* or custom.[22] The malim had no role at all in matters

---

15. H.J.J.L. de Stuers, De Vestiging en Uitbreiding der Nederlanders ter Westkust van Sumatra (Amsterdam: P. N. van Kampen, 1849), II, App. C, pp. 243 et seq., especially p. 251.

16. Hamka, Ajahku, pp. 23-24. Hamka concentrates on the philosophical differences between the two centers.

17. Steijn Parvé, "De Secte der Padaries," p. 252.

18. Ibid., p. 257.

19. H. M. Lange, Het Nederlandsch Oost-Indisch Leger ter Westkust van Sumatra (1819-1845) ('s Hertogenbosch: Gebroeders Muller, 1852), I, p. 16; B..d., "De Padries op Sumatra," Indisch Magazijn, II, No. 1 (1845), pp. 175-176. For the meaning of these gelar, see Hamka, Ajahku, p. 24, ftn. 1.

20. V. d. H., "Oorsprong der Padaries," Tijdschrift voor Neêrlands Indië, I, No. 2 (1838), p. 124.

21. J. Van Der Linden, "Het Inlandsch Bestuur in het Gouvernement van Sumatra's Westkust," Tijdschrift voor Indische Taal-, Land- en Volkenkunde, IV (1855), p. 266. This article is based on an answer to a query from the Resident of Sumatra's west coast and was compiled on July 26, 1833. The original is to be found in the van den Bosch Papers, 394, in the Algemeen Rijksarchief [hereafter ARA], The Hague.

22. Ibid., pp. 257-259 and 262.

The Valley of Alahan Pandjang

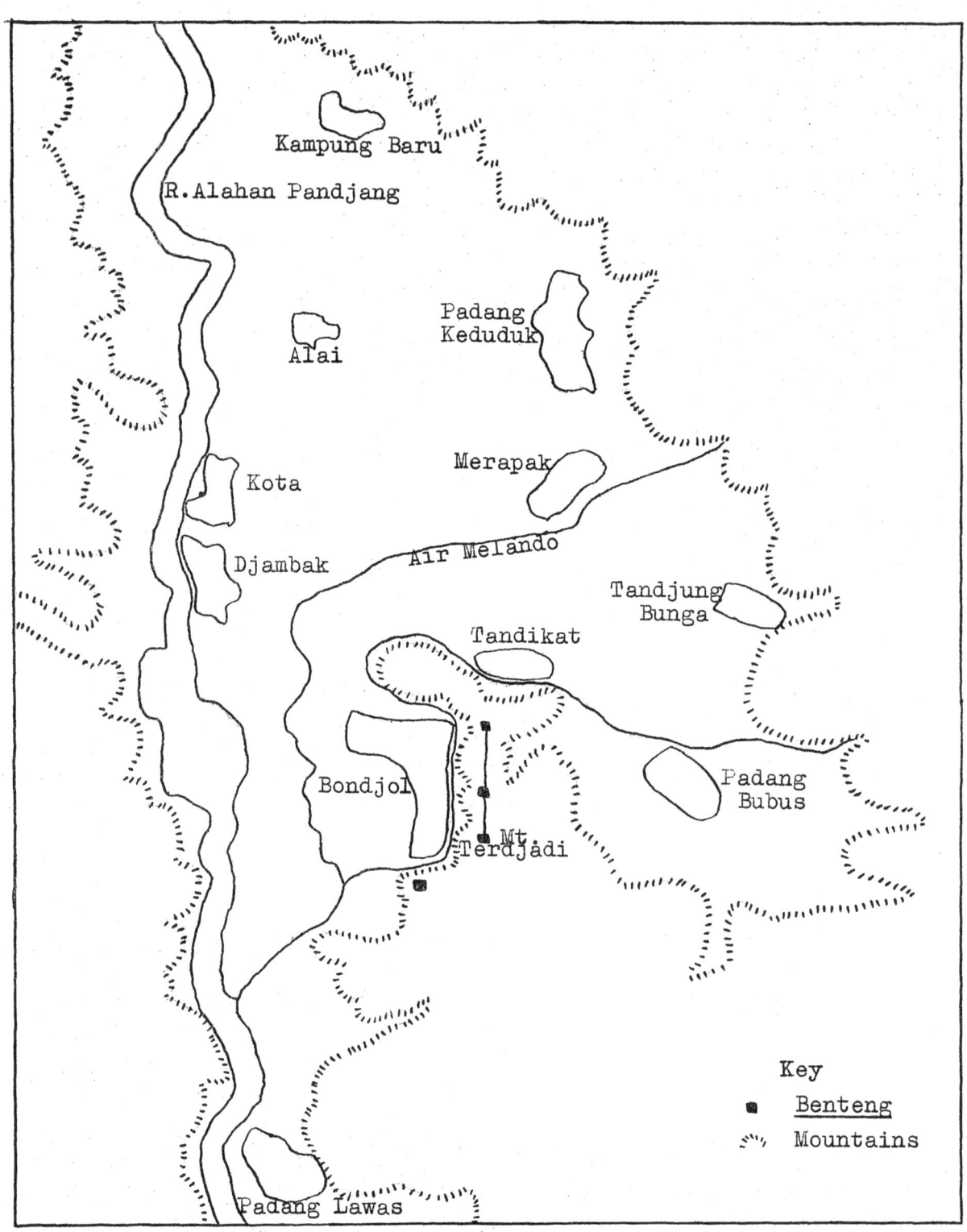

After: Schets van de Positien voor Bondjol,
January 1836 (Baud Papers 494, ARA)

of administration,[23] although an *imam* may have had a voice in the rapat penghulu where religious matters were concerned.[24] In general a malim, if he chose to be a tarikat teacher, lived outside the social hierarchy, gaining his fame and eminence from his influence on his pupils. His only other recourse was to become an "adat-religious," one of the *orang empat djenis* (the people of the four sorts) who assisted the penghulu. In this respect the malim was the only representative of the *sjari'at* (Islamic law) assimilated by the adat. His function outside the circle of the family was normally that of imam or *chatib* in the negeri mosque.[25]

About 1803 there erupted into Minangkabau society three hadji who had returned from a pilgrimage to Mecca.[26] In Arabia they had witnessed the conquests of the Wahhabis, and although it is possible that Wahhabiyah ideas had penetrated Minangkabau earlier, this was probably the first news of their military successes. The Wahhabis arose in Arabia in the mid-eighteenth century and spread their teachings chiefly by the use of force. Their creed was based on the Hanbali school of law, the strictest and most uncompromising of all the schools, and they aimed at a return to the authority of the Koran and the sunna. They saw the main purpose of the Islamic community as applying the law of God, the classical law stripped of all the innovations of intervening centuries. To expand the community they invoked *djihad* (holy war).[27]

---

23. C. Th. Couperus, "De Instellingen der Maleijers in de Padangsche Bovenlanden," *Tijdschrift voor Indische Taal-, Land- en Volkenkunde*, IV (1855), p. 8; G. D. Willinck, *Het Rechtsleven bij de Minangkabausche Maleiërs* (Leiden: Brill, 1909), p. 295. Willinck is not always a reliable source, but he is the only scholar who has tried to give an account of the position of the malim in the pre-Padri period.

24. Van Der Linden, "Het Inlandsch Bestuur," p. 268.

25. Willinck, *Het Rechtsleven*, pp. 218-219 and 296-299.

26. V. d. H., "Oorsprong der Padaries," p. 113.

27. R. B. Winder, *Saudi Arabia in the Nineteenth Century* (London: Macmillan, 1965), pp. 8-11; W. C. Smith, *Islam in Modern History* (New York: Mentor, 1957), pp. 48-51. It has been claimed by two leading scholars of Minangkabau that the Padri were not themselves Wahhabis; see E. B. Kielstra, "Het Ontstaan van den Padrie-Oorlog," *Indisch Militair Tijdschrift*, Part II (1887), p. 227, ftn. 1, and B. Schrieke, "Bijdrage tot de Bibliografie van de huidige godsdienstige beweging ter Sumatra's Westkust," *Tijdschrift voor Indische Taal-, Land- en Volkenkunde*, LIX (1920), pp. 254-255. Kielstra and Schrieke admit, however, that the Padri used Wahhabi methods and were opposed to customs such as tobacco and opium smoking and games of chance which also met with the disapproval of the Wahhabis. It is not possible here to enter into a discussion of Wahhabi doctrine and practices, but it does seem that some of their distinguishing characteristics, such as abhorrence of the reverence for saints and tombs, were absent from Padri teaching. Imam Bondjol himself is known to have been addicted to and skilled in astrology; see Madjolelo and Marzoeki, *Tuanku Imam Bondjol*, p. 65.

The Wahhabis were also concerned to remove corruption from contemporary Arab society, and it was against alleged corruption in Minangkabau--cockfighting, the smoking of opium, the chewing of betel, and the general anarchy in society--that the returning hadji now preached.[28] Tuanku Nan Tua could not be won over to the use of force to spread the work of reform, but a number of his pupils were, and the reform movement split.[29] The main aims of the converts of the hadji--especially the famous "Eight Tigers"--were strict obedience to the tenets of the Koran, in particular the Confession of Faith, the saying of the five daily prayers, abstinence, and circumcision. All customs allegedly not prescirbed by the Koran were to be abolished, the wearing of long white clothes and the veiling of women made obligatory, and cockfighting and the use of betel, tobacco, and opium brought to an end.[30] Gradually the hadji's converts began to fortify their kampung and started to wage war on those kampung which would not voluntarily embrace their creed. In each conquered kampung the penghulu administration was subordinated to the control of two religious heads, the imam and the *kadi* (Muslim judge), who enforced Islamic discipline by fines or death.[31]

The Founding of Bondjol and the Padri War

We now come to the "memoirs" of Imam Bondjol. We know from the investigations of the Dutch scholar van Ronkel that a fuller manuscript of the Imam's life existed in the early twentieth century at Bondjol, where it was designated "*tambo* [story] of the son of Tuanku Imam," and which gave a more complete account of the early days of Bondjol before Dutch intervention.[32] From van Ronkel's paraphrase of this manuscript and from other sources we can piece together some of the early history of Bondjol.

In the early period of the reforms a group of visitors from the valley of Alahan Pandjang journeyed to Agam to see their effect. They were led by an important penghulu, Datuk Bendahara, who had been a student of Tuanku Nan Tua, and by his confidante, the future Imam Bondjol.[33] Imam Bondjol, then known as Tuanku Muda, appears as a pious young man who had totally embraced the new teaching, and

---

28. Steijn Parvé, "De Secte der Padaries," pp. 253-255; v. d. H., "Oorsprong der Padaries," p. 113.

29. Steijn Parvé, "De Secte der Padaries," pp. 253-256 and 259; B..d., "De Padries op Sumatra," pp. 168-169.

30. B..d., "De Padries op Sumatra," pp. 170-171; Steijn Parvé, "De Secte der Padaries," p. 259; Een ambtenaar op Sumatra [Steijn Parvé], "De Secte der Padaries in de Padangsche Bovenlanden," Indisch Magazijn, I, No. 1 (1844), pp. 26-27.

31. Steijn Parvé, "De Secte der Padaries," p. 273; B..d., "De Padries op Sumatra," pp. 171-172.

32. Ph. S. van Ronkel, "Inlandsche getuigenissen aangaande den Padri-oorlog," De Indische Gids, XXXVII, No. 2 (1915), pp. 1099 et seq.

33. Ibid., pp. 1104-1105; B..d., "De Padries op Sumatra," p. 175.

as a faithful servant of his penghulu leader.[34] After accompanying one of the hadji on his journey to spread the new teaching, they returned to Alahan Pandjang within four months. The influence of Datuk Bendahara ran throughout only part of the valley; on the other side of the river Datuk Sati of Merapak was in the ascendant. The latter opposed the new teaching and conflict broke out;[35] it was this conflict, of which Imam Bondjol makes no mention in his "memorandum," which led to the founding of Bondjol.[36]

The actual course of the founding of the negeri is somewhat obscure. Both the tambo and nearly contemporary Dutch authorities ascribe the founding of Bondjol to Datuk Bendahara.[37] However, Imam Bondjol's Indonesian biographers, probably basing their interpretation on some inconsistencies in the Dutch sources, argue that the first "fort" for the defense of Islam was established by Datuk Bendahara near Padang Lawas to the south of Alahan Pandjang, and that it was only after his death that Tuanku Muda established Bondjol to the northeast at the foot of Mount Terdjadi, where it could be better defended.[38] The founding of Bondjol was followed by full-scale civil war in Alahan Pandjang, during which Bondjol was besieged for nine months. Even after the siege was broken up Bondjol continued to be attacked for two and a half years, and during this period Imam Bondjol seems to have played a leading part as a skillful fighter.[39] The Dutch accused him of surrounding himself with a group of fanatical young men as *hulubalang*,[40] and indeed his Indonesian biographers reproduce one of his writings on the supreme joy of holy war and Islamic martyrdom.[41] This would seem to be corroborated by what is known of the campaigns undertaken by the Bondjollers themselves after they felt secure in their own valley, and in which they penetrated north to Rao and then into the territory of the Mandahiling Batak.[42]

---

34. Van Ronkel, "Inlandsche getuigenissen," pp. 1104-1105; v.d.H., "Oorsprong der Padaries," p. 119.

35. Ibid., p. 120; B..d., "De Padries op Sumatra," p. 176.

36. The meaning of Bondjol is somewhat obscure. Literally it means a "projection" and in this sense it was probably used by contemporary Minangkabau to mean a fort. Imam Bondjol, however, seems to have given it the more symbolic meaning of a fort for the defense of Islam; see Lange, Het Nederlandsch Oost-Indisch Leger, I, p. 17, ftn. 1.

37. Van Ronkel, "Inlandsche getuigenissen," p. 1104; v. d. H., "Oorsprong der Padaries," pp. 120-121.

38. Madjolelo and Marzoeki, Tuanku Imam Bondjol, pp. 62-64.

39. Van Ronkel, "Inlandsche getuigenissen," p. 1105; v.d.H., "Oorsprong der Padaries," pp. 121-124.

40. Ibid., pp. 124-125. Hulubalang were the men who led the people in war.

41. Madjolelo and Marzoeki, Tuanku Imam Bondjol, pp. 65 and 72.

42. V.d.H., "Oorsprong der Padaries," pp. 116-117; B..d., "De Padries op Sumatra," p. 177. The tambo admits that women, cattle, buffaloes and even pots and pans were robbed from defeated

The above description relates to that part of the Padri War which took place before European intervention. The war in this period has been described by some scholars as a "social revolution" or a "coup d'etat," because in order to carry out their reforms the Padri had to remove the penghulu, the inherited representatives of the suku administration.[43] Nevertheless Imam Bondjol's memorandum, and what is known of his early life, makes it quite clear to what extent he relied on the penghulu to carry out his wishes.[44] That the penghulu were never totally displaced in Alahan Pandjang is obvious from what the memorandum relates of a penghulu-led revolt against the Imam at the end of 1832, which resulted in three penghulu inviting the Dutch into Bondjol. A change in the doctrinal emphasis of the Padri movement, to which the tambo bears witness, may have been partly responsible for this. At an uncertain date the nephews of the four tuanku of Bondjol were sent to Mecca "to guarantee purity of teaching,"[45] and it seems probable that they returned to Minangkabau as part of a larger group of hadji in 1829.[46] The first Wahhabi empire had ended in defeat in 1818, and the hadji appear to have come under more moderate influences in the holy places; among other things, on their return they recommended the handing back of captured goods to their lawful owners.[47]

The tambo, as paraphrased by van Ronkel, alleges that although now in their decisions the penghulu relied on Islamic law, interpreted by four jurists, in purely "adat matters" the former were the sole arbiters. In the midst of this Imam Bondjol seems to have felt himself too old to abandon the concepts which had molded his youth, and in a Friday sermon he abandoned the future of Alahan Pandjang to the penghulu, who nevertheless asserted that they would continue to revere his judgment.[48] What happened subsequently is well depicted in the memorandum. After his defeat by the Dutch in 1837 the Imam seems to have gone even further in his accommodation with the penghulu. In his last days of freedom in the *rimbu* (forest) he appointed one of his younger sons, Sutan Tjaniago, his successor. Among his parting words to this son were the following: "'One thing more: recognize the authority of the adat-penghulu; if he cannot

    negeri; see van Ronkel, "Inlandsche getuigenissen," pp. 1105-1106.

43. Schrieke, "Bijdrage tot de Bibliografie," pp. 251-252 and 260; Willinck, Het Rechtsleven, p. 301.

44. Schrieke's observations are perhaps more relevant to the situation in Tanah Datar, where a large part of the Minangkabau royal family and a number of penghulu were murdered on the orders of the fiery Tuanku Lintau.

45. Van Ronkel, "Inlandsche getuigenissen," p. 1106.

46. Rapport over de Krijgsverrigtingen te Sumatra's Westkust, pp. 241-242, ARA, Ministerie van Koloniën [hereafter MK], 4136.

47. Van Ronkel, "Inlandsche getuigenissen," p. 1107.

48. Ibid. It is not clear what role the penghulu of Bondjol played in decision making before this time (approximately 1829).

be obeyed, he is not a true penghulu and only bears the title. Abide as faithfully as possible by the Adat, and if your knowledge is not sufficient, then learn the twenty attributes of Allah.'"[49]

The Conflict Over Trade

The other important aspect of the life of Imam Bondjol, his effort to wrest control of Minangkabau trade from foreign hands, is not mentioned in the memorandum and is only touched on by the tambo.[50] The natural outlet for Minangkabau trade was the west coast of Sumatra. For centuries, however, the enterprising Minangkabau had seen the chief ports of their coast dominated by others. In the early seventeenth century the Atjehnese had a monopoly of the pepper trade on the coast.[51] The Dutch, at first welcomed by the Minangkabau as their saviors in the later seventeenth century,[52] established their own monopoly on the coast, and later the English too got a foothold further to the north. Although the Dutch monopoly was theoretically in force throughout the eighteenth century,[53] by the time of Imam Bondjol's birth and youth Dutch hold on the coast was precarious. Among other things the coastal people, despite strict Dutch regulations, were planting cotton and making salt,[54] and cotton fabric was being woven in the darat to help lessen dependence on the Dutch.[55]

The rivers of the east coast, which rose in the heart of Minangkabau, provided an alternative outlet for Minangkabau trade. In the early sixteenth century Tomé Pires declared that the "kingdom" of Indragiri furnished the chief port of Minangkabau.[56] This eastward trade seems to have gradually declined and it was only in the

---

49. Van Ronkel, "Inlandsche getuigenissen," p. 1116. It is difficult to know if these are the exact words used in the manuscript, as in various places van Ronkel paraphrases his source. The publication of this manuscript would be of inestimable value to historians.

50. Ibid., p. 1107.

51. Schrieke, Indonesian Sociological Studies, I, pp. 51-53; J. Kathirithamby-Wells, "Achehnese Control over West Sumatra up to the Treaty of Painan of 1663," Journal of Southeast Asian History, X, No. 3 (1969), pp. 459 et seq.

52. Ibid., p. 469.

53. See the treaties reproduced in J. E. Heeres and F. W. Stapel, Corpus Diplomaticum Neerlando-Indicum (The Hague: M. Nijhoff, 1907-1955), VI, pp. 29-54 and 64-66.

54. Von Erath and van der Stengh to Alting, January 15, 1789, par. 169-171, ARA, Koloniaal Archief [hereafter KA], 3800.

55. Consideratie, Nopens den Handel . . . Padang, December 22, 1789, par. 221, KA 3800.

56. The Suma Oriental, I, pp. 152-153.

late eighteenth century that the Minangkabau were able to find a way out of the Dutch trading net on the west by the founding of Penang in 1786.[57] The Dutch found that the Minangkabau were bringing goods from there into the darat almost as cheaply as they could be brought from the west coast, and the Dutch *opperkoopman* at Padang went so far as to try to persuade the penghulu of Lima Puluh Kota to close the main road from their luhak to the Kampar River.[58] This attempt failed and the Dutch came to regard Penang as a "cancer to trade."[59] The attractive alternatives available to the Minangkabau increased with the founding of Singapore, to which a considerable amount of the coffee of the darat began to be sent.[60] In return for its chief export Minangkabau was supplied by Singapore with Siamese salt, Bengal cottons, and coarse China ware.[61]

After a period of English "control" of the west coast between 1795 and 1819, the Dutch returned to Padang in May 1819. As a result of a treaty with a number of penghulu and representatives of the murdered Minangkabau royal family, Dutch forces made their first attack on a Padri kampung in the darat in April 1821.[62] Considering that the interior of Minangkabau had frequently been in turmoil during the one and a half centuries the Dutch had been on the coast, their motives for entering the darat at this point must remain a subject for further investigation.[63] The ostensible reason was the disruption of trade by the Padri.[64] From Imam Bondjol's account and other evidence, however, there seems to have been a flourishing trade under Padri control in the interior, carried on via channels not subject to foreign control.[65]

Bondjol was well situated for trade with the west coast, as several of the near-by rivers flowing to the coast were navigable.

---

57. Von Erath and van der Stengh to Alting, January 30, 1788, par. 48, KA 3752.

58. *Ibid.*, January 15, 1789, par. 21-31, KA 3800.

59. Consideratie, Nopens den Handel, par. 191.

60. Van den Bosch to Baud, November 16, 1832, in Exh[ibitum] June 5, 1833, No. 70 k/m Geh[eim], MK 4230.

61. Singapore Chronicle, March 1826 and September 1829, in J. H. Moor, Notices of the Indian Archipelago and Adjacent Countries (Singapore, 1837), pp. 98 and 101-102.

62. Rapport over de Krijgsverrigtingen, pp. 1-6.

63. The most important investigation of a problem of this type is R. Robinson and J. Gallagher, Africa and the Victorians (London: MacMillan, 1961), see particularly pp. 17-18.

64. Rapport over de Krijgsverrigtingen, p. 8.

65. The disruption of trade reported by Anderson (See J. Anderson, Mission to the East Coast of Sumatra in MDCCCXXIII [Edinburgh and London, 1826], p. 347) does not appear to have been permanent.

The Bondjollers carried on an active trade in the area between Tiku and Air Bangis, where they were supplied with English and Indian cotton-piece goods and other English goods, chiefly by the Atjehnese. They also made their salt on the same piece of coast.[66] The return of the Dutch put all this commerce in jeopardy. Imam Bondjol's aim now was to press into the lowlands as far south as Pariaman, a place vital to Dutch sea communications, and in May 1823 his forces captured the hinterland of Pariaman.[67] However, for reasons which are obscure--the more so as the episode is unmentioned in the memorandum--on January 22, 1824 the Imam and two other Bondjol tuanku entered into a treaty with the Dutch by which the latter hoped to improve their position on the coast.[68] Apart from the usual clauses of eternal peace, friendship, and mutual assitance, the nucleus of the treaty was an attempt to draw Bondjol firmly into the Dutch trading orbit. The three tuanku promised to do all in their power to encourage their neighbors in Rao, who had been a support of Dutch trade in Company days, to come to Padang or its dependencies to trade (clause Id); to permit the free and unimpeded introduction into Bondjol territory of all articles the Dutch wished to sell (clause Ie); to assist the Dutch to stop "smuggling" (clause If); and to buy their salt from the Dutch at six guilders per *pikul* (clause Ih).

Considering his own aims with relation to the coast between Air Bangis and Pariaman, it is difficult to know what moved Imam Bondjol to agree to this treaty. The Dutch salt monopoly in particular had always been hated, and Dutch salt was 200 percent more expensive than salt coming from the British possessions of Natal and Tapanuli.[69] Perhaps he hoped for a breathing space from Dutch intervention in the darat, and was pleased with the Dutch promise never to interfere with the religion or government of Bondjol's lands, and to see that Bondjol's customs were "respected" throughout Dutch territory on Sumatra (clause IIb). It is difficult to know what would have become of the treaty had its Dutch maker, Lieutenant Colonel Raaff, not died in April 1824, for he was highly respected by the Bondjollers as a brave soldier. But as a result of hostilities which took place in 1824 before de Stuers, the new Resident, could arrive, the Bondjollers returned the treaty to the Dutch.[70] When de Stuers asked for a reconsideration of the agreement, Bondjol insisted first that Dutch posts along the coast should stop at Pariaman, and that Bondjol

---

66. Lange, Het Nederlandsch Oost-Indisch Leger, pp. 187-188; Madjolelo and Marzoeki, Tuanku Imam Bondjol, pp. 21 and 81.

67. Een officier van het Indische Leger, "Episoden uit de geschiedenis der Nederlandsche krijgsverrigtingen op Sumatra's Westkust. II. 1822," Indisch Magazijn, I, No. 2 (1844), p. 229; "III 1823," Indisch Magazijn, I, No. 2 (1844), pp. 7-9. The page numbering is according to the loose numbers of the journal.

68. The treaty is reproduced in Rapport over de Krijgsverrigtingen as a footnote to pp. 146-156. It is printed in de Stuers, De Vestiging en Uitbreiding, I, pp. 78-83, and in Indonesian in Madjolelo and Marzoeki, Tuanku Imam Bondjol, pp. 81-85. I have followed the clause lettering of the ARA manuscripts.

69. De Stuers, De Vestiging en Uitbreiding, I, p. 80.

70. Rapport over de Krijgsverrigtingen, p. 192.

should remain in control of the coast between the river Masang and Air Bangis. These proposals were rejected by the Dutch.[71]

Struggle between the two adversaries for control of the coast now continued for a number of years. An unexpected blow fell in 1825 when the Dutch resumed control of Air Bangis from the laxer British, and also gained possession of the British posts of Natal and Tapanuli further north. Their aim was to channel trade to the coast ports they controlled, and *pelakat* (proclamation) after *pelakat* was issued to the Minangkabau forbidding trade at all places other than Bengkulu, Padang, Natal and Tapanuli.[72] During the period of the Java War, however, Dutch forces on Sumatra's west coast were virtually halved, and it was only in 1830 that they once again were able to take the offensive. By this time Imam Bondjol had gained in the Atjehnese an ally in the struggle for the coast, although he makes no mention of them in his memorandum. Moving northwards, in April 1830 he attacked and destroyed all of Natal apart from the fort in alliance with the Radja of Trumon, who assisted from the sea.[73] Early in 1831 he led 3,000 men against Air Bangis for four days and nights; two-thirds of the garrison had been killed before the Bondjollers retreated.[74] He then joined forces with the Atjehnese pirate Saidi Marah, who in 1829 had destroyed the Dutch fort at Tapanuli,[75] and once again blockaded Natal from land and sea, only retreating after the Dutch managed to send reinforcements.[76]

From now on, however, reinforcements kept arriving from Batavia and the Dutch were able to take the offensive. Towards the end of 1831 they attacked and captured Katiagan, one of the chief centers of Bondjol's trade.[77] In the house of a merchant there they found 100 large bales of cotton and 1,000 pikul of rice, together with iron and coffee.[78] After the capture of Katiagan the Dutch advance northwards, supported by sea power, was relentless. The leading coastal kampung fortified by Bondjol to protect their trade, extending to the north of Natal, were taken and burnt.[79] The tide now turned against the Bondjollers. After the fall of Lintau in the interior in 1832, the defeat of Bondjol was regarded as the chief aim

---

71. De Stuers, De Vestiging en Uitbreiding, I, pp. 102-103.

72. Elout to Clifford, May 6, 1831, No. 1/109 in Exh. September 26, 1831, No. 28, MK 810.

73. Ibid.

74. Rapport over de Krijgsverrigtingen, pp. 269-270; J. C. Boelhouwer, Herinneringen Van Mijn Verblijf op Sumatra's Westkust, Gedurende de Jaren 1831-1834 (The Hague: Erven Doorman, 1841), p. 21.

75. Rapport over de Krijgsverrigtingen, pp. 244-245.

76. Ibid., pp. 272-273; Boelhouwer, Herinneringen, pp. 19-20.

77. Rapport over de Krijgsverrigtingen, pp. 296-303.

78. Boelhouwer, Herinneringen, pp. 49-51.

79. Rapport over de Krijgsverrigtingen, pp. 303-307.

of Dutch arms on Sumatra's west coast.[80] By June 1834 the Dutch had taken Matur and were on the banks of the Masang. The slow decline in Bondjol's fortunes is well depicted in the memorandum.

It should perhaps be noted that while the Dutch were occupied with enclosing the west coast, the Bondjollers could always find an outlet for their trade by way of the east. It appears that Imam Bondjol made conquests on the Rokan, the Kampar Kanan, and the Kampar Kiri, all rivers flowing to the east.[81] A tributary of the Kampar Kanan was navigable to the mountains near Bondjol, and on it stood the prosperous market town of Kota Baru. It seems probable that this town was Bondjol's window on the east coast world. Goods were loaded there and sailed down to Pelalawan, a leading emporium half-way down the Kampar Besar, the journey taking thirteen to sixteen days. From Pelalawan trade continued in large vessels to Penang or Singapore, the crossing to the latter lasting about six days.[82] But once their hands were relatively free, the Dutch were eager to prevent this trade too, and during the Governor-Generalship of Johannes van den Bosch it became Dutch policy--though it was long before it could be brought to fruition--to seal up the outlets for this trade by occupying the mouths of the leading east coast rivers. Quite early in his administration van den Bosch flattered himself "that the trade of the whole island will soon be brought under our supervision. . . ."[83]

Flight, Capture, and Exile

The memorandum gives an account of the Dutch siege of Bondjol, and of the last days before its fall; however, it devotes only a few lines to Imam Bondjol's flight, capture, and exile. For much more information we can turn to the tambo, paraphrased by van Ronkel, which gives an extensive account of the latter part of the Imam's life,[84] part of which is corroborated by Dutch sources.[85] The description of the aged Imam's flight into the forest in the tambo is moving in its simplicity. He left Merapak with the words: "'As long as I can be buried in Alahan Pandjang I will continue to fight against the company;[86] my sons and I will carry on this struggle; may my

---

80. Van den Bosch to Baud, August 26, 1833, in Exh. January 10, 1834, No. 11^k Geh., MK 4232.

81. Madjolelo and Marzoeki, Tuanku Imam Bondjol, p. 76.

82. S. Müller, Berigten over Sumatra (Amsterdam, 1837), pp. 26-29.

83. Van den Bosch to Elout, December 26, 1830, Geh., in Exh. September 26, 1831, No. 28, MK 810.

84. Van Ronkel, "Inlandsche getuigenissen," p. 1109 et seq.

85. Nota betrekkelijke de gevangen neming van den Toeanko Imam von Bonjol, November 9, 1837, in Exh. March 19, 1838, No. 162, Geh., MK 4249 [Hereafter referred to as Nota].

86. The Minangkabau continued to refer to the Dutch as representatives of the "company" well after the demise of the Dutch East India Company.

prayer to Allah and his messenger be answered: to die in the fight against the company.'"[87] He took eighty people with him into the rimbu, though some deserted him due to the lack of food and the monotony. Finally, after having sent one of his younger sons to Bukit Tinggi to discuss Dutch terms, he decided to give himself up before his family died from privation. His parting words of advice to his son concerning his future conduct and friendships are Shakespearean in their beauty and simplicity.[88]

Tuanku Imam Bondjol surrendered to the Dutch at Palupuh (VII Lurah) on October 28, 1837. His first night in captivity was passed without sleep, filled with worry over the fate of the women and children he had left behind in the rimbu.[89] However, he was permitted to stay at Palupuh until he could be reassured that his family had been safely conducted back to the valley of Alahan Pandjang, and it was not until November 5 that he was taken to Bukit Tinggi.[90] It was decided by the local Dutch authorities that the Imam could not be considered a common criminal as he was not a subject of the Netherlands Indies Government; he must therefore be regarded as a prisoner of war[91] and accorded the respect due to a statesman and soldier.[92] There was also some discussion among local officials over whether it would be safe to allow him to live the rest of his days at Padang, or whether he should be removed forever from Sumatra.[93] However, the Supreme Government at Batavia determined on his removal to the Preanger Regency on Java.[94] Imam Bondjol had barely entered Padang when he was taken to the mouth of the river and saw to his terror that a boat was ready to receive him. He and his companions realized "that they would have to cross the great ocean, and would never again see Alahan Pandjang."[95]

His departure from Padang marked the beginning of many years of exile and wandering. At the end of 1838 the Resident of the Preanger Regency expressed his dislike of having a prisoner with Imam Bondjol's history under his authority. It was decided that it was inadvisable for influential Padri to come into close contact with the inhabitants of the interior of Java, and the Imam was removed to Ambon.[96] There he was given a monthly sum of 65 guilders and a ration of rice, and was permitted to rent a house. Two years later he was again moved,

---

87. Van Ronkel, "Inlandsche getuigenissen," p. 1110. Again it is impossible to know if these are the exact words of the tambo.

88. Ibid., p. 1116.

89. Ibid., p. 1117; Nota, MK 4249.

90. Nota, MK 4249.

91. Michiels to Francis, November 9, 1837, No. 323/93, in Exh. March 19, 1838, No. 162, Geh., MK 4249.

92. Nota, MK 4249.

93. Ibid.

94. Besluit Buiten Rade, January 23, 1838, No. 3, MK 2578.

95. Van Ronkel, "Inlandsche getuigenissen," p. 1118.

96. Geheim Besluit, January 19, 1839, L^{a}F, MK 4504.

this time to Menado in northern Sulawesi, and here he seems to have been treated with less respect and kindness by the local officials.[97] He lived out the rest of his life in Menado, cultivating a small piece of land, and died there in 1864.[98] He was buried in his last place of exile, never having seen the valley of Alahan Pandjang again.

MEMORANDUM OF TUANKU IMAM CONCERNING THE COMING OF THE DUTCH TO SUMATRA'S INTERIOR AND THE WAR THEY CARRIED ON THERE

Translated From The Malay[1]

There was a man named Tuanku Muda, son of a priest called Tuanku Radjanuddin, born in Alahan Pandjang, from where his forefathers originated. When he was thirty-five years old[2] he decided that, as all the necessities of life were difficult to come by at his dwelling place and even water had to be brought from a considerable distance, he would seek a better place for himself and his family. Through God's especial goodness he came with his wife, two brothers, and two sisters to a secluded spot at the foot of Mount Terdjadi, where he built his house and planted the ground with rice, palm and other fruit trees, and established a breeding place for cattle, horses, etc.

When Tuanku Muda had lived there a year and a half he discussed with the chiefs[3] and people of Alahan Pandjang the building of a fort and a prayer house; after this had been decided upon, all hands set to work and a fort was erected of fifteen *tumbak*[4] square, within which subsequently were built a temple[5] and six houses, which, after

---

97. Van Ronkel, "Inlandsche getuigenissen," pp. 1245-1246.

98. This is the date given by Madjolelo and Marzoeki, Tuanku Imam Bondjol, p. 166. See, however, E. B. Kielstra, "Sumatra's Westkust van 1836-1840," Bijdragen tot de Taal-, Land- en Volkenkunde, XXXIX (1890), p. 177, where the date of the Imam's death is given as November 6, 1854.

1. The memorandum was translated from Malay into Dutch. See de Stuers, De Vestiging en Uitbreiding, II, App. B, pp. 221-240. General de Stuers gained access to this memorandum from his brother, General F. de Stuers, to whose gouvernement Imam Bondjol was finally exiled. I have used some of de Stuers' original footnotes and added some of my own. The round brackets in the text contain de Stuers' interpolations. The memorandum is written in the third person.

2. 1807.

3. Here "chiefs" refer to the penghulu. Elsewhere in the memorandum "chiefs" are mentioned who are obviously Padri-appointed tuanku.

4. One tumbak equals 12 feet.

5. The Dutch generally referred to mosques or surau as "temples."

everything was completed, received the name of Bondjol, indicating that this fort was erected for the maintenance of the just institutions of Islam, to oppose all evil and unlawful actions, and to recommend to everyone to practice nothing that is not fair, just, and good.

After this it was decided to appoint judges or administrators over this place, and with universal consent Tuanku Muda, Tuanku Hitam, Tuanku Gapuk, and Tuanku Keluat were so named.[6] Tuanku Muda was then called Tuanku Imam by the people. These four judges followed the holy institutions of Muhammad, and all their decisions bore the mark of justice. After five years under the administration of Tuanku Imam this place had expanded so much that it became very extensive, and its prosperity was so great due to increasing industry and trade that many people went there because of the cheapness of foodstuffs, since rice, cattle, and horses were plentiful.

On report of this many people from the surrounding negeri flocked there, and soon the place was filled with a lot of people from far and wide.

In course of time, and on the occasion that a son was born to Tuanku Imam, who received the name of Umar Ali, it was decided in a general consultation of chiefs and the population, which meanwhile had grown to about 500 men capable of bearing arms, to build a bigger fortification and a bigger prayerhouse; to execute this plan about 15,000 men came by invitation from the surrounding places to help, and immediately all hands were set to work, the necessary stones were hauled half a mile from a big river and the people placed in a row from there to the fortress, in order to bring the stones by passing them from hand to hand; the work was carried on day and night for fourteen days without pause, except for periods for eating and prayers, when the fortification and prayerhouse were completed. The fort was 200 tumbak long, 100 tumbak broad, 7 *kasta*[7] high and 5 kasta thick; in it were built 40 big and 3 small houses.

Then the people were sent out to look for arms and ammunition and each brought his contribution to the strengthening of the fort; the above-mentioned four regents and the other chiefs then had prickly bamboo[8] planted round the fort. Meanwhile, Tuanku Gapuk, Tuanku Keluat, and Tuanku Hitam died one after another, and Tuanku Imam was left to carry on the administration alone.[9]

Then Tuanku Imam had another son, who was called Jusuf, and after a year a third, called Ali; he also had three wives and seventy

---

6. They were called the Berempat, i.e., the four.

7. One kasta equals one cubit, i.e., 18 to 22 inches.

8. Bambu duri.

9. The treaty of January 22, 1824 was signed by a Tuanku Hitam and a Tuanku Gapuk, though it is possible from the evidence of the tambo that these were the successors of the original bearers of the gelar.

slaves, both male and female.

When the people had been relieved of all care for the building and arming of the fort, they confined themselves exclusively to trade; with the enjoyment of peace and unity the prosperity of negeri Bondjol increased more and more, and merchants came there to trade from the neighboring places.

For twenty-five years the inhabitants of this place enjoyed all the satisfactions which unity, peace, and prosperity always bring, and no one committed injustice or wanton deeds, but each exerted himself at all times to practice virtue and to cultivate the fullness of justice by concord.

In the midst of this joy and internal content and prosperity, a man from Sungai Puar called Pada Bongsu arrived unexpectedly with the news that the Dutch, under the command of Colonel Raaff, were in negeri Simawang;[10] that Balimbing had been subjected to them after a fight of three days in which many people had lost their lives;[11] that they had conquered and burnt negeri Tabat Sawah Tengah, and the inhabitants had fled far and wide; that Sipajang too had been taken by the Dutch troops after one day's resistance by the population, and the inhabitants had fled in all directions;[12] that, as soon as the inhabitants of Lima Puluh[13] had heard the news, they had marched with a force of 3,000 men against the Dutch troops, which with native auxiliaries were 5,000 strong, and after making a stand for twenty-four hours they had had to give way to superior force and flee; that the Dutch troops, after having erected a fort on Mount Tendikir[14] between Lima Puluh and Tanah Datar, had burnt negeri Tandjung Alam to the ground which caused the inhabitants to take flight, and that they had then erected a fortification on Batu Sangkar[15] in the territory of the Sultan of Minangkabau, where they had remained and made peace with the people of Tanah Datar.

Following this, a certain man from Lintau, called Tuanku Ketjil, came to kampung Bondjol and related that the people of Lintau had marched against the Dutch troops in Tanah Datar, but had been beaten back by them;[16] that the Dutch troops were advancing on Agam; that they had conquered Kota Lawas[17] and Pandai Sikat, and the inhabitants,

---

10. Raaff arrived at Padang on December 8, 1821. His early campaigns were in Tanah Datar, directed against Tuanku Lintau.

11. February 1822.

12. June 1822.

13. Lima Puluh Kota, a "federation" of 50 negeri, making up one of the three luhak of Minangkabau.

14. June 1822.

15. Fort Van der Capellen. It was close to one of the old Minangkabau capitals, Pagarrujung. The fort was erected in 1822 and completed in 1826.

16. March 1822.

17. July 1822.

after three days' resistance, had fled far and wide to the lands of Danau,[18] Alahan Pandjang, and elsewhere; that the Dutch troops had erected a fortification there, at a place called Guguk Sigandang; that on the arrival of the Dutch, Menumpu and Kurai in Agam had made peace with them and the troops had erected a fortification on the mountains there.

Then the troops marched against Kota Baru; here they met fierce resistance from the people who fought courageously under their chief Tuanku nan Rintjeh, so that the Dutch had to beat a retreat and return to the fort, with great losses and leaving behind a piece of artillery.[19]

After some time the Dutch troops went to fight against Kapau, but also encountered here such fierce resistance that they retreated to the fort with much loss on both sides.[20] Subsequently, they marched against negeri Lintau[21] to conquer it as well; the population, after having resisted for seven days without pause, received support from the people of Labau. The latter attacked the rearguard, so that the Dutch troops were caught between two fires. Only after both sides had suffered great losses did the Dutch troops return to fort Batu Sangkar, leaving behind four pieces of artillery, four barrels of powder, four lanterns, and many guns and swords. It was on this occasion that Tuanku nan Rintjeh, the chief of Kota Baru, lost his life.[22] Meanwhile, Colonel Raaff had died at Padang,[23] and Colonel de Stuers arrived unexpected at Padang as his replacement,[24] and subsequently came to Minangkabau; later he also stayed at Batu Sangkar and exerted himself to restore tranquillity to these lands, so that the people began to live again, as it were, and often went to visit Padang once more. After about five years Colonel de Stuers returned to Batavia.[25]

Colonel Elout, Commandant for the Company, who replaced Colonel de Stuers,[26] came to Batu Sangkar, and after some time he went with his troops to fight against Kapau (1831);[27] the inhabitants, although

---

18. Lake Manindjau.

19. September 1822.

20. August 1822. This is one of the many examples in the text of Imam Bondjol's confusion of dates.

21. April 1823.

22. This is incorrect, as Tuanku nan Rintjeh was alive at a later date. I do not know the date of his death.

23. April 1824.

24. November 1825.

25. December 1829.

26. Actually H. MacGillavry was Resident for one year after Colonel de Stuers; Colonel Elout arrived at Padang in March 1831.

27. Actually, this was in April 1832.

supported by the people of Tilatang, nevertheless had to surrender after fierce resistance. Then the Dutch troops proceeded with their conquest in the direction of Kota Tua, in the land of Agam. On receipt of an invitation Tuanku Samei, the chief of that land, appeared before the above-mentioned officer, and soon peace was made with that district, and the Dutch troops erected a fort there which was named Kota Godong Batu.

Then the Dutch troops went to Magek, also in the land of Agam; the inhabitants submitted to them, and, with the making of peace, the piece of artillery left behind by the Dutch troops in the battle of Kota Baru was returned; peace was also made with the people of Tilatang, and the troops erected a fort in the middle of Tilatang.

Next the Dutch troops once again attacked Lintau (1832). After three days' fighting a certain man of Lintau, called Tuanku Limbu, came to offer his submission to the Government and guided the Dutch troops into Lintau, and after it was captured the Dutch erected a fort in the middle of Balaitengah.[28] Subsequently the Dutch marched against Kamang, in Agam district; the courageous inhabitants put up fierce resistance lasting two days and both sides had many dead and wounded.[29] Then a paramount chief of the land of Suliki, in Lima Puluh, named Alam Putih, came to the help of the Dutch with his people; travelling by way of uncultivated areas, they attacked the inhabitants of Kamang in the rear and set their fortifications on fire, so that they scattered far and wide, while some submitted to the Dutch.[30]

Then the Dutch marched on Matur, in the land of Agam. The population offered fierce resistance; the battle continued undecided for seven days, while many men fell and were killed on both sides; finally the Dutch troops retired. After a cessation of hostilities for fourteen days the Dutch troops resumed battle, upon which Matur, after having suffered great losses, had to surrender.[31]

Next the conquest was pursued to Lawang, in the land of Duabelas;[32] after a day's fighting the Dutch troops won a victory over the population. Thereupon a man called Tuanku Tinggi, from Sungai Puar in the land of Duabelas, came to offer his homage to the Dutch Government; a general peace was concluded with the people of Duabelas, and the troops were led into Sungai Puar, where they camped in the marketplace.[33] After three days a letter was sent to the land of Kumpulan and another to Alahan Pandjang. On learning the news of the presence of the Dutch at Sungai Puar there arose confusion among the population of Alahan Pandjang, as Sungai Puar is only twelve hours on foot from there. Many were afraid, while many others showed their courage. Some

---

28. July 1832.

29. July 1832.

30. July 1832.

31. September 1832.

32. XII Kota.

33. September 1832.

wanted to take flight and others prepared themselves for resistance. In the midst of this situation there arrived a certain emissary from Colonel Elout, called Pandita Sari, with the above-mentioned letter; it was handed to the Penghulu Datuk Bendahara.

After the departure of Pandita Sari for his land Pasir Lawas, Datuk Bendahara assembled in the marketplace the Penghulu Datuk Sati, Tuanku Imam, and all the heads and people of Alahan Pandjang; when they had gathered together, the letter from Colonel Elout was broken open by a certain Tuanku Labai and read out; it contained the following:

> This letter comes from the Colonel of the Dutch troops Elout to the Penghulu Datuk Bendahara and Datuk Sati and to Tuanku Imam, in the land of Alahan Pandjang.
>
> I, Colonel Elout, inform you that the Dutch Government now claims your Country; if you will surrender the Country peacefully, let all the chiefs come to us in Sungai Puar to make peace; but if you will not surrender your Country, then be on your guard, because we will soon march against your Country.

When Tuanku Labai had stopped reading and everyone had understood the contents of the letter, a quarrel arose among the chiefs and people; some wanted peace and others resistance; but the majority wanted peace, which was also the choice of Datuk Bendahara. Only Datuk Sati opposed this: "I will not make peace," he said, "because our Land is too small and too sparsely populated to be able to perform the Government's services."

Then Tuanku Imam rose and said: "Let there be no discord among you, but be of one mind and loyal to each other, lest calamity befall us."

However, this warning of Tuanku Imam was not well received, and discord spread increasingly among the people. Hereupon Tuanku Imam considered and spoke to himself: "What is the use of my remaining longer in Alahan Pandjang, as the penghulu are disunited and without them I can command nothing; let me rather leave here with my wife and children." No sooner had he thought of this than he went home and sent for Tuanku Sabar, to whom he revealed his resolution and stated that he wanted to go to Lubuk Sikaping. At the same time he entrusted to him full powers over Bondjol and part of his goods, house, and cattle, and he requested him to inform him of the arrival of the Dutch so that he could make peace with them.

A day later Tuanku Imam left Alahan Pandjang with all his family and part of his goods for Lubuk Sikaping; he arrived there after a day's journey and took up residence at the house of Datuk Sati. Three days after his departure from Alahan Pandjang the penghulu Datuk Bendahara, Datuk Baginda Arab, and Datuk Baginda went to offer their submission to the Government of the Dutch. Appearing before Colonel Elout, they concluded peace with him on the condition that all the Government's commands should be obeyed, provided that the Dutch troops did not move into fort Bondjol, and no infringement was made on the religion, manners, and customs of the people.

When this was all confirmed with promises on both sides, the Dutch troops were led inside Alahan Pandjang by the above-mentioned three people;[34] on their arrival there the people had already prepared *atap* (thatch) to build dwellings at a certain place called Medan Saba, but the Dutch refused to live there and moved into the temple and the houses in Bondjol, after having chased away the inhabitants, thus making the temple and the houses of the population into their barracks.

During the month and a half that the Dutch troops lived there, they appropriated by force the fruit, cattle, and fish in the ponds belonging to the people, without making any payment.

Three days after Tuanku Imam had gone to Lubuk Sikaping, his brother, named Radja Manang, came to bring him the news that the Dutch troops had moved into fort Bondjol and had made a barracks of the place of worship, while some of the Javanese soldiers had taken up residence in the house of Tuanku Imam, and that he had been charged by Colonel Elout, who was living in the house of Tuanku Ketjil, to request Tuanku Imam to come to him. "All right," replied Tuanku Imam, "I shall go to Colonel Elout."

The following morning about five o'clock Tuanku Imam set out for Alahan Pandjang with his son Jusuf, Paduka Madjalelo, and Radja Manang. With feelings of fear and shame towards the Malays there, they journeyed towards it along unbeaten paths.

On arrival in Bondjol Tuanku Imam with his son Jusuf immediately went to Colonel Elout, and the following conversation took place between them:[35]

"Where is Tuanku Imam?" asked Colonel Elout.

"That's me," he replied.

"Come inside, Tuanku Imam! Into the room," resumed the Colonel, whereupon Tuanku Imam entered the room with his son Jusuf, and then at the request of Colonel Elout sat down next to the latter. Then the following conversation began again:

"How are you, Tuanku Imam?"

"Well, Sir."

"Where are you living now, Tuanku Imam?"

"I am living at present at Lubuk Sikaping, because I fear the Dutch troops, as I am not yet familiar with them."

"You must not be afraid; the Government will do you no harm." Then he asked: "How old are you now, Tuanku Imam?"

---

34. September 1832.

35. An Indonesian version of this conversation is to be found in Muhamad Radjab, Perang Paderi di Sumatera Barat (1803-1838), (2nd edition; Djakarta: Balai Pustaka, 1964), pp. 160-162.

"Sixty."

"And I am sixty-one," resumed Colonel Elout, "so we are the same age."[36] Meanwhile Colonel Elout ordered some refreshments and tea. After consuming these, Colonel Elout continued the conversation and said: "It would be better for Tuanku Imam to go home for the time being; he can come and speak to me this evening."

"Where shall I go to spend the night?" replied Tuanku Imam. "My house is filled with Javanese and Malays."

At this Colonel Elout resumed: "It would be better for Tuanku Imam to sleep for a time in the house of Tuanku Sabar."

"Good," replied Tuanku Imam. Then with his son Jusuf he said good-bye and went to the house of Tuanku Sabar, where he stayed. In the evening there came a messenger from Colonel Elout to request Tuanku Imam to visit him; thereupon the latter with his son Jusuf appeared before the Colonel and greeted him. Colonel Elout ordered Tuanku Imam to sit down, which he did at once. Then Colonel Elout sent a request for Tuanku Muda and the Lieutenant to come to him. When they had appeared and sat down next to Colonel Elout, he began the following conversation with Tuanku Imam:

"You are old now, Tuanku Imam! You must burden yourself with no more activity; it would be better for you to enjoy tranquillity and contentment in your old age, and leave the worry of affairs to the young."

"Good," replied Tuanku Imam. "I shall follow your advice and wise opinion, Colonel, and submit myself to your decree!"

"Then you can," pursued Colonel Elout, "choose one from among you who is capable of being your successor."

At this Tuanku Imam answered: "I shall obey your will, Colonel, because I know no one capable of succeeding me other than the person you choose!"

"If Tuanku Imam leaves me that power," replied Colonel Elout, "then it will give me pleasure to name Tuanku Muda here as Regent[37] of the district of Alahan Pandjang; because Tuanku Muda is the favorite of Tuanku Imam, has good judgment, and is able and courageous, isn't he?"

"Very good," said Tuanku Imam, "I shall conform to your advice."

Then Colonel Elout proposed that the following morning all the penghulu and hulubalang and people of Bondjol should be assembled to name Tuanku Muda Regent of the district of Alahan Pandjang, after which Tuanku Imam and his son Jusuf said farewell to Colonel Elout, and returned to the house of Tuanku Sabar.

---

36. It is difficult to account for this statement. Elout was born in 1795, and was thus 23 years younger than Imam Bondjol.

37. The Dutch appointed Regents on the Javanese pattern from their first entry into Minangkabau.

At about six o'clock the next morning Colonel Elout had all the chiefs and people called together by a young man called Achir Ali. When they had all gathered in Bondjol, Tuanku Muda was appointed Regent of Alahan Pandjang. On this occasion Colonel Elout consulted with the chiefs and people present about going to conquer the district of Sundatar in the land of Hulu Rao; when this was decided on, the troops set off there; Colonel Elout left behind Lieutenant Laba (?) [sic] and forty men to guard fort Bondjol.

Tuanku Muda showed the way to Sundatar; Colonel Elout and three men (officers) followed behind.

After a day's journey they arrived in Sundatar; the population came to pay homage to the Dutch troops, and soon peace was made. They stayed here a day; the next day the troops marched further towards Rao, and against Padang Mantinggi, where there was a fort called Bondjol. When they were half-way there a certain Hadji Mahmud Saman, son of a Radja of Lubuk Lajang in the land of Rao, came to pay homage to the Government, and a peace treaty was made with him; then this Radja Mahmud Saman led the troops into Padang Mantinggi, and a general peace was concluded with the population.

When Colonel Elout and his men, who had all lodged as they pleased in the houses and the place of worship, had sojourned here for ten days, he left behind about one hundred soldiers under the command of ten officers to guard the place, while he returned to Alahan Pandjang and Bondjol with Tuanku Muda and the rest of the men. After remaining here for ten days, he went with his men to Agam, on the high mountains; here he conquered in succession nearly the whole land of Lima Puluh; then, having led his men back to Batu Sangkar, Colonel Elout returned first to Padang and then to Batavia.[38]

After some time Lieutenant Laba, who was guarding Bondjol, was replaced by another officer from Batu Sangkar, and he left for fort Bukit Tinggi.[39]

The Dutch troops continued to live in the mosque at Bondjol and in the houses of the inhabitants, whose occupants they expelled, and they brought dogs and all sorts of filth inside, and disposed of the fruit and cattle of the inhabitants as they pleased, and even forced on the residents all sorts of work and burdensome deliveries of rice and *padi* without payment, and punished them daily. On one occasion some government goods were brought from Sipisang to Bondjol to be transported from there to Lubuk Sikaping. Twenty Alahan Pandjang men had to carry these goods under an escort of a sergeant and twelve soldiers. When they had arrived at Sungai Silasung, which was half-way there, they requested permission to stop for as long as it took to satisfy their hunger and say their prayers, but they were not allowed to. However, when one of the twenty bearers, named Darusalam, insisted on satisfying his desires despite this refusal, one of the soldiers immediately fired at him and hit him in the chest, so that he lay there dead, while the others were hurried on with the cane. So they ran in great terror for the whole day, and after the

---

38. Colonel Elout did not leave for Batavia then.

39. Fort de Kock was erected in 1825-1826.

goods had been brought to Lubuk Sikaping and stored in the temple there, they returned to Alahan Pandjang.

By the time they returned, the Commandant had left for Sipisang, and although each went back to his dwelling place, this occasion did not go unremarked.

The severe and arbitrary actions of the troops caused universal grumbling in Alahan Pandjang, and led the inhabitants to meet together in Tandikat, where many cases were raised which had been extremely unjust and arbitrary, the more so as the population had become reconciled to the Government with mutual promises. These agreements had not only been thrown to the winds but, instead of a peaceful and tranquil administration which they had expected from the Government, they had suffered oppression and mistreatment. The result of all this was that they had definitely decided to rebel and to die rather than stand it any longer. Letters were immediately sent to all the districts, and it was agreed that each would raise a general rebellion and kill all the soldiers in their districts on the third of the month Radjab (January 1833).

On the morning of the third of the month Radjab,[40] on a Friday, twenty hulubalang, led by two paramount chiefs called Tuanku nan Garang and Radja Lajang, unexpectedly marched into Bondjol, and when they had entered the temple, ran amuck among the soldiers and within half an hour murdered all the European and Javanese soldiers. When he heard of this, the Regent Tuanku Muda rushed to the scene of this frightful massacre, but he was immediately greeted by one of the hulubalang with a spear which wounded him in the back so that he ran home bleeding.

Then one of the chiefs mentioned above, Tuanku nan Garang, went to the house of Tuanku Imam, and drew his sword to murder him; whereupon Umar Ali, one of the sons of Tuanku Imam, placed himself between them, and addressed Tuanku nan Garang in this manner: "If you want to murder my father, first let us see which of us two is the victor." When he heard this courageous language, Tuanku nan Garang's resolve immediately vanished. At Sipisang, where the Commandant of Bondjol had gone, there had also been a similar running amuck of which many soldiers had been the victims, and only the Commandant Roman[41] succeeded in saving himself and some of his men by flight.

Eight days later Tuanku Muda died from the effects of his wound. At the end of a month everyone was in a position to resist on all sides; the *benteng*[42] were fortified and the population provided with arms.

Six months later the Dutch troops with native auxiliaries marched against Alahan Pandjang, commanded by Commandant Rampang, Lieutenant Laba, Major Lebas, and another officer.[43] Before they had got close

---

40. January 11, 1833.

41. Lieutenant Colonel Vermeulen Krieger.

42. Forts.

43. This was in September 1833, not June as de Stuers says (De Vestiging en Uitbreiding, p. 232, ftn. 3). The four officers mentioned here are Commissioner-General van den Bosch, who

to the district, the hulubalang Bendahara Langit and Tuanku nan Garang, who, with their people, had stationed themselves on the road from the land of Lima Puluh, went to meet the Dutch troops;[44] the fight had only lasted three hours when night fell and separated the combatants. The following day the fight was resumed with renewed fury; towards evening Tuanku nan Garang was shot right in the head by a bullet, which mishap was quickly followed by his death, while three men were wounded; the fight lasted until towards midday on the third day, when the Dutch troops withdrew to the land of Lima Puluh, in fact to Pajakumbuh.[45]

After this Bendahara Langit got news from Bondjol that the troops from Rao[46] had marched against kampung Alai. On learning this, he divided his people and sent some of them there to give support to the inhabitants of Alai, while some held station at Batu Bidara. The fight had already started when Bendahara Langit's men arrived; they immediately rushed to the aid of the people of Alai; the fight lasted the whole day and until noon of the following day, when the Dutch troops retreated to Rao.[47] After this there was a cessation of hostilities for a whole year.[48]

After this time had passed the Dutch troops once again marched against Alahan Pandjang from the land of Agam; coming to Matur[49] on the way, they encountered fierce resistance; only after fighting for three days did the inhabitants of Matur surrender, whereupon peace was concluded. A fort was erected here, after which there was again a general cessation of hostilities for some time.

During this time of peace the people of Alahan Pandjang again began to make provision for their sustenance and they cultivated their ricefields as before. At harvest time a man from Sipisang arrived unexpectedly with the news that the Dutch troops had been at work waging war on Sipisang in the land of Lima Puluh,[50] led by Colonel Bauer and Lieutenants Karab[51] and Lang,[52] with a considerable

---

      personally led an attack on Matur; Colonel Elout, who led a column along the coast; Major De Quay who started out from Lima Puluh Kota; and Major Eilers who led a column from the north.

44. The column of Major De Quay.

45. September 1833.

46. The column led by Major Eilers.

47. September 1833.

48. Actually from early October 1833 to June 1834. In February 1834 Lieutenant Colonel Bauer took over command of the Dutch forces.

49. June 1834.

50. Actually Sipisang is in Tudjuh Lurah. It was attacked in April 1835.

51. Probably Captain Krafft. See Lange, Het Nederlandsch Oost-Indisch Leger, II, p. 83, ftn. 1.

52. Not Lieutenant-adjutant Lange, as stated by de Stuers (De Vestiging en Uitbreiding, II, p. 233, ftn. 5) but Lieutenant B. J. De Lange.

force of native auxiliaries from Tanah Datar and Agam. On this occasion Datuk Baginda and Datuk Baginda Kali had taken up station there. The battle lasted three days: finally Datuk Baginda and Datuk Baginda Kali could hold out no longer against the greatly superior forces and retreated to Kumpulan, while at the same time the troops pressed forward. Baginda Kali still tried to hold his own but some of his people and Baginda deserted him and fled to Alahan Pandjang. However, after holding out a considerable time and losing many men, he fled to Alahan Sati.[53] After all the houses and the mosque had been reduced to ashes, Kumpulan was immediately occupied by the Dutch troops, whereupon a cessation of hostilities followed for a month.

After this time had passed, Colonel Bauer sent a letter to Tuanku Imam, asking him and all the hulubalang whether they wanted to be reconciled with the Government or not. On receiving this letter Tuanku Imam assembled all the oldest men and the inhabitants of Bondjol and put this question to them, upon which they declared that they would leave the decision to Tuanku Imam and readily acquiesce in his decree. Then Tuanku Imam proposed to them that they should be reconciled to the Government and undertake to obey all its laws and commands, provided the Dutch troops remained in Kumpulan and did not settle in Alahan Pandjang; this proposal was universally accepted and communicated to Colonel Bauer by letter. The Colonel sent no answer, but informed Tuanku Imam and the population of Alahan Pandjang by word of mouth that they would have to be on their guard, as he was planning to march against them with his army. On this occasion, Tuanku Tinggi of Sungai Puar sent a letter to Tuanku Imam, exhorting him to pay no heed to the proposals of the Government but to make ready for resistance, which would have his support and for which he was already sending some gunpowder and ammunition as provisions.[54]

Meanwhile the Dutch troops, supported by native auxiliaries and commanded by Colonel Bauer and lieutenants Karab and Lang, had arrived at the plain Padang Lawas, before Alahan Pandjang.[55] It was about five o'clock in the morning. The population, which was ever ready for battle, offered fierce resistance; both armies suffered many dead and wounded. Some of the Dutch troops got close to Bondjol; but a heavy canonnade from Tuanku Imam made them shrink back to Padang Lawas again. Finally the people of Alahan Pandjang had to leave the battlefield and each returned to his dwelling. The Dutch troops remained there and put up their huts, after which there was a cessation of hostilities for a month.

Meanwhile the people of Alahan Pandjang built five forts on the top of Mount Terdjadi. Then the Dutch troops once more marched against Bondjol;[56] half-way there they encountered the people of Alahan Pandjang who held them to a stand; the battle was so intense

---

53. This should read Alahan Mati.

54. Tuanku Tinggi was much trusted by the Dutch and had performed important services for them. See Lange, Het Nederlandsch Oost-Indisch Leger, II, p. 90, ftn. 1.

55. June 1835.

56. July 1835.

that the fighters could not distinguish friend from foe. Meanwhile
the forces of Tuanku Muhamad Saleh, Tuanku Nabaga, Ompai, and Imam
Parang attacked the Dutch troops in the rear, which caused such confusion among them that they fired at one another; towards evening the
battle ceased, after both sides had lost many men. About five o'clock
the next morning the Dutch troops advanced on the benteng Lubuk
Beringin; after fierce resistance the men of the garrison, only twenty
in number, had to leave the fort; they fled to the benteng Medan
Saba, which was on the river. The Dutch troops immediately entered
the abandoned benteng; heavy firing was kept up between this benteng
and the benteng Medan Saba over the river; by nighttime the garrison
of Medan Saba decided to leave this fort as it could not be defended
further, whereupon they went to Bondjol; the abandoned benteng was
immediately occupied by Dutch troops. At this point the fighting
was suspended for some time, whilst the participants busied themselves
with restoring the posts and erecting new forts. The people of
Alahan Pandjang erected two more forts on the above-mentioned Mount
Terdjadi. When the things mentioned were ready the Dutch troops,
under the command of Lieutenant Karab, marched against Bondjol on a
certain day about five o'clock in the morning. Having arrived at a
small river in the neighborhood of Bondjol they shelled the latter
with five big guns. Tuanku Imam was saying his morning prayers;
when he had finished he went to his guns and both sides kept up
heavy firing till evening. In the course of that night and four
consecutive nights the native troops erected a fort about 150 fathoms
from Bondjol. When this was ready, heavy firing commenced between
both forts, while in the meantime Lieutenant Karab sent a considerable
force to capture Njamka [possibly Djambak]. These troops had to return to their fort at Bondjol by midday, having been unable to endure
the courageous resistance of the inhabitants of that kampung.

Meanwhile the war between the inhabitants of Bondjol and the
Dutch troops was carried on incessantly day and night for a month.
In the meantime some of the troops were sent to conquer Lubuk Masang;
the population of this kampung fled partly to Njamka [Djambak?] and
partly to Bondjol. Next the capture of kampung Baru was attempted;
but the inhabitants put up fierce resistance, and despite the death
of their paramount chief, the hulubalang Linggang Sepadi, they held
their ground so well that the Dutch troops finally had to return to
their cantonments.

After some time the Dutch troops marched against one of the
forts on the high mountain range, the garrison of which was commanded
by the penghulu Kali Balang, Tuanku Sabar, Ampalima Sutan, and
Baginda Talabai. Fighting was so fierce that after half a day the
enemies were in hand-to-hand combat. Finally the garrison could hold
out no longer; they fled to Bondjol, after which the Dutch troops
entered the fort and took up station there. Subsequently some troops
were sent to capture kampung Padang Bubus. These troops arrived at
the above-mentioned place about five o'clock in the morning: a
fierce fight developed, which was undecided for a considerable time
until finally, after the lapse of half a day, the Dutch troops could
hold out no longer and retreated to their fort on the mountain range.

After the lapse of some more time, the Dutch troops marched
against Baru; the people of this kampung had marched out to wait for
the enemy; about seven o'clock the two armies met. While the Dutch
troops were erecting a fort at Tarebati, heavy fire was maintained

from both sides, which killed and mutilated many.

In this way the fighting lasted a whole year, with short intermissions; the chiefs and hulubalang of the surrounding land of Agam and other regions which had been conquered by the Dutch troops sent letters from all sides to Tuanku Imam to inspire him with courage and to urge him to make a stand, while they came to his assistance with men, gunpowder, and ammunition, which permitted him to offer such a strong resistance.

After some time Colonel Bauer left for Batavia[57] and General Cleerens came in his place, bringing with him fresh troops and a number of pieces of artillery and arms; after his arrival the war was carried on without pause. During this time Tuanku Imam received a letter from the Resident of Padang, Francis, suggesting that he be reconciled to the Government. Tuanku Imam let it be known that he first wished to assemble the population, who were scattered far and wide in the fields, to talk about the matter and to deliberate together, and that he therefore requested seven days cessation of hostilities, whereupon he immediately ordered the white flag to be run up, which the Dutch troops also did. However, before the seven days had elapsed the Dutch troops once again fired at the benteng Sungai Lama; the garrison offered fierce resistance; after half a day the fighting was again discontinued by both sides. The flags of peace were now hauled down, which caused surprise, as the seven days had not yet elapsed. The battle with kampung Bondjol was resumed with renewed fury, as a result of which there were many dead and wounded on both sides. After the lapse of some time General Cleerens returned to Batavia.

Then General Cochius came from Batavia[58] bringing with him a number of soldiers; the fighting continued on both sides; the Dutch troops shot burning bullets which fell on the prayerhouse and dwelling of Tuanku Imam and set both alight; this increased the fury of the population and they fired in deadly earnest.

About three o'clock one morning, when the people of Bondjol, exhausted by the incessant firing and fighting, were snatching some moments' rest, the Dutch troops, who still continued to shoot without intermission, took the opportunity of entering Bondjol through the breached part [of the wall].[59] Some African or Buginese soldiers totally unexpectedly penetrated the place where the women of Tuanku Imam were sleeping and wanted to drag some of them off. On this occasion the youngest son of Tuanku Imam, called Mahmud, was stabbed in the stomach, while one of the women had her buttock cut through, from which she died, and a second women was also wounded in the buttock. All the women were screaming fearfully; Tuanku Imam, awoken

---

57. Bauer handed over command to Cleerens on May 3, 1836.

58. He arrived before Bondjol on April 12, 1837.

59. The Dutch had concentrated on breaching the wall with their artillery fire. This reconnaissance of the Dutch inside Bondjol, led by Captain Vogel, took place on the night of December 2-3, 1836. Thus Imam Bondjol is inaccurate in dating it to the period of Cochius' command. See Lange, Het Nederlandsch Oost-Indisch Leger, II, pp. 159-163.

by this, took his sword and, accompanied by his son Umar Ali, went to the dwelling of the women from where the screaming could be heard. On encountering the soldiers he was wounded by a shot in his buttock; but he continued to run amuck among the soldiers, together with his son. The latter was shot in the side; the bullet remained in the flesh and, not being able to bear the violent pains, he went home with his wound bleeding. Tuanku Imam, although quite alone, continued to wield his sword right and left, until finally the soldiers retreated from Bondjol. Tuanku Imam followed them outside Bondjol with his sword; here the soldiers stabbed him with a bayonet so that he fell to the ground. When they stabbed him a second time, he got up at once and again wielded his sword right and left among the soldiers, whereupon they fled to their cantonments; Tuanku Imam, exhausted and suffering dreadfully from thirteen wounds which were bleeding continuously, was carried home by the inhabitants of Bondjol.

About five o'clock the next morning the Dutch troops came very near the breached part of Bondjol, and attacked there;[60] the population, prepared for this, defended themselves bravely; even the women took up arms to help their men; the battle was so fierce that the two armies could not distinguish one another, and the shouts on both sides echoed to the sky. This lasted until twelve noon when the Dutch troops retreated to their forts; the number of dead and wounded was great on both sides.

Lieutenant Lang sent some of his soldiers and Mr. van Draha (?) [sic] to capture the fort of Baginda Madjalelo on Mount Terdjadi. After having kept up heavy cannon fire for two days they got to within a gunshot of the fort; they fired, threw missiles, and struck one another with white-hot fury. Baginda Madjalelo fell with a gunshot in the head; his brother, called Sutan Suleman, succeeded him as chief and the battle was continued with vigor. When it was still undecided after two days, Lieutenant Lang came in the night and had two barrels of gunpowder placed in a prepared hole at the foot of the mountain, where the fort was. About seven o'clock the next morning the powder was ignited and a piece of the mountain, with part of the fort, plunged from the cliff; one man lost his life and another was buried beneath the rubble, but, as he was still alive, was taken up and cared for by the soldiers; thereupon Sutan Suleman and the garrison abandoned their fort and came to Bondjol, whence they were pursued by the Dutch troops. Thereupon the entire population of Bondjol, both men and women, marched out of their fortifications to go to meet the soldiers. After a fierce fight of only half an hour, on which occasion the women too used guns, the Dutch troops retreated to Sutan Suleman's fort. The population of Bondjol pursued them to a certain distance, and then returned to Bondjol. The soldiers rebuilt Sutan Suleman's fort and provided it with the necessary armaments; subsequently they shot at Bondjol from it with fire-bullets, which caused frightful devastation among the buildings and trees. For a month fierce firing was kept up between this fort and Bondjol.

Subseqently Lieutenant Lang came in the night with his soldiers to about ten and a half fathoms from Bondjol and erected his fort

---

60. This attack of December 4, 1836 also took place under the command of General Cleerens.

there, which was followed by a furious fight; after two days he
moved his battery to about four and a half, and then eight days later
to one and a half fathoms; meanwhile the battle continued with increasing fury; nothing could be heard but the incessant firing and
shouting which accompanied it, and everything was covered in thick
smoke. The Dutch troops succeeded in making breaches at various
places and setting alight by fire-bullets the bamboo which was
planted around Bondjol. While the battle was continued with terrible
fury, the opposing sides exchanged coconuts and other small objects.[61]
On both sides the number of dead was appalling:[62] in Bondjol there
still remained fifteen hulubalang, who stood fast day and night for
two and a half months.

About this time, three hulubalang called Kali Madjalelo, Imam
Parang, and Tuanku Maharadja, who lived in Alahan Pandjang outside
Bondjol, came in the night to Tuanku Imam in Bondjol and suggested
that he leave the kampung and go with them to kampung Merapi[63] in
order to deliberate there over what was to be done in these perilous
times, as Bondjol had suffered such damage and the batteries had collapsed and all the houses and trees had burnt down and fallen to the
ground. Tuanku Imam consented to that proposal but wanted to wait till
the next evening, as he first wanted to make the necessary arrangements
for the women and goods; upon this the three people mentioned returned
to their kampung promising to come to fetch Tuanku Imam at the appointed time.

The very same evening Tuanku Imam sent his women and children and
all the other women and slaves, from Bondjol, where meanwhile the battle still continued, to kampung Merapi [Merapak]. They arrived at
the above-mentioned kampung and took up residence at the house of
Sutan Lima Kota. When, after two days, the above-mentioned three
people had again come to Tuanku Imam in Bondjol, he left for kampung
Merapi [Merapak] with one of his sons, the latter's teacher, and a
slave, and put up with his family at the house of Sutan Lima Kota.

The next night, after the departure of Tuanku Imam, the fourteen
hulubalang still remaining in Bondjol also left and joined Tuanku
Imam in kampung Merapi [Merapak].

When the Dutch troops saw that kampung Bondjol had been abandoned
they immediately occupied it,[64] repaired the collapsed batteries and
brought them into a good state again. Two days later the Dutch troops

---

61. The tambo confirms that even in the heat of battle the Bondjollers
    gave young coconuts to the soldiers, and the latter gave their
    opponents Javanese tobacco; see van Ronkel, "Inlandsche
    getuigenissen," p. 1108. The original Padri abhorrence of tobacco
    seems to have been forgotten!

62. According to Lange (Het Nederlandsch Oost-Indisch Leger, II, p. 231,
    ftn. 1), Dutch losses between July 7 and August 7, 1837 were 12
    dead and 27 wounded.

63. This is an error for Merapak.

64. August 16, 1837. It was subsequently named Kota Generaal Cochius
    by the Dutch.

marched to kampung Merapi [Merapak]; the population, on hearing this, marched out to meet them. After only one hour's fighting the Dutch troops retreated to Bondjol, while the inhabitants of Merapi [Merapak] returned to their houses. With this the war was at an end.

After a lapse of two days peace negotiations were concluded at Bondjol between two delegates of Tuanku Imam and the Government.

Later Tuanku Imam was invited by a letter from the Resident of Padang to go to the fort on the mountain and meet the Resident there. Having arrived at the above-mentioned mountain and not finding the Resident there, he was brought to Padang with his son and three followers, under escort of a captain, an officer, and twelve men, from where he was subsequently transported to Batavia; he remained there four months, in the house of the Commandant of the Balinese; then he was moved to Tjiandjur. After eleven months he was again sent to Batavia and was transported from there to Ambon by warship.

Written at Ambon, September 13, 1839

Tuanku Imam Bondjol

(Source: de Steurs, De Vestiging en Uitbreiding, I, opposite p. 163)

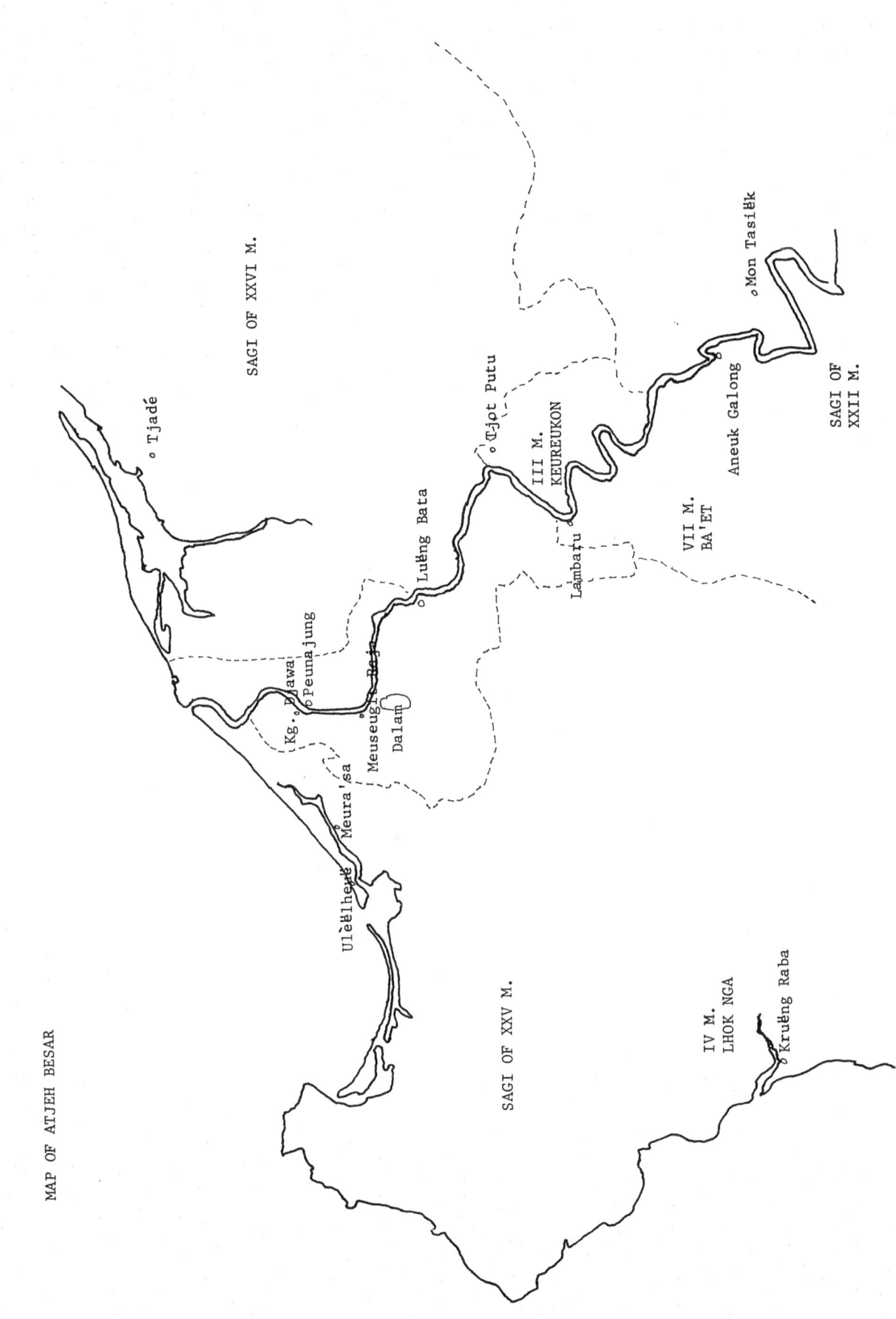

HABIB ABDUR-RAHMAN AZ-ZAHIR (1833-1896)

Anthony Reid

Despite his undoubted services to Atjeh, Habib Abdur-Rahman has never been a candidate for the honor of *pahlawan nasional* (national hero), the title given to leaders of the later stages of Atjeh's long war against the Dutch (1873-1912). Habib had submitted to the Dutch, and when the struggle was revived a few years later, he was branded as a traitor who had abandoned the anti-colonial cause too soon.

There is a more fundamental reason, however, why it would be inappropriate to regard Abdur-Rahman as a hero of nationalism. His whole life was a testimony to Islamic internationalism. Not only was he responsible for reviving the historical claim of Turkish suzerainty over Atjeh; he also made clear time and again that he acknowledged no loyalty to any particular country or people but only to the house of Islam, of which he was an aristocrat.

Abdur-Rahman was brought up among the emigrant Hadhramaut Arabs, who had settled in all the ports of the Indian Ocean during the nineteenth century. They were primarily a trading people, whose commercial and shipping links were tightest between the Red Sea, South India, and Singapore. From mid-century, however, European steamships began to destroy most of their shipping business,[1] probably including that of Habib's father. The Hadhramaut Arabs became small traders, retailers, religious teachers, and financiers. They married into the local aristocracy, with some of them becoming rulers and founding dynasties. Others became advisers and ministers.

In spite of their local ties, they retained their solidarity as an international community, comprising one important strand in the broad and multicolored belt of Islam, stretching from Constantinople to the Moluccas. Yet few reflected this mobility and freedom as well as Habib Abdur-Rahman. According to his own account Atjeh appeared to be the first country in which he began to establish real roots. Yet even his stay there was broken by two extensive foreign journeys and was punctuated by constant restless movement within the country. He needed to be honored. His visits were privileges bestowed on the local Muslim communities. If they failed to be appreciative, he invariably served notice that he would depart. His pride could not tolerate a setback or a slight to his honor.

His movements in the most difficult period of his life--the two years following his return from Turkey--are a good illustration of this trait. He never had any illusions that Atjeh could win a war with the Dutch. If the great powers proved unwilling to intervene on Atjeh's behalf, the only solution would be to seek an honorable peace with the Dutch. Arriving in Singapore in March 1874, he set

---

1. L.W.C. van den Berg, Le Hadhramaut et les Colonies Arabes dans L'Archipel Indien (Batavia: Government Printer, 1886), pp. 148-149.

about opening negotiations, both directly and by invoking the mediation of the British governor. When the Dutch refused to have anything to do with him and his lack of success began to be painfully apparent, his recourse was to leave in November 1874 for his former haunts on the Malabar coast. Returning to Penang in May 1875, he immediately faced the same dilemma. He again found his creditors and benefactors losing faith as he failed to obtain satisfactory terms from the Dutch. After much talk of returning to India, Mecca, or Constantinople, Abdur-Rahman went to Kedah as a royal guest at the end of November 1875. When he finally returned to Penang three months later, he was clearly at the end of his tether. Reluctant as he was to return to fight a losing war, it seemed the only remaining way to restore his credibility and his bargaining power.[2]

One of the elements in Habib's mobility was the frequency of his marriages. Besides the five mentioned in his biography, he contracted at least one more in Singapore in August 1874--to a Pahang Arab woman related to Sayyid Junied.[3] The daughters of *sayyid*[4] could not marry below their station, which created a considerable demand for spouses of the correct lineage. Most of Habib's marriages were undoubtedly of this type, making allies and hosts of one family of Hadhrami sayyid in the new town he was visiting. Only his marriage to Potjut in Atjeh appears certain to have been part of a different tradition, that of the Arab marrying into the ruling family of an Indonesian state to strengthen his bid for power.

None of these six wives appears ever to have travelled with him. While in Penang and Kedah his retinue included a concubine and two servants or slaves, of whom one was a Turkish Circassian.[5] Habib brought two young Circassians back with him from Constantinople,[6] and, according to Snouck Hurgronje, had earlier brought Hindu slaves to Atjeh from India.[7]

---

2. These moves are described more fully in Anthony Reid, The Contest for North Sumatra: Atjeh, the Netherlands, and Britain, 1858-1898 (Kuala Lumpur: Oxford University Press, 1969), pp. 158-180. Reference should be made to this work wherever no specific source is given below. The ultimate sources for most of Habib's moves in the Straits Settlements are the full reports of the Dutch representatives in Penang and Singapore, both of which are filed in Algemeen Rijksarchief (hereafter ARA) Consulaats-archief, Penang, 46 and 99-102.

3. Maier to Governor-General, August 23, 1874, ARA Consulaats-archief, Penang, 46.

4. The term sayyid is generally used for descendants of Muhammad through his grandson Husain. Habib is an honorific applied to sayyid in Malabar and elsewhere and apparently was introduced to Atjeh by Abdur-Rahman himself.

5. Laviño to Governor-General, May 27, 1875 and March 16, 1876, ARA Consulaats-archief, Penang, 101-102.

6. Heldewier to Gericke, December 20, 1874, ARA Kabinets-archief (hereafter Kol. Kab.), N^{16}, dossier 6044.

7. A.W.S. O'Sullivan (trans.), C. Snouck Hurgronje's The Achehnese (Leyden: E.J. Brill, 1906), I, 23n.

Unlike the majority of his compatriots, Habib believed in style. His dress, his horse, his entourage, his bearing, all had to show he was a man to be respected. For solemn occasions he wore a splendid Turkish sword of honor. To greet the Dutch *Djambi* mission of 1871 he wore the Turkish Medjidie decoration which had been bestowed on Sultan Ibrahim twenty years earlier. In May 1875 he created a spectacle in Penang by the magnificent costume and richly-attired horse with which he paid his first visit to Lieutenant Governor Anson in the government house on Penang Hill.[8] He believed, with apparent justification, that only by such a display of grandness could he ensure that Indonesians and colonial authorities alike would pay him the respect due someone of his station and office.

But this style could only be maintained by constant subventions from his supporters. Undoubtedly the wealth of Atjehnese pepper growers with their willingness to support religious causes was one of the attractions of Atjeh for Habib. In 1875 he told Lavino that he had received about $36,000 a year while in Atjeh.[9] Though this figure is undoubtedly exaggerated, it should be compared with the sums he claims to have gathered to build the Great Mosque--if indeed he made a clear distinction between the two causes. His considerable expenses as envoy in Constantinople were provided mainly by Teuku Paja, whom the Dutch knew to have sent at least two telegraphic credits to Constantinople totalling $6,000. In the Straits Settlements Abdur-Rahman was frequently forced to appeal to the leading Arab merchants or to T. Muda Njak Malim of Simpang Ulim for further support for his diplomatic efforts.

It is disappointing, but scarcely surprising, to find that, when the righteous cause of promoting Atjeh was abandoned as hopeless, the need for money remained. In 1875 Abdur-Rahman asked the Dutch for a reward of $50,000, or $500 a month for life, if he successfully negotiated a Dutch-Atjeh peace. This was refused. After leading the war effort for a time he successfully demanded twice the amount-- $1,000 per month for life. On this princely pension he lived extravagantly at Mecca. He maintained three houses and a well-provided harem there, and strove to maintain his standing by giving frequent lavish feasts.[10]

Abdur-Rahman's two essential assets were the sacredness of his descent from the Prophet and his religious learning. Sayyid were honored throughout the Muslim world but nowhere more than in Atjeh where a position of respect and comfort was assured even the most unimpressive members of the sacred lineage. The fact that Abdur-Rahman also had a good knowledge of Muslim law immediately established him as a religious leader. During his early years in Atjeh he became

---

8. Lavino to Governor-General, May 27, 1875, ARA Consulaats-archief, Penang, 101.

9. Lavino to Governor-General, June 24, 1875, ARA Consulaats-archief, Penang, 101. Throughout this introduction and the translation which follows, the currency referred to is the Mexican silver dollar, valued in this period at 4s. 3d. sterling.

10. De Vicq (Jidda) to Karnebeek, November 12, 1886, ARA Kol. Kab. C^{13}, dossier 6169.

particularly influential as an upholder of a relatively strict line opposing such sins against Islam as gambling, opium smoking, and pederasty. Most Atjehnese were ready to admit the scandalousness of these common practices and to support, in principle, movements of reform and religious revival as long as they were pursued with the high degree of common sense and flexibility which Habib displayed.

As Snouck Hurgronje and James Siegel have both pointed out,[11] Habib Abdur-Rahman formed part of a recurring pattern of religious reformers who were able to bring direction to the divided Atjehnese. Even for the strong Sultan Ibrahim, traditional alignments and suspicions among the *ulèëbalang* (district chief) placed severe limits on the ability of the sovereign to lead his people effectively. After 1870 the Sultanate was a minimal force. But a religious leader could appeal on the basis of a higher loyalty, by portraying the work to be done as a religious duty rather than a secular command. Habib's ability to exhort the Atjehnese to common effort in this way "was nothing short of prodigious."[12] He raised enormous sums for mosque construction and other public works, for his elaborate diplomatic ventures, and for the war. He settled feuds which had endured for decades and he brought a larger force of Atjehnese into the field against the Dutch than any of the military leaders after 1878.

Even though traditional respect for his birth and his learning were among Habib's greatest assets, he himself was a man of the modern world. When the Sultan of Serdang consulted him about the credentials of a certain sayyid, Abdur-Rahman's immediate response was an offer to telegraph Mecca.[13] He appeared to be as much at home with European statesmen as with Atjehnese *ulama* (Islamic teachers and scholars).

Nothing could be further from the truth than van den Berg's claim[14] that most Europeans who met him gained the impression of "un énorme fanfaron." Time and again skeptical Dutch and British officials, to say nothing of highly-placed Turks,[15] were forced

---

11. Snouck Hurgronje, The Achehnese, I, pp. 158-164; James Siegel, The Rope of God (Berkeley: University of California Press, 1969), pp. 49-51 and 60-67.

12. Snouck Hurgronje, The Achehnese, I, p. 164.

13. Lavino to Assistant Resident of Deli, August 6, 1875, and reply August 19, 1875, ARA Consulaats-archief, Penang, 101.

14. L.W.C. van den Berg, Le Hadhramaut, p. 200.

15. A grudging acknowledgement by the Russian Ambassador Ignatiev, the strongest opponent of Habib's cause in Turkey, is indicative of the way in which the Atjehnese envoy impressed Turkish leaders: "They say he is of Arab origin and very intelligent. He possesses, moreover, an education which strikes the Turkish ministers quite as much as his diplomatic cast of mind." A. Guber, G. Levinson, and V. Mazaev, eds., Politika Kapitalicheskikh Derzhav i Natsional'no-Osvoboditel'noe Dvizhenie v Iugo-Vostochnoi Azii, (1870-1917). Dokumenty i Materialy (Moscow: The Science Publishing House, 1965), I, p. 53.

after meeting him to acknowledge his acute intelligence, political insight, and understanding of the Western world.

Habib's greatest success was in Constantinople, where he was lionized by the pan-Islamic press and created real concern in European capitals that Turkey would intervene forcefully in the war. It is significant, however, that his strongest supporters in Turkey were not the courtiers seeking to flatter the Sultan's vanity but liberal reformers like Midhat Pasha who were to overthrow Abdul Aziz in favor of a parliamentary constitution three years later. Despite the consistent pragmatism with which he had greeted Western advances before 1873, Abdur-Rahman had to overcome a reputation in Dutch circles as a fanatic troublemaker after his Constantinople mission. Dutch consuls who met him successively in Jidda, Singapore, and Penang were nevertheless all won over by him. Maier in Singapore and Lavino in Penang, in particular, became converts to his moderate peace plans once they had given him a hearing.

Similarly, Habib was able to persuade one British official after another that British mediation was the only way to peace in Atjeh. After meeting him, successive Governors of the Straits Settlements, Sir Andrew Clarke (1873-1875) and Sir William Jervois (1875-1877), alarmed the Dutch with their confident insistence that Atjeh was prepared for peace only on the basis of British guarantees. In the case of Jervois, at least, there is little doubt that his meeting with Abdur-Rahman in Penang on June 23, 1875 changed his position fundamentally on the Atjeh question. Anson, the Lieutenant Governor of Penang, was particularly anxious to assist Habib's efforts to bring about a peaceful settlement, even though he had not been notably sympathetic to Atjeh before the envoy's arrival.

Habib's success with both Atjehnese and Westerners was in large measure due to the direct and forceful methods he frequently used, in contrast to the traditional politeness of Indonesian court circles. Snouck Hurgronje relates[16] that if Atjehnese displeased him by arriving very late for a meeting or addressing him in an improper fashion, "he would smite, kick, or even spit upon them by way of correction." He made use of the favorite Atjehnese *mupakat* (public discussion), whereby "his weaker opponents are terrorized, while the stronger are flattered, and finally many are won over and even persuaded that they themselves were the originators of the proposed plan."[17] While the forceful, aggressive style which Habib adopted at such meetings would have been highly dangerous for most Atjehnese, in a foreigner as revered as Habib it was a sign of strength and authority.

To Europeans likewise he spoke forcefully and directly, in a manner which always commanded respect. His reply to Kraijenhoff's[18] mission of "friendship" in 1871, when Habib was at the height of

---

16. Snouck Hurgronje, The Achehnese, I, p. 163.

17. Ibid., p. 76.

18. Controleur Kraijenhoff represented the Governor of Sumatra's West Coast, through whom relations between Atjeh and Batavia were to be conducted according to the 1857 Treaty. He came on successive Dutch missions to Atjeh in September 1871, May 1872, and October 1872.

his power in Atjeh, is a fair example:[19]

> Atjeh lives in friendship with England, France, Turkey, and other countries, because it is not injured by these powers. On the other hand, Holland, which now wanted to tighten the bonds of friendship, had not refrained from periodically seizing states from the Atjehnese kingdom, as had happened only recently. What sort of friendship was that! He knew only one sort, namely:
> > Salah di larang,
> > Benar di ikut,
> > Di undju lepaskan,
> > Kasu karau di talong.[20]
>
> If Holland sincerely meant well, she should give back what she had taken, namely Singkel, Baros, Sibolga, and Nias, with the neighboring islands, as well as the petty states of the East Coast, while she must support the Sultan against the princes on those borders who wish to break away.

A later quotation, recorded by Anson's secretary in 1875,[21] shows Habib's style at a much more desperate moment for both himself and Atjeh, when he was struggling to persuade the Dutch, through Lavino, to accept his ultimate concession to them.

> The Syed said he had now come to state for the last time what he was ready to do, and if the Dutch would not trust him he would then leave Penang. He could easily get to Achin [the coast of Achin was blockaded by eleven Dutch men-of-war], and if the Dutch Government would not have anything to do with him, he could go to Achin, and bid them fight on. The war could be continued for three years more. He knew in the end the Achinese would be beaten, but what would the Dutch get? a desert, all the pepper destroyed, and the country desolate. If peace were brought about, 1000 Dutch soldiers would suffice to hold Achin, and two or three hundred the other places. He desired peace more than any one, and prayed that there might be an end to the slaughter. He would prefer to see the country under the Dutch, as he would profit greatly by it. The Dutch would make roads and improve the country. In every way it was to his interest to bring about a settlement. He was not an Achinese. What was Achin to him? If he brought about a settlement would not he be a great man.

---

19. As summarized in E. S. de Klerck, *De Atjeh-oorlog* (The Hague: Martinus Nijhoff, 1912), p. 347.

20. The first two lines of the quatrain might be translated "falsehood is forbidden; truth is upheld." The following two lines appear to have been wrongly copied.

21. A. E. H. Anson, *About Others and Myself, 1745 to 1920* (London: John Murray, 1920), pp. 326-328.

The Dutch would highly honor him, and he would get stars and medals. If he wished he could go to Europe and entirely give up Achin. He was well known to distinguished statesmen. It was clear what his interests were, and yet the Dutch would not trust him.

As for his intentions, he had shown on several occasions that he intended well towards the Dutch, and was anxious to bring about peace. The first occasion was when General Kaupmann,[22] just before the war began, consulted with him. He then fully explained his views and advised the General the best way to bring about terms. Instead of listening to him, they had taken up Panglima Tibang, his enemy, a man of no position; and then this war had begun. He had told the General how they should proceed: at first offering favourable conditions, and by degrees establishing their supremacy as the English have always done in India. In that way they could have got Achin without any bloodshed. He had proposed the terms for a treaty, but the Dutch, instead of following his advice, or trusting him, had at once made war, thinking to conquer the place directly. Then he had gone to Constantinople to try to get the Turkish Government to intervene to stop the war, but they would not. He had seen the Dutch Consul at Jedda, and again he had shown to him how anxious he was to bring about terms. Failing at Constantinople, he had returned to Singapore, and from there had addressed the Governor-General, so the Dutch had plenty of opportunity of knowing his good intentions. It was true he had encouraged the Achinese to fight when the war had once begun, and since then, of course, he had assisted them, but he was none the less anxious for peace and an end of the slaughter.

What he now proposed was this: he would go on board a Dutch man-of-war, and not land at all. They would anchor off Kloewang, and he would send for the leader of the Achinese. Then in the presence of a number of Dutch officers and surrounded by a guard, he would, in Malay, openly give advice to the chiefs. In the first place, after explaining the situation, he would get them by word of mouth to engage to agree to terms. To make this more binding, he would then get them to agree in writing and lastly would have them solemnly to swear on the Koran. After that they could not go back, and terms could be arranged. Meanwhile there would be a suspension of hostilities. This was what he would do. He was the key by which the Dutch could alone enter Achin. If they threw away the key they could not get into the box without smashing it. They had thrown away the key, and had battered the box with a crowbar. It had made a great noise, but the box was not broken by it. The key was there, and they would not try it.

---

22. Colonel Koopman, of the 1871 Djambi mission.

About the Text

This autobiography is unfortunately only second hand. It was written by Captain I. D. I. van der Hegge Spies, the commander of the Dutch warship *Curacao*, which carried Abdur-Rahman and his party from Atjeh to Jidda. During the voyage, lasting from November 24, 1878 to January 28, 1879, the captain appears to have taken down the story of Habib's life as it was told to him. Although the manuscript he left is in third-person Dutch, it reads as though very little altered from notes taken directly from Habib. A copy of the manuscript of van der Hegge Spies was made available to me by James Siegel, to whom I am extremely grateful. The original is in the Instituut voor de Tropen, Amsterdam.

In 1880 this manuscript was used as the basis for an article in *De Indische Gids*.[23] The author, Alexander, in fact made only minor rewording from the manuscript, most of which takes the meaning still further from what Habib appears to have intended. I have commented in footnotes on the very few points at which Alexander added something to the manuscript, possibly as a result of further information from van der Hegge Spies.

THE TEXT IN TRANSLATION

Born in Hadhramaut (Temir) in the year 1249 [1833-1834],[1] Habib went to Malabar at the age of two with his father, Muhammad Az-Zahir, who remarried there.[2] Habid had no brothers or sisters. At the age of five (1837) his father sent him to Egypt to learn reading and writing, and at the same time to study the Koran. His education was later continued in Mecca.

In 1842 he returned to Malabar; next he was sent to Calicut to study further there. When, at the age of sixteen (1848), he had sufficient learning and was at home with the Koran, his father let him travel with one of his ships called the *Yeddul Manan*, not as master but rather as supercargo, principally to learn about trade.

---

23. Alexander, "Korte Levensschets van den Arabier Habib Abdoe 'Rahman Alzahir, naar zijne eigen opgaven saamgesteld," *De Indische Gids*, 2, Part II (1880), pp. 1008-1020.

1. Spies gives the Muslim year 1249 and the Christian year 1832, which do not correspond. I have assumed it is the Muslim date which derives from Habib and have omitted what I take to be Spies' miscalculation. The Christian years mentioned in the following two paragraphs appear to be derived by Spies from his original miscalculation. I cannot locate Temir. Anson (*About Others and Myself*, p. 328) claims that Abdur-Rahman was born "in the British territory of Aden."

2. Alexander ("Korte Levensschets," p. 1009) adds that Habib's mother died shortly after his birth.

After having made various voyages with this ship, visiting the coasts of India, Ceylon, and Arabia, Habib came to Mocha. At that time a daughter of the deceased ruler was living there, whose possessions had been taken by others after the death of her father. Habib, although not knowing her personally, took her cause to heart, spoke and dealt in her interest, and succeeded in getting these possessions returned to the girl. Out of gratitude she asked him to marry her, having previously rejected various other claimants to her hand. Later, when Habib was staying in Atjeh, he received news of her death.

After having lived at Mocha for a year and a half, he went to Mecca; from there to Constantinople; and then back to Malabar. After marrying again in Malabar and staying there some months, he went to Calicut, where he also took a wife by whom he had a daughter named Sjarifa Fatima, who is still alive.

After having lived in Calicut for a couple of years he moved to Hyderabad, where the Hindu religion was professed.[3] As the ruler of this region had no children, although he greatly desired them, Habib gave him a potion with the result that he saw his desire for children fulfilled. Habib was now able to persuade the ruler to go over to Islam, while the ruler, out of gratitude, appointed him Djamidar, or commander of 1,000 soldiers.

After having filled this position for eleven months he asked to be released and proceeded to Calcutta. There he appears to have established himself as a goldsmith, or rather as a worker in gold, a gilder, while at the same time he purified the raw gold or ore which came to the market. Whatever the real basis of this occupation was, it appears to have yielded great profits. Habib related that he earned $100 a day at it, while he lived in a villa called Golkat which cost $600 a month in rent.

After staying there for some years, earning and putting away a lot of money, the lure of travel overcame him, and particularly the desire to see Europe. On this journey he visited Italy, Germany, and France, and then returned to Mecca via Constantinople.[4] Next he travelled through British India and visited Bombay, where he stayed for three months; Hyderabad, where he spent seven months; and Calicut, where he remained only three months.

Then he went to Singapore, where he stayed eleven months and got to know the Maharadja of Johor, whose service he entered for a salary of $2,000 a year. Habib says of Johor that there was much to

---

3. This probably refers to Hyderabad in the Deccan, which had a thriving Hadhramaut colony. Its ruler, the Nizam, had for over a century been a firmly Muslim as his counterpart in the other Hyderabad (Sind). Habib may have served in one of the Hindu samasthans, semi-autonomous princely domains tributary to the Nizam, or with one of the Hindu or Shi'ite noble families.

4. Alexander ("Korte Levensschets," p. 1010) adds that Habib was received with great honor in Constantinople because of his learning and birth, and then digresses to dwell upon Habib's broadmindedness which extended to drinking wine.

be done at the time of his arrival. Many buildings and roads needed to be constructed, and the internal government also needed to be organized; the responsibility for all this belonged to Habib.[5]

After having been there about one and a half years, he asked the Maharadja for his release and obtained it with a written testimony of satisfaction over the services he had performed. Thereupon he proceeded to Atjeh. On his way there he stopped at Pulau Penang where he stayed about a month, going from there to Pidië as a passenger on a schooner belonging to Teuku Main of Ajer Labu [Iĕ Labeuĕ] and on to Atjeh in a sampan.

On arrival there he remained for three days in Kampung Djawa, and then moved to the house of Habib Mohammad Mahaldi in Kampung Langsepong. This took place in Djumadil Awal 1281[6] [October 1864]. The above person brought him to the Sultan, Ibrahim Mansur Shah, to whom he showed the testimony of the Maharadja of Johor. He was well received by the Sultan on the strength of this. Here, too, Habib married again. Meanwhile the Sultan appointed him head of the Great Mosque.[7]

At this time in Atjeh there was great confusion in the government and much discord among the chiefs, while the authority of the

---

5. Habib arrived soon after the accession to the Johor throne of Abu Bakar (1862-1895), a modernizing ruler who introduced a number of educated Singapore Malays into the Johor administration. Early in his reign Abu Bakar also brought some prominent Singapore Arabs into key positions in the state. Some public works did take place at Johor Baru during these years (1862-1864), but Habib's claim to control "internal government" is certainly exaggerated. C.H.H. Wake, "Nineteenth Century Johor: Ruler and Realm in Transition" (Ph.D. thesis, Australian National University, 1966), pp. 241-247, and additional information kindly supplied by Dr. Wake.

6. The Spies text gives the Muslim year 1261 (which Alexander renders 1221) and the Christian year 1864. Since the former cannot be correct, I assume it is a slip of the pen for 1281. An anonymous Dutch source states the less likely possibility that Habib arrived in Atjeh from Malabar about 1283H (1866). "Aanteekeningen over Atjehneesche aangelengenheden," Tijdschrift voor Nederlandsch-Indië, nieuwe serie, No. 3, II (1874), p. 405. This source is primarily based on an undated memorandum on Abdur-Rahman in ARA Kol. Kab. E[24], dossier 6052. Langespong was about a mile upriver from the dalam, on the left bank in the territory of Panglima Meuseugit Raja. The wife Habib took here was an Arab, presumably a relation of Mahaldi, and she continued to live in Langespong. "Aanteekeningen," p. 409.

7. This position was probably a purely religious office such as the imam of the mosque and should not be confused with the hereditary Atjehnese offices of Panglima Meuseugit Raja or Kali Malik'ul Adil, both of which had become secular ulèëbalangships with jurisdiction in the neighborhood of the palace and Great Mosque, and had lost their original religious significance. Snouck Hurgronje, The Achehnese, I, p. 121.

Sultan was greatly weakened. The Sultan consulted Habib frequently, as a result of which the state of affairs improved very much and more order was introduced to the government.

The Sultan, already having the intention to bring the succession back into the legitimate line after his death, wished to have Tuanku Mohamud [Mahmud], son of the deceased Sultan Suleiman Iskandar, near him in the Kraton. Mahmud was then in the hands of Teuku Muda Ba'et in Lamtengah.[8] On a certain day the Sultan consulted Habib about how he might bring this about. Habib requested, and immediately received from the Sultan, authority to deal with this matter as circumstances demanded. The Sultan also put 2,000 men at his disposal. With these he went straight to the III Mukim Tjot Putu and raised still more men and chiefs there. His force having grown to 12,000 men, he proceeded to Kampung Lamtengah. Close to the Kampung, on the near side of the river he called a halt and sent an envoy named Sjeich Abdul Rachman to the house of Teuku Muda Ba'et to try to bring Tuanku Mahmud to him.

On arrival the envoy found that Teuku Muda Ba'et was not at home, and it was no trouble for him to get Tuanku Mahmud to flee with him to Habib. Thereupon Habib went via Tjot Putu to Pagar Ajer, whence he sent a messenger to the Sultan in Kota Radja to inform him of the satisfactory outcome of the mission. The Sultan had several uleëbalang collect Tuanku Mahmud and from then onwards kept him close at hand.

Teuku Muda Ba'et, who was incensed that Tuanku Mahmud had been brought to Kota Radja refused to follow the commands of the Sultan as did various chiefs and uleëbalang of the three Sagi.[9] Once again Habib requested the Sultan to give him authority to bring them to obedience. Having obtained this, he campaigned through the three Sagi with an evergrowing force, persuading the recalcitrant chiefs to follow him to Kota Dalam (Kraton)[10] partly by force and partly

---

8. Both by tradition and in terms of the men he could command, the uleëbalang of the VII Mukim, Ba'et was second only to Panglima Polem in the Sagi of the XXII Mukim, and one of the most powerful men in Atjeh. In the major succession dispute of 1850-1857 between the young heir Suleiman and his uncle and erstwhile guardian Ibrahim (Mansur), Teuku Muda Ba'et took the side of Suleiman. This alliance was cemented by Suleiman's marrying Ba'et's sister, who was then still a child. Suleiman never succeeded, however, in recovering his capital, and the conflict ended with his death in 1857. Ba'et remained unreconciled to the Sultan and continued to protect Suleiman's wife and infant son Mahmud, born about 1854. K.F.H. Van Langen, "De Inrichting van het Atjehsche Staatsbestuur onder het Sultanaat," Bijdragen tot de Taal-, Land- en Volkenkunde, 34 (1888), pp. 397-398; Reid, Contest, pp. 16 and 80.

9. The three Sagi (corners) into which all of Atjeh Besar outside the capital and environs was divided. They were known by the conventionalized number of Mukim they once held, i.e., XXV Mukim (west of Atjeh river), XXVI Mukim (east of Atjeh river), XXII Mukim (upriver).

10. Atjehnese called the royal enclosure the dalam, whereas the Dutch wrongly referred to it as the kraton, the term used on Java.

by means of his fluency. He then proceeded to Lamtengah, took Teuku Muda Ba'et captive, and thereupon marched to the territory of Teuku Nanta,[11] the only uleëbalang who had still refused to go with Habib to the Sultan. Becoming fearful, this chief then joined the others who were coming to offer their submission to the Sultan, whereupon Habib returned to Kota Dalam.

In eight days time Habib had through cunning and force brought all uleëbalang both to the Sultan's presence and to obedience to their ruler. As a reward for services rendered, Habib was appointed by the Sultan head of religion[12] and of the Great Mosque, as well as chief of Tjot Putu in the III Mukim.[13]

In order to strengthen his position in Atjeh, Habib, who was a foreigner, now contemplated establishing kinship ties with an influential chief through marriage. As Teuku Muda Ba'et was now with the

---

    Kota Dalam and Kota Radja were expressions sometimes used by Atjehnese to refer to their capital, although Banda Atjeh Daru's-Salam was historically a more correct name. The Dutch adopted the usage Kota Radja.

11. Teuku Nanta Setia succeeded about 1848 in wresting control of VI Mukim near the capital which had formerly been part of the domain of Teuku Nek of Meura'sa. These two families remained bitter rivals thereafter. In the succession dispute of 1850-1857, Nek sided with Ibrahim while Nanta provided Suleiman with his principal base. Van Langen, "De Inrichting," pp. 406-408; Snouck Hurgronje, The Achehnese, pp. 126-127.

12. Snouck Hurgronje (The Achehnese, I, pp. 161-163) states that Habib was put in charge of a new court, the balè meuhakamah, created to enable him to try all cases according to Islamic law. Although such courts appear to have been instituted on earlier occasions in Atjeh's history, their religious significance had seldom outlasted the ruler concerned, and most disputes were settled by uleëbalang according to adat. Because of his consummate political skill as well as his religious prestige, Habib was able to use his office to settle a wide range of disputes and to attack such acknowledged abuses as opium and gambling. Ali Bahanan, who reported to the Dutch on a visit to Atjeh in 1867, noted that Abdur-Rahman had already made powerful enemies in his new position because of the stiff fines he imposed and his levies for mosque construction, not to mention the other ulama resentful of this newcomer. "Aanteekeningen" (pp. 405-406) suggests that the Sultan accepted Habib's offer to resign sometime in 1866-1867.

13. The III Mukim Keureukon was a territory on the border between the Sagi of the XXVI and XXII Mukim, though belonging directly to the Sultan rather than to either Sagi. Snouck Hurgronje,(The Achehnese, I, p. 124) refers to a famous ulama in Tjot Putu in a slightly earlier period, and it may be that Habib took over the déah (religious school) which this teacher had built. The III Mukim Keureukon and parts of the adjoining XXVI Mukim remained the basis of Habib's most direct support in Atjeh Besar, although he was obliged to march against Tjot Putu in late 1871, when one of Tuanku Husein's supporters settled there. "Aanteekeningen," p. 411.

Sultan in Kota Radja, after Habib's armed expedition described above, Habib asked and obtained from him, for a payment of $400, his sister Potjut as a wife. By this marriage Habib became a considerable person within the Atjehnese state, for Potjut was not only the sister of one of the foremost chiefs but at the same time the widow of Sultan Suleiman Iskandar.

However, after returning to his own domain, Teuku Muda Ba'et refused to allow Potjut to go to Tjot Putu. At first he promised to let Habib have her after three months but in the end declared that Habib would not get her except by force. Habib, therefore, decided to go to Tjot Bada with a great force and compelled Teuku Muda Ba'et to let him have Potjut, whom he now brought to Tjot Putu. From this point dates the friendship between Habib and Teuku Muda Ba'et which has continued until today.

The Sultan was exceedingly surprised at this war Habib had carried on with results so favorable to himself, while Habib's enemies, among whom Teuku Kali[14] was foremost, slandered him and attempted to make him suspect in the eyes of the Sultan. They said that Habib only waged war in order to have ever more men at his command and intended to make war on the Sultan himself. At this time, however, the Sultan placed no trust in these accusations.

On the contrary, Habib's proposal to build another large mosque was accepted by the Sultan, who gave him authority to requisition the various uleëbalang and other chiefs to deliver the necessary wood, which was collected and sent to Penajung by Habib. Having accumulated a sufficient stock of timber there, Habib gave a great feast in which almost the whole population of Atjeh Besar, chiefs and commoners, took part. Thereafter a start was made on building the *missigit*,[15]

14. His full title was Teuku Kali Malikon Adé, from the Arabic Kadhi Maliku'l adil, meaning "judge of the righteous king." Although in the seventeenth century the official with this title appears to have administered both Islamic and adat law, his hereditary successors became entirely secularized, and more learned men were appointed to judge religious questions. In the nineteenth century the Kali Malikon Adé managed to acquire a fief of twelve villages near the capital, and thus became in almost every respect an uleëbalang, as symbolized by his use of the title Teuku. The last title holder, Teuku Kali Njak Tjut (d. 1885) could neither read nor write, yet he was still a very important adviser to the ruler and presided over a council of "court uleëbalang" who judged some secular questions. Van Langen, "De Inrichting," pp. 42-43; Snouck Hurgronje, The Achehnese, I, pp. 97-101.

15. Atjehnese meuseugit (cf. Arabic, Masdjid), mosque. The mosque in question was the meuseugit raja Beit ur-Rahman, the great mosque of the capital, said to have been founded by Sultan Iskandar Muda (1607-1637). It was burned down in the reign of Nuru'l Alam (1675-1678) and was in very bad repair again in Habib's time. The mosque reconstructed by Habib was destroyed by the Dutch in 1873, but a painting purportedly of it, as recollected by Tgk. Sjeich Ibrahim (b. Sjeich Maraban), now hangs in the balai of the Governor of Atjeh. Its inscription states that it was built on Habib's initiative in 1867, at a cost of $13,000. In reality, however, the work does not appear to have been complete until 1870.

for which $3,000 was given by the Sultan himself.

Habib went in person to visit the various petty states on the West Coast of Atjeh to collect money. He succeeded in getting $33,000 and reported this success to the Sultan.

Meanwhile, each of Habib's absences was used to slander him with the Sultan. During his stay on the West Coast, for example, it was said that he had gone there to buy weapons, etc. Although the Sultan initially paid no attention to these suggestions, they were repeated so often that he finally began to waver in his good opinion of Habib--perhaps it could be true that this foreigner was a bad man. Habib's enemies, jealous of his wealth, also grew in number. In this way his position in Atjeh became untenable.

He successfully asked for his dismissal and left from Pulau Penang for Mecca,[16] where he received letters of recommendation from: (1) the Great Sherif Abdullah Basjah;[17] (2) the Sherif of Jidda, Mohamar Basja;[18] and (3) his former teacher Habib Tadlak.

---

16. According to "Aanteekeningen," pp. 406-408, Abdur-Rahman had attempted to leave for Jidda when he first fell into the Sultan's disfavor, but found the port barred to him. He therefore went to Keureukon for about six months, before returning to the capital where he was seized by Teuku Kali. He was saved from execution by the Sultan, who made arrangements for him to leave Atjeh. Two days after embarking for Jidda, however, he was taken off the vessel in the roads by people from Keureukon. For two years more, the "Aanteekeningen" asserts, Habib agitated against the Sultan from Keureukon. He departed for Jidda via Simpang Ulim only when it became clear that Panglima Polem would not support a march against the dalam, probably in 1868.

17. Grand Sharif Abdullah Pasha (1858-1877) of the Devi or Abadila family, which was relatively open to western ideas. Abdullah appears to have been unusually interested in the Djawah, as Indonesians were known in Mecca, especially for the support they might give to his anti-Turkish maneuvers. Zohrab (Jidda) to the Foreign Office, London, March 17, 1880 and February 8, 1881, FO 78/3130 and 3314 respectively; Snouck Hurgronje, Mekka (The Hague: Martinus Nijhoff, 1888), I, pp. 168-173; G. de Gaury, Rulers of Mecca (London: Harrap, 1951), pp. 249-253. According to Turkish government sources, Habib was "blood relation" of Sharif Abdullah and always visited him when in Mecca. Heldewier to Gericke, May 25, 1874, Buitenlandse Zaken (hereafter B.Z.), dossier Atjeh.

18. Mouhamar Pasha was the Turkish wali (Governor General) of the Hejaz, resident in Jidda. He exercised limited powers in this period. Late in 1868, the Porte received a petition addressed to Mouhamar Pasha and signed by 65 Atjehnese "notables," which declared that the Atjehnese considered themselves Turkish subjects and begged for military protection against the Dutch. It appears likely that this petition was inspired by Habib's visit to the Hejaz. The signatories may have been his leading supporters in Atjeh. Translations of the petition are in E.S. de Klerck, De Atjeh-oorlog, pp. 461-462, and Anthony Reid, "Indonesian Diplomacy: A Documentary Study of Atjehnese Foreign Policy in the Reign of Sultan Mahmud, 1870-1874," Journal of the Royal Asiatic Society, Malayan Branch, 42, No. 2 (1969), pp. 75-76.

With these letters of recommendation, Habib boarded a sailing vessel and departed for Atjeh directly.

After anchoring in the Atjeh roadstead, he informed the Sultan of his return by letter, adding that the only reason he had come was to get his wife Potjut and that he would return thereafter to Mecca. At this time the Sultan sent two envoys on board to talk to Habib. Habib repeated to them what he had written to the Sultan, but he also gave them the three letters of recommendation so that the Sultan could examine them. As soon as the Sultan realized the contents of these three letters, he sent his envoys back on board with instructions to invite Habib to come to the Kraton. The Sultan personally stood on the beach to await him and brought him to the Kraton out of fear that Habib's many enemies would kill him.

The Sultan gave him back his former positions as head of religion and of the Great Mosque and chief of Tjot Putu. Habib continued to grow in the favor of the Sultan and was eventually appointed his *Wazir* (minister). In this role Habib succeeded in bringing more peace and order to Atjeh, while the Sultan's revenues increased because Habib was energetic in raising the *hasil* (tax). The ulèëbalang, on the other hand, became increasingly hostile toward Habib. They could no longer get to see the Sultan because he always referred them to Habib.

Meanwhile, Habib proposed to the Sultan that he allow the Dutch into Atjeh to trade and thereby establish a good relationship with them. Habib believed such relations were in the interests of the Atjehnese kingdom. Before taking a decision, the Sultan wanted to know the opinions of some leading chiefs, namely Teuku Kali, Teuku Imam Longbata, and Teuku Nek Mara'sa.[19]

In the discussions the Sultan had with chiefs in Habib's presence about this proposal, they fully agreed with Habib, and it was concluded that Habib would go to Batavia with Teuku Kali and Teuku Nek Mara'sa as envoys from the Sultan to the Governor-General of Netherlands India. The steamship *Patty*, and Captain Roura[20] were to be hired for this purpose. After the chiefs left the Kraton, however, they openly said that Habib intended to sell Atjeh to the Dutch.

While these discussions and deliberations were taking place, His [Netherlands'] Majesty's steamship *Djambi* arrived at Atjeh roads, bringing a letter from the Governor-General of Netherlands India and some presents. Habib was deputed to go to the *Djambi* with Teuku Kali

---

19. As ulèëbalang of territories close to the capital, T. Imam Longbata (Luĕng Bata) and T. Nek Mara'sa and T. Káli Malikon Adé were frequently consulted "court ulèëbalang." Van Langen, ("De Inrichting," p. 421) names these three and two others as members of a sort of judicial council for Sultan Ibrahim.

20. Captain Edouard Roura, of Marseilles, had been trading in pepper between Penang and the West Coast of Atjeh since the 1850's. He was particularly friendly with Abdur-Rahman, who corresponded with him and used his ship the Patty to travel to Penang in 1872.

and Teuku Nek Mara'sa.[21] When he left the shore, and also later when he left the *Djambi*, he was given a thirteen-gun salute.

The Commander of the *Djambi* spoke to Habib in detail about his mission, with the result that the two other envoys muttered that Habib was busy selling Atjeh. When later the Commander came ashore at Kota Dalam he held discussions with Panglima Tibang (Habib's enemy).[22] On hearing this, Habib was very disturbed.

After the *Djambi's* departure the following events occurred. Tuanku Zainal Abidin,[23] son of Sultan Ibrahim Mansursjah, learning that his father intended to designate Tuanku Mahmud as his successor, resolved to murder his father. In fact, he tried to do so by firing at his father with a pistol but did not hit him. This conflict between the Sultan and his son was patched up by Habib.

Shortly thereafter Tuanku Zainal Abidin died of a short-lived but serious illness. Sultan Ibrahim followed his son soon after.[24] Before his death, however, he made a written will in which Tuanku Mahmud was designated his successor and Habib Abdur-Rahman was named regent during his minority.

Meanwhile there was disagreement among the ulèëbalang about the succession. While some wanted Tuanku Mahmud as Sultan, there was another party which wanted to see Tuanku Husein,[25] the son of

---

21. Habib's chronology is confused here. The Djambi was in Atjeh roads during September 19-30, 1871, after the death of Sultan Ibrahim. The Djambi carried a letter from the Governor of Sumatra's West Coast, not from the Governor-General. The basic task of Controleur Kraijenhoff, who led the Dutch mission, was to establish whether Dutch objectives in Atjeh might be obtained peacefully. The mission achieved nothing initially, being constantly put off by the Shahbandar, Panglima Tibang, until Habib arrived from a six-month sojourn on the West Coast on September 24. Two days later a five-man Atjehnese delegation was received by the Djambi with thirteen guns. It was composed of Habib and Teuku Kali as the joint regents of Atjeh, and three "court ulèëbalang"-- T. Aga Imam, T. Luëng Bata, and T. Meura'sa. De Klerck, De Atjeh-oorlog, pp. 344-349.

22. Panglima Muhammad Tibang had come to Atjeh as a child performer from South India, but stayed and became a Muslim. He became a confidant of Sultan Ibrahim, who appointed him Shahbandar (port-officer), a post he continued to hold under Mahmud. Dutch accounts of the Djambi visit, however, emphasize how completely Habib dominated the negotiations and how competently he put the Atjehnese case. Only later did the Dutch take Tibang more seriously.

23. Sultan Ibrahim had two sons: Pangeran Hussein, who died in 1869, and Tuanku Zainal Abidin, who died in 1870. Tuanku Mohammad Daud, who succeeded to the throne as a minor in 1874, was the son of Zainal Abidin.

24. Sultan Ibrahim died in 1870. His tomb within the dalam is undated.

25. Tuanku Husein was the second son of Tuanku Abas, who in turn was the younger brother of Sultan Ibrahim and the son of Sultan Jauhar al-Alam (1795-1823). Because of the death of both Ibrahim's sons,

Tuanku Abas and grandson of Sultan Mohamadshah, appointed successor to the dead Sultan Ibrahim. In the meantime Habib carried on the government during the minority of Tuanku Mahmud (one year) as guardian of the minor and regent of the state.

At the end of this year Tuanku Mahmud was elevated to the position of Sultan[26] with the forceful help of Panglima Polem,[27] who came to Kota Dalam personally for that reason. Habib governed the kingdom as Grand Vezir[28] for and in the name of the Sultan.

After another year, when he judged the authority of the new Sultan sufficiently established, Habib made a voyage to the West Coast states with an authorization or *tjap* (seal) of the Sultan to levy the hasil. He succeeded in collecting a sum of $12,000 hasil plus $9,000 which was provided by the people for the expenses of the missigit.

Meanwhile the chiefs and people of the XXVI Mukim were still disinclined to follow the commands of Sultan Mahmud. They were encouraged in this behavior by Panglima Tibang, who bore a great hatred for Habib since, having formerly been the adviser of the late Sultan Ibrahim, he had lost all his influence on the ruler after Habib's arrival. The Panglima even tried to do him to death with poison.

On his return from the West Coast, Habib made use of the money he had raised there to force the XXVI Mukim into obedience to the Sultan by force of arms. He succeeded in this after marching on Tjadé with a large army.[29]

Meanwhile Panglima Tibang continued to make trouble within the Atjehnese polity and tried to ingratiate himself with Sultan Mahmud. To this end he made particular use of Habib's absence when he went yet again to the West Coast.

---

and the youth of Suleiman's son Mahmud, the sons of Abas were the closest adult males in the line of succession. The older son, Tuanku Abdul Medjid, was without support as he was an opium addict who had fallen foul of Habib.

26. "Aanteekeningen," p. 409, states that Mahmud was declared Sultan about November 1870, Ibrahim having died in July of the same year.

27. Panglima Polem was the Panglima Sagi of the XXII Mukim, and as such had more men at his command than any other uleëbalang.

28. Habib's title was Mangkubumi (administrator). Teuku Kali Maliku'l Adil appears to have been designated to share the office, though in a distinctly secondary capacity.

29. According to "Aanteekeningen," pp. 410-412, this expedition was directed against those in the XXVI Mukim who continued to support Tuanku Husein's candidature for the Sultanate. Husein himself was living with the uleëbalang of Tjadé but fled before Abdur-Rahman's advance. This expedition took place after Habib's return from the West Coast and the Djambi visit at the end of 1871.

During this absence His [Netherlands] Majesty's Steamer *Maas en Waal* arrived in Atjeh roads.[30] The negotiations which then took place were conducted by Panglima Tibang without Habib's knowledge, since Tibang had won the Sultan's favor. Such was the state of affairs when Habib returned to Kota Radja from the West Coast. Habib already realized that war with the Dutch was unavoidable.

Unwilling to share the government of Atjeh with Panglima Tibang and unable to exercise any constructive influence over the course of events, Habib left Atjeh to return to Arabia.[31] He took ship for Penang on the steamer *Patty*, and left from there for Mecca by the mail.[32] Having stayed there for some time with the Sjarif, Abdullah Basjah, he travelled on to Constantinople. There he was given an audience with the Sultan, who received him very well and bestowed on him the Commander's Cross of the Osmanie Order. Then he returned to Mecca.[33]

---

30. Habib was absent on the West Coast during a second visit by the Djambi in May 1872 and also during the visit of the Maas en Waal in late October 1872. Panglima Tibang was also absent during both visits, attempting to elicit British support in the Straits Settlements. Kraijenhoff, who conducted both these Dutch missions, found the Atjehnese very reluctant to undertake any discussions in Habib's absence. De Klerck, De Atjeh-oorlog, pp. 364-370.

31. Habib and Tibang appear to have returned to the capital in November 1872 to learn that Kraijenhoff had announced an impending high-level Dutch mission to Atjeh. Tibang had already contacted Schiff, the Resident of Riau, who was to lead this Dutch mission during his visit to the Straits Settlements. Without consulting Habib the Sultan was persuaded to send Tibang back to plead with Schiff for a delay in the mission. Tibang, supported by Teuku Kali and the few other "court uleëbalang" who shared his jealousy of Habib, was no match for Abdur-Rahman in terms of support in the country. The Arab may have felt, nevertheless, that he had lost control of Atjehnese relations with the Dutch at the very moment these were becoming critical. His departure was dignified by a royal commission to appeal to Turkey and other European powers for help against the Dutch.

32. A report of January 6, 1873 from Penang stated that Habib had left there "on the last mail" for Europe. His intention was thought to be an appeal to the French government, which had been suggested to him by Roura. Van de Putte to Gericke, March 14, 1873, B.Z., dossier Atjeh.

33. It seems unlikely that Habib could have visited Constantinople in February or March 1873 without this being noticed by the Dutch at the time or mentioned in the extensive coverage of his moves after April. Habib had a private audience with Sultan Abdul Aziz to present his papers on May 15, 1873. In December 1873, at the end of his Constantinople mission, he was given the the Osmanie Order of the second class. According to Dutch sources the higher honor of Grand Cross of the Osmanie Order was denied him, as was a formal interview with the Sultan, because of pressure from the Western powers, especially Russia.

On arrival there he received news that war had already broken out between the Netherlands and Atjeh and that Sultan Mahmud had died.[34] At the same time he received a joint letter from the chiefs of the three Sagi, in which they gave him authority for a seven-year period to negotiate on their behalf with other countries for help in the war in which Atjeh had become involved.

Habib accepted this commission, travelled again to Europe, and visited Constantinople and Paris,[35] where he made fruitless attempts to persuade these governments to offer assistance to Atjeh. The Turkish government promised moral support by sending a letter to the King of Holland, though he was later informed by a letter from Murad Effendi that Atjehnese affairs were governed by written agreements among European governments, so that Turkey did not feel entitled to interfere in the war.[36]

Habib also appealed indirectly for the intervention of England by making use of an earlier acquaintance in Singapore with Sir Rutherford Alcock,[37] who at that time had been Ambassador to China and Japan, and now a member of the Upper House.

Because Habib travelled in very great style, the costs were considerable; however, the necessary funds were regularly forwarded by Teuku Paja of Pulau Penang.[38]

After making all these attempts in vain, Habib returned to Singapore.[39] There he addressed a letter to the Governor-General of Netherlands India, in which he offered His Excellency his services

---

34. Holland declared war on Atjeh on March 26, 1873. Sultan Mahmud died in January 1874, and it was at his plenipotentiary that Habib acted in Turkey.

35. Habib arrived in Constantinople from Suez on April 27, 1873 and remained there lobbying very effectively for Atjeh until December 18, when he sailed for Suez and Jidda. He had intended to visit France but did not do so, presumably because his overtures were flatly rejected by the French.

36. For the diplomatic outcome of Habib's mission, see Reid, Contest, pp. 119-129 and 145-153.

37. Sir Rutherford Alcock (1809-1897) was Britain's first Consul-General in Japan (1858-1865), and Minister-Plenipotentiary in China (1865-1871). He took an extended home leave in 1862-1864, and probably met Abdur-Rahman in the suite of the Maharadja of Johor while passing through Singapore. If Habib wrote to Alcock in 1873, however, this appeal does not seem to have reached Whitehall.

38. A wealthy pepper trader and uleëbalang of Tandjung Samuntoh in eastern Atjeh, Teuku Paja was in Penang on business at the outbreak of the Atjeh war. His nephew accompanied Habib to Constantinople. T. Paja fell into debt to the extent of $70,000 by 1874, largely because of his constant support of Habib's extravagant mission. He returned to Atjeh soon after Habib and took a prominent part in the war.

39. He arrived by the S. S. Jeddah on March 13, 1874.

of mediation to restore peace in Atjeh. Habib said that he never received any answer to this letter.[40]

Habib left Singapore for Pulau Penang[41] with the intention of embarking from there for Atjeh. He stayed in Penang about three months, dined many times during his stay with the Lieutenant Governor, Colonel Anson,[42] and repeated to the [Dutch] Consul[43] the written offer he had made to the Governor-General.

However, because the government was evidently not then willing to negotiate with him, he decided to return to Atjeh and offer his help to the Atjehnese in the war against the Dutch. Meanwhile the Consul, Mr. Lavino, tried in all possible ways to prevent his going there. He had him trailed by a spy wherever he went.

One day he managed to elude the vigilance of this spy. After he had cut his hair, shaved his beard, and dressed entirely as a Kling [South Indian], he took an unnumbered vehicle in which he rode to the beach. There he met the Atjehnese Njak Barun, went with him in a sampan to a small steamer preparing to sail to Atjeh, gave himself out as a Kling, and booked for Idi without revealing himself to anyone on board. Throughout the voyage he pretended to be a lunatic.[44]

When it anchored at Idi the steamer was ordered by a warship in the roadstead to avoid any communication with the shore until the ship was inspected. At this Habib managed to hail a small Atjehnese sampan which was nearby, had himself lowered into it, and put ashore at Padawa Pantong. Njak Barun, who had stayed on board, also reached Padawa at night and procured for Habib an escort of 50 men, with which he set off for Atjeh Besar. In every place he came to--Idi Ketjil, Tandjung Samuntoh, Simpang Ulim--honor was paid to him. He

40. Habib's extensive activity in Singapore to promote a Dutch-Atjehnese settlement is described in Reid, Contest, pp. 158-175.

41. Habib left Singapore secretly in late November 1874 for Ceylon and South India. He resided mainly in Calicut, but appears also to have visited Madras and Bombay in the hope of influencing British officials. He arrived in Penang from India on May 14, 1875. Maier to Loudon, December 1, 27, 1874; January 11, February 9, 23, March 8, 1875; ARA Consulaats-archief, Penang, 99.

42. Colonel A.E.H. Anson (1826-1925) was Lieutenant Governor of Penang since 1867. Anson (About Others and Myself, pp. 324-329), recalls his discussions with Habib with delightful vividness.

43. George Lavino had the full-time post of Agent of the Netherlands Indian Government for Acheen affairs at Penang, though he became Consul in 1881. Anson brought him and Habib together for negotiations against strong resistance from Batavia.

44. On March 7, 1876 Lavino's spies lost track of Abdur-Rahman, who boarded the Penang Chinese steamer Batara Bayoo Sree the same day. Lavino's account of his movements confirms Habib's precisely, except that his companion becomes Njak Harun. Lavino to Van Lansberge, March 16 and 22, 1876, ARA Consulaats-archief, Penang, 102.

stayed in Simpang Ulim several days. Radja Teuku Muda Njak Malim[45] gave him $5,000 for the costs of the war as well as 500 barrels of gunpowder. His force was augmented to 2,000 men. From there he went to Kerti [Keureutoë] where his force was again increased considerably and he was given $5,000 by the various uleëbalang. In Peusangan he received $1,000, in Pidië, $5,000, in Gigiëng from Bintara Kambangan [Keumangan][46] $1,000. By the time he reached Pidië his force comprised about 10,000 men.

From there, he addressed a letter to the chiefs of the three Sagi, notifying them of his arrival and asking whether they wanted him in Atjeh with the force he had assembled, and if so in what capacity. He received the reply that they were anxiously looking forward to his coming. Then he went to Indrapuri, summoned all the uleëbalang of the three Sagi, and put the same question to them in person that he had put in writing. They unanimously told him they would elect him their commander and war leader. Next he went to Missigit Mon Tasiëk, called the chiefs together once again, and put the same question to them, to which he received the same reply. Habib then told them he was prepared to accept this commission if each one promised obedience to him and if he received an appointment in writing signed jointly by the chiefs.

After receiving this commission Habib assumed the leadership of the war; however, he still had to contend with the disunity of the uleëbalang, of whom only one section obeyed his orders while another section acted entirely according to their own lights without any considered plan.

When Habib assumed the conduct of affairs, Kajulah, Bilul, and Lambaru were already under the control of the [Netherlands Indies] government. As commander he led the Atjehnese against the government four times: three times in the XXVI Mukim[47] and once, the last time, in IV Mukim [Lhok Nga]. Before the attack on the [IV] Mukim took place Habib tried to persuade the various uleëbalang to submit to the government because he was well aware that Atjeh was bound to lose out in the war, not only because it was no match for the government, but more importantly because there was no unity and his commands

---

45. Radja Teuku Muda Njak Malim was the most energetic and successful uleëbalang of the East Coast before the war, with the largest pepper exports in the country, a small fleet of schooners, and considerable investments in Penang. Together with Teuku Paja, he was the staunchest financial supporter of Habib.

46. Teuku Bintara Keumangan was the leader of the federation of six uleëbalang of Keumangan (or Gigiëng) in the Pidië district. He followed Habib to the war front and seconded his attempts to unite the Atjehnese.

48. Kajulah, Bilul, and Lambaru were among the points taken in February 1876, during the first serious Dutch attempt to extend their occupation eastwards of the Atjeh river into the XXVI Mukim. Habib reached Atjeh Besar by July 1876, but he devoted his efforts to strengthening his own position and supervising fortifications in the XXII Mukim rather than initiating attacks. A renewed Dutch offensive in late 1876 ended in March 1877 after the occupation of most of the XXV and XXVI Mukim. Atjeh Besar then remained curiously peaceful until April 1878, when Abdur-Rahman began the attacks here mentioned.

were so badly carried out. Panglima Polem had entirely withdrawn from the war out of enmity for Habib,[48] and even refused to give financial assistance from the money collected from the people for that purpose. He let Habib have only a very small proportion--$500.

Nevertheless, the majority of the chiefs were still in favor of the war. Habib therefore decided to try to bring the conflict to a decision by attacking the IV Mukim and threatening Kota Radja and Uleëlheue.[49] But now again the (Radja's) troops which he called up presented themselves in very deficient numbers.

When General Van der Heijden then attacked him from various sides he fled to Missigit Mon Tasiëk. At this he again assembled the various chiefs and urged them to submit; however, they still wanted to continue the war. There followed the taking of Sinalob. The whole Atjehnese army retreated to Missigit Mon Tasiëk, and although Habib considered this fortress was strong enough to make resistance possible, this was not to be the case.

Once Missigit Mon Tasiëk had fallen into our [Dutch] hands,[50] Habib once more convened a gathering of the chiefs, where he bluntly told them that their cause was completely lost and that they would be wise to submit with him to the government. As for himself, he wanted to be released from the task with which they had entrusted him, because he intended to take leave of them and offer his submission. Of the twelve chiefs who participated in this meeting,[51] seven were inclined towards submission, whereas five chiefs still desired to continue the war.

---

48. Polem had in fact withdrawn from the war in 1874 in despair at Atjehnese disunity but rejoined it as one of Habib's leading supporters in 1876. The quarrel mentioned here must have arisen in 1877-1878.

49. This major operation began immediately after the Dutch commander Van der Heijden had sailed for Geudong with a large part of his force on June 15, 1878. The Dutch post at Kruëng Raba in the IV Mukim Lhok Nga (West Coast of Atjeh Besar) was cut off and seriously threatened until it was relieved on June 25. Habib twice offered to allow the 100-man garrison to leave if they destroyed their fort. Meanwhile he mobilized some thousands of men who put Kota Radja itself in danger until Van der Heijden's return with his men on June 23-24. Habib's offensive brought an end to Dutch passivity. Van der Heijden was reinforced and allowed to conquer the whole of the Atjeh valley. E. B. Kielstra, Beschrijving van den Atjeh-oorlog (The Hague: Van Cleef, 1885), III, pp. 219-247.

50. July 28, 1878.

51. This is probably a reference to the uleëbalang jang duabelas--the twelve uleëbalang, composed of four from each of the three Sagi of Atjeh Besar, who traditionally had the power of election to the throne. Abdur-Rahman made a similar statement to Lavino in 1875, saying that five out of twelve chiefs of Atjeh Besar were on his side. Lavino to Van Lansberge, May 27, 1875, ARA Consulaatsarchief, Penang 101. These references are among the most striking evidence for the strength of the institution which Snouck Hurgronje (The Achehnese, I, p. 138) plays down.

In this state of affairs a letter fell into Habib's hands addressed to Teuku Muda Ba'et by the Governor of Atjeh and dependencies, in reply to a previous letter sent by the chief to the governor. In Teuku Muda Ba'et's absence, this letter was answered by Habib, and once the reply was sent Habib wrote himself to the Governor. The correspondence which ensued resulted in the submission of Habib, which took place in Kota Radja on October 13, 1878, after the conditions he advanced were accepted.

While negotiations were being conducted between Habib and the government he still saw to it that the building of new fortifications continued day and night. He did this in the first place so as not to be unprepared if the negotiations with the government failed, but also to avoid arousing the suspicion of the population. For although Habib had informed the ulèëbalang of his intentions, he had done this in such general terms that the submission itself, as well as its timing, was unknown to them. Indeed, many perhaps regarded his statement as intimidation.

His journey to Aneuk Galong, where he was awaited on the above date by Chief of Staff Major Gey van Pittius and Assistant Resident Sol, always took place at night, for fear of being hindered by hostile elements.[52]

The above was noted down and put into writing by me as a result of various conversations I held with Habib and questions I asked him. The native writer Mohamud Arif has assisted me by giving information. As far as possible I have taken note of facts which I believed were not generally known, but above all I have envisaged providing a contribution to the knowledge of the character of a man who has played an important role in the Atjeh war.

---

52. Alexander ("Korte Levensschets," pp. 1019-1020) closes his narrative with details of Habib's journey to Jidda aboard the Curacao in November and December 1878. Abdur-Rahman lived on his pension in Mecca until his death in 1896. Although he was avoided by most Atjehnese because of what they regarded as his betrayal, he still believed in 1884 that he could restore peace if the Dutch would allow him to do so. Snouck Hurgronje knew him in Mecca (1884-1885), and was obviously impressed (The Achehnese, I, pp. 76 and 158-164). In 1886 he was appointed Sheikh es-Sadat (superior of the sayyid of Mecca) by the Turkish wali Osman Pasha. A month later, when Osman was replaced, he was relieved of this office by the Grand Sharif Aun al-Rafiq. Typically, Habib responded to this humiliation by withdrawing to Malabar for some months. De Vicq to Karnebeek, November 12 and December 23, 1886, copies respectively in ARA Kol. Kab. C^{13}, dossier 6169, and dossier 6170.

ARUNG SINGKANG (1700-1765):
HOW THE VICTORY OF WADJO' BEGAN

J. Noorduyn[1]

One of the most colorful figures in the history of Southwest Celebes is the man who was elected Chief King of the Buginese state of Wadjo' in 1737 and remained in this office until 1754.[2] His personal name was La Ma'dukelleng and his title is usually given as Arung (i.e., Prince of) Singkang, though he is also called Sultan of Pasir and Arung Peneki. He was probably born about 1700 and was of noble Wadjorese descent. When still a young man he was forced to flee his country, and he went to the east coast of Borneo, where there were already many Buginese settlers. Little is known about him during this time. He engaged in many activities and became known as a leader. He assembled a group of dedicated followers who manned his fleet of warships and in 1726 he conquered the towns of Kutai and Pasir. In 1737 he reappeared in Wadjo' with his own ships and troops and succeeded in rallying Wadjo' in a successful war against the mighty neighboring state of Bone. Within a few years he was able to bring most of the other Buginese states to his side, and in February 1739 an allied army under his command marched to Makasar with the avowed purpose of attacking the Dutch fort there.

Although they captured Goa, the Makasarese capital, they were unable to conclude successfully their bold expedition. Arung Singkang's following slowly began to dissolve at this critical juncture and his offensive power proved inadequate. Beginning on May 16, 1739, Arung Singkang launched four attacks on the fort but they were repulsed. Finally, on July 20, the Dutch troops defeated them decisively and put them to flight. Arung Singkang returned to Wadjo' to await the Dutch counterattack which came in January 1741, but the Dutch were equally unsuccessful in their efforts to subdue Wadjo'. After some inconclusive battles and fruitless negotiations, they departed again on March 29. After that time Wadjo' remained almost completely outside Dutch influence for nearly a century and a half. Arung Singkang's

---

1. I am most grateful to the Netherlands Institute for Advanced Study at Wassenaar for providing the excellent facilities enabling me to finish this paper, and to Dr. L. Andaya for his generous assistance in improving the English expression in this paper. Any remaining errors are, of course, my own.

2. The most recent description of the former principality of Wadjo' and its institutions is "Hiérarchie et Pouvoir Traditionnels en Pays Wadjo'" by Christian Pelras in Archipel, 1 (1971), pp. 169-191. Older works are B. F. Matthes, Over de Wadjorezen met hum Handels- en Scheepswetboek (Makasar: P. van Hartrop, 1869) and J. Noorduyn, Een achttiende-eeuwse kroniek van Wadjo' (The Hague: H. L. Smits, 1955).

position in Wadjo' did not remain unchallenged, however. His term of office ended in civil war. After his retirement in 1754, he returned to the town of Peneki and to his private war against Bone. He died in 1765.

The short Buginese story which is published below in English translation is concerned with a small part of Arung Singkang's career, viz. how he succeeded in going ashore in Wadjo' in 1737.[3] The importance of this story does not lie in its value as a historical source because there are other Buginese texts which describe the events of his time more accurately and in greater detail.[4] These other sources usually restrict themselves to mentioning facts, dates, the course of official negotiations, etc. and do not contain opinions nor such unhistorical things as prophecies.[5] Our short story, on the other hand, may give some insights into how the Wadjorese of that time viewed Arung Singkang and his exploits.

The central theme of the story and the climax to which it gradually leads is the idea that Arung Singkang was the man who liberated Wadjo', his native country. The Buginese term which the text here uses is derived from the same word which two centuries later became the slogan of the Indonesian revolution: *maradeka* (in Indonesian, *merdeka*). But, if concepts and events lying two centuries apart may be compared, there is one distinctive difference between the slogan of 1737 and the one used in 1945, viz. that Sabang and Merauke were still completely beyond the author's horizon, and, what is more, even Southwest Celebes as a totality did not come into his view. It is Wadjo'--a small part of a small region--whose victory is commemorated in the story. That Arung Singkang succeeded in liberating Wadjo' from the oppressive interventions of adjacent

---

3. The Buginese text is to be found in Ms. No. 126, pp. 1-14 of the loan collection of Makasarese and Buginese Manuscripts of the Netherlands Bible Society in the Leyden University Library, cf. J. Noorduyn, "Een Boeginees Geschriftje over Arung Singkang," Bijdragen tot de Taal-, Land- en Volkenkunde, CIX (1953), pp. 144-152.

4. The most detailed Buginese account is to be found in Cod. Or. 1923 VI, pp. 11-46 in the Leyden University Library. A summary of this text and some supplementary data from different chronicles are given in Noorduyn, Een achttiende-eeuwse, pp. 126-138. The story of Arung Singkang as it is contained in one of these chronicles has been published in full in Noorduyn, Een achttiende-eeuwse, pp. 278-299. Recently, some additional data about Arung Singkang's parentage and early years have been published by A. Zainal Abidin, S.H. in "Memperkenalkan beberapa Pahlawan Sulawesi Selatan Diperantauan (Istimewa La Maddukelleng Sultan Pasir)," Bingkisan Jajasan Kebudajaan Sulawesi Selatan & Tenggara, I, No. 7 (1967), pp. 6-14.

5. Notes on Buginese and Makasarese historical literature are to be found in: A.A. Cense, "Enige Aantekeningen over Makassaars-Boeginese Geschiedschrijving," Bijdragen tot de Taal-, Land- en Volkenkunde, CVII (1951), pp. 42-60; A.A. Cense, "Old Buginese and Macassarese Diaries," Bijdragen tot de Taal-, Land- en Volkenkunde, CXXII (1966), pp. 416-428; J. Noorduyn, "Origin of South Celebes Historical Writing," in Soedjatmoko, ed., An Introduction to Indonesian Historiography (Ithaca: Cornell University Press, 1965), pp. 137-155.

states is considered his great achievement, although this is but a small feat compared with the grand scheme which he had in mind and the ultimate object which he pursued but did not and could not attain at that time.

Under the strong leadership of Arung Singkang, Wadjo' came to occupy an unprecedented position of power in Southwest Celebes by bringing both large and small Buginese states under its banner through force or persuasion. In this process it naturally came into conflict with the Kingdom of Bone, which had become under Dutch patronage the most powerful state in Southwest Celebes after Makasar was conquered by the Dutch in 1669. The prominent position of Bone is the reason why Bone and its Queen Batari Todja figured as the principal opponents of Arung Singkang even before he had returned from Borneo to Wadjo'. The rulers of Bone made a sevenfold charge against him, tried to prevent him from returning to his country, and in vain laid an ambush for him when he did enter Wadjo'. It is this persistent but unsuccessful opposition of Bone which is stressed by the author of our story. The reader can almost sense the author's delight in recording the Queen of Bone's concession that Arung Singkang's retorts to her charges were irrefutable, even though they were in fact far from strong, if not completely beside the point. The author or his source even exaggerated Arung Singkang's offenses against Bone. According to our story he was accused of having killed a certain Topasarai, and he himself acknowledged this as a fact. It is known from other sources, however, that Topasarai was not killed but merely robbed. It seems as if the antagonism between Bone and Arung Singkang was deliberately overemphasized to accentuate clearly the latter's superiority. The same exultation in Arung Singkang's superiority can be sensed in the passage where the assembled princes of Bone are reported to admit that Arung Singkang's fleet was unrivalled and that it was senseless for Bone even to consider attacking him at sea.

Such small differences of fact or merely of emphasis contain certain clues as to the intentions of the author. Another detail in which the story differs from what actually happened is the sequence of events. For example, Bone's accusations were brought against Arung Singkang, contrary to what our story relates, *after* he and his troops went ashore and not before.

The true sequence of events is fairly well known from other Buginese sources.[6] On his way back to Wadjo' Arung Singkang arrived off Palette, on the coast of Bone, on April 8, 1737. There he was refused admittance to the river which he could have used to get to Wadjo' and therefore, went a few miles to the north, to Doping on the coast of Wadjo'. One of the messengers from Bone who came to see him in Doping was I Djakkolo', the Gellareng of Bontoala'. He arrived after Arung Singkang had been waiting off Doping for forty days. He informed Arung Singkang that Bone gave him permission to go ashore in Wadjo'. Two days later, on May 24, Arung Singkang went ashore and immediately proceeded to Singkang, where he stayed for thirty days. While he was in Singkang a conference of Bone and Wadjo' was held in Tosora, the capital of Wadjo', in which Bone brought seven accusations against Arung Singkang. The latter was invited to the conference and was given the opportunity to defend

---

6. Cf. the literature mentioned in note 4.

himself. He did so successfully and apparently was acquitted. After that, however, the Chief King of Wadjo' asked him not to continue staying in Singkang but to go to some place on the coast. He then went to Peneki, which lies to the south of Doping. He drove out the Bone troops which were garrisoned there and thus committed an open act of hostility. This was the immediate cause of the war between Wadjo' and Bone in which Arung Singkang soon came to play the leading role.

On examining this summary of events, one finds it difficult to believe that Arung Singkang, when he was in Doping, desisted from his plans (as our story wants us to believe), went away to the other side of the gulf, and only returned after a prophetic figure had urged him to do so. It is true, Arung Singkang could have gone away in the period of forty days in which he was lying off Doping, but he does not seem to have had a good reason for doing so since he was waiting in Doping to get permission to go ashore. The Chief King of Wadjo', it is true, did request him to leave. This request, however, was made only after Arung Singkang had entered Wadjo' and had already been for some time in Singkang. Furthermore, he was not requested to leave Wadjo' but merely to stay nearer the coast.

It seems indisputable that the interesting story of Arung Singkang's meeting with the enigmatic "big scabby" prophet on the island of Padamarang is fiction rather than fact. This does not make the story less interesting, for it clearly expresses the author's belief that Arung Singkang's strong conviction was based on an auspicious prophecy and that his incredible acts were authorized by a supernatural sanction.

It is obvious that the prediction "you shall liberate Wadjo'," which according to our story was acted upon by Arung Singkang, is in fact a prophecy *post eventum*. This implies that the story itself was not written before Arung Singkang had really accomplished Wadjo's liberation, i.e., at least a few years after the events described in the story took place. It is quite possible that the differences of fact we noticed in the story are also to be ascribed to this distance of time. Nevertheless, there is evidence that these words and the special emphasis of the story were a reflection of contemporary public opinion. There clearly was a difference of opinion between Arung Singkang and his compatriots concerning the object of their enterprise, and in this matter our story seems to side with the latter rather than with Arung Singkang. There is no doubt that his ultimate aim was the termination of foreign dominance in Celebes, which is clearly shown by the words he is recorded to have spoken in a conference of Bone, Wadjo', and Soppeng in October 1737: "Wadjo' wishes that you, Bone, make the Dutch depart, because as long as they are here our countries will be in ruin." It is also certain that many, even among his closest associates, did not share these views, and only reluctantly followed him on his march to Makasar. Just before he departed for Makasar at the head of the combined armies of Bone, Wadjo', and Soppeng, the leaders of these countries decided against the expedition. It was only Arung Singkang's own forceful personality which finally persuaded them to go. "Return to your own countries," he is reported to have said to the leaders of the three countries. "I shall go myself to Makasar with my own troops." After these words they went with him.[7] But

---

7. Cf. Noorduyn, Een achttiende-eeuwse, pp. 131, 133, 291.

this fundamental difference of opinion about the common goal and about the means to attain it became one of the main reasons of his ultimate failure. Those who had not been totally persuaded in his convictions soon abandoned him when the decisive hour had come.

One may conclude that Arung Singkang was a fighter for freedom ahead of his time. In his eyes, the liberation of Wadjo' was not an end in itself but a necessary stage on the road to the real end. His contemporaries, however, expected less of him. They were satisfied when Wadjo' had gained its independence, and they honored the man who had liberated Wadjo' for what he did achieve. We do not know how many people held this opinion. The author of the following short story at least was among them, and, therefore, it is not difficult to understand why the theme of his story is "The Victory of Wadjo'."

THE TEXT IN TRANSLATION

This is how the victory of Wadjo' began.

When the King of Pasir was in Wadjo', the Queen of Bone sent a messenger to him. She sent the Gellareng of Bontoala' as the spokesman. The King of Pasir had been declared guilty of crimes committed far and wide, and so the Three Allied Countries had designated him as an evildoer. When it became known that the King of Pasir was in Wadjo', ways and means were contrived to drive him out of Wadjo'. In that state of affairs the Queen of Bone, the Arung Pitu,[1] and all descendants of King Mappadjunnge arrived at a unanimous decision. After this the Gellareng of Bontoala' departed.

Upon his arrival the King of Pasir was informed that a messenger from Bone had come. The messenger entered briskly, dressed in a white Bone court dress and a black cap. He went quickly into the audience hall and sat down before the youthful King. To fulfill his mission of speaking for Her Majesty the Queen of Bone, he turned to the King of Pasir and said: "Her Majesty the Queen of Bone has sent me to say: The young Prince of Pasir has committed seven treansgressions against Bone and by so doing he neglected to maintain *adat* and failed to comply with its prescriptions. First, he killed Topasarai at Tobonio,[2] who belonged to the royal house of Bone. Secondly, he killed a messenger of Bone. Thirdly, he came to Mandar, made the Selimpao[3] fight, placed his artillery in position, and frightened the King of Mandar, who is an ally of Bone. Fourthly, he passed by Balang-lompo,[4] which is a possession of Bone, and set fire to it.

---

1. The Arung Pitu (Seven Princes) were the highest advisory board in the kingdom of Bone.

2. Tobonio is a village on the southeast coast of Borneo.

3. Selimpao is apparently the name of Arung Singkang's fighting cock.

4. Balang-lompo and Balang-tja'di are small islands in the roads of Makasar.

Fifthly, he went by Makasar and fired on the castle[5] which belongs to a great friend of Bone. Sixthly, he entered the River Tjenrana[6] aboard very strange ships and frightened the Arung of Bone, who is a woman. Seventhly, he gave orders to go to Kera[7] and to kill La Selle', who was the son of Topalagai, together with two well-to-do people and three from the lower class."

The Monarch of Pasir replied: "The words which Bone has spoken are true. But if you say that I killed Topasarai at Tobonio, I must reply that a Wadjorese man was killed by Bone people in Pasir. I sought for Bone people in the country of Pasir but there were none. Then it was said that there was a man from Bone at Tobonio. Therefore, I gave orders to kill him. I know very well that Topasarai belonged to the royal house of Bone, but I also know that the Three Allied Countries administer justice in a righteous way: A murderer is killed only when he and his victim are of equal birth. Well, the man who was killed by the Bone man was of noble blood in Wadjo'. Therefore, I killed Topasarai at Tobonio. You should acknowledge that we are on even terms now because he belonged to the royal house of Bone.

"When you say that I killed a messenger of Bone, I must reply that only some of my subjects who went fishing at sea had an encounter there. And when an encounter takes place at sea the law of the fishes is applied, namely: The vanquished is devoured.

"And, messenger of Bone, as to the fact that I stopped in Mandar, conquered the king, and made the Selimpao fight, I staked one thousand dollars against the king. I was afraid that the Selimpao would kill and that the king would still say that we were even. Therefore, I placed my guns in position because I reasoned that the king might claim that we were even in this cockfight. Being merchants, we try to be on our guard the best we can.

"And, Gellareng, as to my going to Balang-lompo and Balang-tja'di, it was only some of my subjects who went ashore to get fresh water. They said to me: 'Lord, there are houses but no people.' I said: 'Set fire to them. They will be idol houses. May this redound to our merit in the hereafter.'

"As to my passing by Makasar, since they fired at me I fired at them.

"And, Gellareng, as to my entering the River Tjenrana, I did not see anybody change his ship. No *pantjaleng* entered the river, nor any *padewakeng* or *padjala*. How then could I have changed my ships? I had only *binta'*, *pantja'dja'* and *kanaikeng*.[8]

---

5. This is Fort Rotterdam which was the seat of the Dutch East India Company in Makasar.

6. The River Tjenrana was the border river between Bone and Wadjo', but its mouth (with the town of Tjenrana) was in the possession of Bone.

7. Kera is a village in the north of Wadjo'.

8. The pantjaleng and padjala are types of fishing ships, the padewakeng is a commercial ship and the binta', pantja'dja and kanaikeng were used by pirates.

"When you say, Gellareng, that at Kera I killed La Selle', the son of Topalagai, together with two well-to-do people and three from the lower class, I must reply that Tjellaloa from Bone killed a man from Wadjo'. I was convinced that all would agree that he had to be revenged."

After that the Gellareng of Bontoala' returned to Bone. There the Arung Pitu happened to be assembled in the royal palace--sitting so close together that the knots of their headdresses touched each other--before Her Majesty the Divine Queen of Bone. The Queen of Bone turned to them and said: "In my opinion, the best thing to do is to send a messenger to the Chief King of Wadjo' because I think the arguments of the King of Pasir are irrefutable. If the Chief King should speak to his grandson, it would only be proper that the King of Pasir should concede."

The Arung Pitu respectfully payed their homage and said unanimously: "Whatever is the wish of our Divine Queen we will all execute."

Then the one who was sent to the spokesman departed. The noble Chiefs of Wadjo' happened to be assembled--sitting so close together that the knots of their headdresses touched each other--before the one who is called the pillar of the state, the Chief King of Wadjo'. The Chief King turned to the spokesman from Bone and said: "What is the message which the Divine Queen of Bone has entrusted you with?"

The one who was sent to be spokesman said in reply: "The Queen of Bone has sent me to say: Your grandson should not be allowed to remain in your country because it is very unpleasant for her to hear things about him, since he is guilty of a blood debt with regard to the Three Allied Countries."

Then the King of Pasir was summoned. The Chief King of Wadjo' said to him: "King of Pasir, you must leave Wadjo' because you have committed crimes towards the Allied Countries according to what Bone says."

The King of Pasir said: "I shall not go away if it is only Bone which says so."

Then the Chief King of Wadjo' said: "Wadjo' has concurred in this, King of Pasir. You must leave Wadjo'."

The King of Pasir said: "Only if you think that it is good for Wadjo' shall I agree to leave."

The Chief King said: "Yes, it is good for Wadjo' if you leave."

So the King of Pasir accepted that it was good for Wadjo' if he left. He then went away and again put out to sea. Near Palette he steered his course eastward for the isle of Padamarang.[9] There in Padamarang he stopped and went ashore. He went to the river to take a bath. There he happened to meet a big scabby man.[10] This man said

---

9. Padamarang is an island on the other side of the gulf of Bone, off the coast of Southeast Celebes.

10. In a story of the founding of Wadjo' a princess with a skin disease occurs and a similar figure is also known from Malay histories. In the present case the skin disease is of the type called ichthyosis, which was considered an "honorific" disease by the inhabitants of

to the King of Pasir: "You must return. You will liberate Wadjo'."

The young Prince of Pasir quickly boarded his golden ship again in order to sail to Doping and to go ashore there.

Seven days after his arrival in Doping the inhabitants of the country of Bone knew about it. The Arung Pitu and the Queen of Bone also knew it. The Queen had the Arung Pitu summoned. When all of them were seated before the Queen, she turned to them and said: "Is it true, my Princes, that the King of Pasir has returned?"

The Arung Pitu unanimously confirmed it, saying: "It is true, my Lady. We are sure because he is at Doping about to go ashore."

The Queen of Bone said: "What is your opinion, Princes, about the landing of the King of Pasir at Doping?"

The Arung Pitu unanimously replied: "It would be senseless to engage in battle with the King of Pasir if it should be on ships since his ships are sailing forts with breastworks. In Bone there are no ships of this type."

The Queen of Bone said: "Well, my Princes, if he should go ashore, then you will be able to meet him in battle."

The Arung Pitu confirmed this. The Queen then said: "Gellareng of Bontoala', go to the King of Pasir and convey to him our favorable decision that he is allowed to go ashore."

Then the Gellareng of Bontoala' departed, accompanied by the Arung Pitu and over three thousand men. When they reached Lamarua[11] the Bone army went into hiding there. The Gellareng of Bontoala' arrived at the ships of the King of Pasir. There were more than ten of them. The King of Pasir already saw the Gellareng of Bontoala' when the latter was still in the distance. He went quickly into his bedroom and dressed himself in a Bone court dress and a black cap.

When the envoy had taken his place, the young Prince, the King of Pasir, also entered the audience hall and sat down opposite the envoy. He turned to the envoy and said: "What is the message you have been sent to convey?"

The Gellareng answered: "Our Divine Queen of Bone has instructed me to go to the King of Pasir and say to him: I approve of your going ashore. When you go ashore all will be well with you and not bad; you will live and not die."

The young Prince of Pasir replied: "I am extremely glad of your words, my friend. But I say to you: If there is a liana obstructing me when I go ashore, I will cut it through."

Twice he repeated these words, that he would cut any liana obstructing him. The envoy agreed.

Then the young Prince tied a knot in the folds of his waistband, turned to the envoy and said: "You may return. I certainly shall not fail to go ashore."

Southeast Celebes. Therefore, the prophetic figure in our story was presumably derived from the culture of Southeast Celebes.

11. Lamarua is situated on the coast of Wadjo', just south of Doping.

DIPANAGARA (1787?-1855)

Ann Kumar

Dipanagara is too well known to students of Indonesian history to need introduction. Yet in spite of the amount of attention he has received, a certain cloud of ambiguity seems to hang about the man and his motives. Thus, de Klerck, who completed Louw's work *De Java-oorlog*[1] has written: "Dipa Negara had counted upon his accession. He was therefore bitterly disappointed, and as disappointment is often synonymous with shame in the minds of natives, it sometimes leads to despair and even to crime. This was to be the case with Dipa Negara. . . ."[2] Elsewhere, however, de Klerck has claimed: "There is not a stitch of evidence to prove his dissatisfaction with the course of events, nor did he make any appeal to the Government. He seemed to have a real preference for a life of retirement, in which he could devote himself to meditation."[3] This inconsistency is perhaps an extreme example, but it does illustrate well the lack of any definitive interpretation of this period and its personalities. But answering the unresolved questions will be a formidable task in view of the enormous amount of material to be examined. The quantity of Dutch-language material is evident from Louw's magnum opus, and the number of Javanese works dealing with the events of the period can be seen in Pigeaud's *Literature of Java*.[4] Louw does use both Javanese and Dutch material, but a more detailed comparison of the differences between the main Javanese accounts would certainly be interesting.

The two best-known Javanese accounts of the period are the so-called *Buku Kedung Kebo*, written by the Regent of Purwaredja, Tjakranagara, who fought on the side of the Dutch government against Dipanagara in the Java War,[5] and Dipanagara's own account, written in Menado (Minahassa) during his exile.[6] Louw uses this autobiographical *Babad Dipanagara*, sections of which he translates in their entirety, with other passages paraphrased and parts he regards as unimportant omitted. He also makes occasional references to the *Buku Kedung Kedo* (which he refers to as the *Babad Tjakranegara*).

---

1. P.J.F. Louw, <u>De Java-oorlog</u>, 6 vols. (Batavia: Landsdrukkerij, 1894-1909).

2. E.S. de Klerck, <u>History of the Netherlands East Indies</u>, (Rotterdam: W.L. & J. Brusse, 1938), II, p. 47.

3. <u>Ibid.</u>, p. 157.

4. Th. Pigeaud, <u>Literature of Java</u>, 3 vols. (The Hague: M. Nijhoff, 1967-1970).

5. See Pigeaud, <u>Literature of Java</u>, I, pp. 167-168, and II, pp. 35, 78 and 869.

6. <u>Ibid.</u>, I, pp. 167-168, and II, p. 392.

The extract translated here is from the autobiographical *Babad Dipanagara*, for which I have used a text printed (in the Javanese script) by Albert Rusche of Surakarta in 1917.[7] It is obviously very close to the text paraphrased by Louw, and I have found his work very useful. Most of the differences between these texts are minor but some are significant: for example, in Louw's text Dipanagara's father is shown to favor the succession of his younger son, while in the printed text this preference is not clear.[8]

Probably the greatest difficulty in understanding the events described in this extract is that our interpretation of Dipanagara's motives and reactions is dependent upon the interpretation of a series of prior events, which in turn hinges upon some rather disputable factors--sometimes upon text readings, and sometimes upon the implications which may be read into the text. For example, Louw sees in Dipanagara's description of the conflict between his father and his grandfather indications that Dipanagara himself was attempting to manipulate the course of events to ensure his own succession. However, not everyone would agree with this interpretation, and Louw's rationalization of Dipanagara's attitude at successive stages,[9] based on considerations of Javanese *adat*, is not entirely convincing. Nor is it only the Javanese sources which present difficulties. One of the most important factors in assessing Dipanagara's motives is the promise said to have been made to him by Raffles, and this remains problematic because of the lack of concrete evidence.[10]

A brief resumé of the main events of Dipanagara's life before the events described in the extract may be useful. In about 1787, the grandson of the first Sultan of Jogjakarta, Amangkubuwana I (Sultan Swargi) had a son by a wife of lower rank. This son, Dipanagara, was largely brought up under the care of his great-grandmother, the Sultan's wife, who bore the title Ratu Ageng. When his grandfather, Amangkubuwana II (Sultan Sepuh), succeeded to the throne in 1792, the Ratu Ageng and Dipanagara lived at Tegalredja, northwest of Jogjakarta in the Magelang region. Here, under the Ratu Ageng's guidance Dipanagara first became seriously concerned with religion, a concern which was to remain with him and acquire a mystical character. In 1810, Amangkubuwana II incurred the disfavor of Daendels (Governor-General of Java, 1808-1811) to such an extent that he was deposed in favor of his son, Amangkubuwana III (Kangdjeng Radja), Dipanagara's father. When, however, the Dutch government lost Java to the English, Amangkubuwana II took the opportunity to resume the reins of government, and in fact went so far as to have his Patih, Danuredja (II), put to death for having countenanced this deposition. Dipanagara's father remained heir-apparent, but Amangkubuwana II hoped to replace him in this position by a more favored son, Mangkudiningrat. This gives some indication of the atmosphere of Jogjakarta at the time of Raffles' arrival on December 27, 1811. Raffles accepted Amangkubuwana II's resumption

---

7. It was apparently first printed in 1909. <u>Ibid.</u>, II, p. 392.

8. Cf. Louw, <u>De Java-oorlog</u>, I, p. 103 and <u>Babad Diponagoro</u>, (Surakarta: Albert Rusche, 1917), I, p. 27.

9. Louw, <u>De Java-oorlog</u>, I, pp. 109-112.

10. See footnote 52 of the translated text.

of the throne, and a treaty was concluded between Jogjakarta and the British government. The treaty, however, was soon broken, and in June 1812 General Gillespie marched on the *kraton*. Amangkubuwana II was deposed for the second time and exiled to Penang. Dipanagara's father was restored.

In November 1814, Amangkubuwana III died. He was succeeded not by his elder son, Dipanagara, but by the thirteen year-old Mas Ambjah, whose mother was the Sultan's queen. He became Sultan Amangkubuwana IV (Sultan Djarot). This succession was in accordance with established custom: in the *Babad*, Dipanagara says that the English (specifically "Djan Kerapet," that is, the Resident of Jogjakarta, John Crawfurd) had offered to make him heir-apparent when they restored his father, but that he refused on account of Mas Ambjah's stronger claim.[11] However, there is enough evidence to suggest that Dipanagara had been promised the throne if his brother died while still a minor or after having conducted himself improperly.

Amangkubuwana IV did in fact die while still a minor in 1822; however, he was succeeded not by Dipanagara but by his three year-old son, under a Regency council, of which Dipanagara was a member. The explanation usually given for this succession is that the restored Dutch government was ignorant of any promise made during the British interregnum, as well they might have been, since both Dipanagara and a Dutch contemporary assert that the relevant document was burnt by those whose interests ran counter to his. It appears, however, that Dipanagara, himself, could have made no effort to inform the Dutch of this promise.

Three years later Dipanagara broke completely with the government of Jogjakarta and the Java War began.

The Text

The following extract consists of a short piece on his youthful religious life (pp. 1-5 of the printed text) and a much longer section covering the period from the accession to the throne of Amangkubuwana IV up until the opening scene of the war (pp. 79-112 of the printed text). The intervening passage, though interesting, has been omitted because of its length. It describes the following events:

> the arrival of Daendels at Jogjakarta (p. 6);
> the revolt of Radèn Rangga Prawiradirdja of Madiun (to p. 10);
> Daendels' replacement of Amangkubuwana II (Sultan Sepuh) by
>   by his son (Kangdjeng Radja) (p. 11);
> the arrival of Raffles and defeat of the Dutch under Janssens
>   (p. 12);
> the execution of the Patih, Danuredja (II), on the orders of
>   Sultan Sepuh (p. 13);
> the abdication of Kangdjeng Radja, on the advice of his son
>   Dipanagara, in favor of Sultan Sepuh (pp. 19-22);
> further moves against Dipanagara's father (p. 24);
> negotiations with the English Resident, John Crawfurd, on his
>   behalf (p. 28);

---

11. *Babad Diponagoro*, p. 38.

Raffles' arrival at Jogjakarta (p. 29);
Sultan Sepuh's decision to seek an alliance with Surakarta against the English (p. 32);
Raffles' decision to depose Sepuh and replace him by Kangdjeng Radja (p. 37);
Dipanagara's refusal to become his father's heir-apparent, on account of the prior claim of his younger half-brother, Mas Ambjah (p. 38);
the signing of the agreements with Raffles (pp. 41-42);
the English attack on the kraton (pp. 43-49);
the installation of Kangdjeng Radja as Sultan, with Mas Ambjah as Crown Prince (p. 53);
the marriage of Dipanagara, which took place five years after the above events and forms rather a nice vignette (pp. 63-75);
the death of the Sultan, leaving Dipanagara to care for Mas Ambjah, who is to succeed (pp. 76-77);
the circumcision and marriage of the young Sultan (Amangkubuwana IV), the account of the former presenting an interesting sidelight on the Resident's life at Jogjakarta (p. 79).

Note on the Translation

I have tried to present a translation as close as possible to the original and have generally followed the Javanese original line for line. I have noted any places where the order of the lines has been altered. Amplifications necessary for the sense appear in square brackets, and I apologize for the plethora of these; poetry, and especially poetry where the metric requirements concerning the number of syllables per line are strictly observed, is rarely as explicit as prose. Footnotes, especially in the numbers found here, impose something of a burden on the attention of the reader. Nevertheless, he is asked to refer to them, since otherwise the text can be hard to follow; for instance, the title Ratu Ageng was borne by three different women during the period covered by the extract. The Javanese original is written in the third person, which quite commonly replaces the first person in *tembang* verse, and I have retained this in the translation.

THE TEXT IN TRANSLATION

p. 1
Let the meter of this first part be Sinom,[1]
serving our purpose of honoring
the work written by the Noblest of Men,
famed throughout the land of Java,
that is
the exalted Prince Dipanagara,
now departed,

---

1. This work is written in <u>tembang matjapat</u>, and Sinom is one of its meters. It is considered appropriate for describing scenes of youth because of its association with <u>nom</u> (young).

recording his own story,
beginning from the time when he began to give himself up to
    the practice of religion.

We tell of his great-grandmother,
the Ratu Ageng.
She lived at Tegalredja[2]
and after the death of his great-grandfather[3]
she remained at that place.
The Prince grew ever more devoted
to matters of religion,
and it was his wish to protect
all his servants and followers, so that their hearts might be
    at ease.

It seems it was the will of God
that Prince Dipanagara
desired only to join
his great-grandmother
in devotion to religion,
and so he came to be at variance
with his grandfather, the Sultan,[4]
and seldom visited the capital,
except at the Garebeg[5] celebrations, when his presence was
    required.

Even though he was forced
to incur such a great sin[6]
out of fear of this grandfather
and of his father,[7]

p. 2 yet in his own heart
he thought only of his religion.
Now at Tegalredja,
during the reign of his grandfather,
there were many who strictly observed the commandments of
    their religion[8]

---

2. The text has "Tegalardja" throughout, but I have used the more common orthography.

3. Sultan Amangkubuwana I (Sultan Swargi), the first Sultan of Jogjakarta.

4. Sultan Amangkubuwana II, usually called Sultan Sepuh.

5. There are three Garebeg celebrations: the Garebeg Mulud, on the twelfth day of the third lunar, commemorating Mohammad's birth and death; the Garebeg on the tenth day of Sawal, celebrating the end of the fast and sometimes called Lebaran Puwasa; and the Garebeg of the tenth day of the twelfth month (that is, the month of the pilgrimage).

6. Attendance at the Garebeg celebrations would not, of course, itself be a sin; presumably the reference is to the accompanying festivities and their taint of worldliness.

7. His father was the son of Sultan Sepuh and was the Crown Prince.

8. The text reads ibadah (to be strict in the performance of one's religious obligations, in particular of the commandment to perform five daily prayers).

and many who performed asceticism.
The Prince
changed his name[9]
when he journeyed through the countryside,
calling himself Sheik Ngabdurahkim.[10]
At the capital
he was "Prince Dipanagara,"
so he had two names.
At that time he had reached his twentieth year.

His only pleasure
was in leading the life of a fakir,
and he was constantly mindful,
both day and night,
of how little time we have in this world,
and so his heart served
the First of Souls.[11]
But his human character was an impediment,
and he was often tempted by women.

Whenever he was mindful
of the purpose of our creation
he would journey through the countryside
visiting the mosques.
There he would be one with
the multitude of the *santri*,
and lead a life of great asceticism.
He went in disguise,
so that it was seldom that anyone knew him.

If he was recognized
by the teacher of the santri
Sheik Ngabdurahkim would leave,
for he desired only
to be one of the ordinary santri,
one of the poor and lowly
at the mosque schools,
and so he went from one to another.
When he did not want to be at the mosque schools he would
    go to the jungles,

to the mountains and ravines, cliffs and caves,
or sometimes follow the coastline.
During the fast month
he would sit in a deserted cave.
Now we tell
that it was beneath a tamarind tree,
where Sheik Ngabdurahkim
was sitting in a lonely cave.
When midnight had passed God sent him a trial.

---

9. The two lines are reversed in the translation.

10. The Javanese form of the Arabic Abdu'l-Rahīm.

11. The text reads purbaning Suksma (that is, God).

    Apparitions in a multitude of shapes
    came to try him.
    Now Sheik Ngabdurahkim
    was not distracted from his concentration
    and his inner gaze was still upon the All-Disposer.
    The apparitions disappeared
p. 3 and then came
    someone who stood before him,
    a man with a radiance like that of the full moon.

    His name was Hjang Djatimulja,[12]
    and he was Sunan Kali[13] in reality.
    Sheik Ngabdurahkim looked at him in amazement.[14]
    He said quietly:
    "Oh Ngabdurahkim,
    God has determined
    that in time to come
    you will be a king." He gave this warning and disappeared
      from sight.

    After the disappearance of the revered Pandita
    Ngabdurahkim was left uneasy
    and exceedingly amazed,
    so that he did not continue with his devotions,
    leaving that place in the morning.
    He went straight to the mountains,
    thinking nothing of the dangers around him.
    He had no concern for his physical body
    thinking only of God's love.

    He went deep into the jungle,
    climbed mountains and descended into ravines.
    He journeyed to no destination,
    being exceedingly perplexed of heart.
    When he had travelled far,
    he slept wherever he might be.
    He arrived at Bengkung,[15]
    Sheik Ngabdurahkim,
    and stopped there for seven days.

    Sheik Ngabdurahkim went down
    to the mosque at Imagiri,[16]
    wishing to join in the Friday prayer.
    He happened to arrive at the same time

---

12. Louw refers to him as Hjang Djatisukma.

13. Sunan Kali-Djaga, one of the wali of Java, and associated with the founding of the realm of Mataram.

14. Two lines condensed into one.

15. Bengkung may be a place name, but it is not to be found in Ch. F. H. Dumont, Aardrijkskundig Woordenboek van Nederlandsch Oost-Indië (Rotterdam: Nijgh & Van Ditmar's, 1917). Louw's text has: "He arrived at a cave. . . ."

16. The place of the royal burial ground, in the mountains south of Jogjakarta.

as the *djuru kuntji*,[17]
who were all coming to the prayer.
They were startled to see
their lord, and were rendered speechless.
Then they crowded around him and made their greetings.

After the Friday prayer
all the djuru kuntji
paid honor to him by making offerings
of whatever they were able to give.
He slept one night
in the Djimatan mosque
and in the morning he left.
Sheik Ngabdurahkim set out
following the river and then went up into the mountains.

He came to a cave, a place of spirits,
and slept there for one night.
In the morning he set out
following the interior of the mountain.

p. 4   Then he arrived,
Sheik Ngabdurahkim,
at a cave called Sagala-gala.
He went inside,
and slept two nights there.

On the next morning he set out
up the steep mountain,
intending to go to a cave called Langsé,
heedless of difficulties before him.
He travelled until he reached
the cave called Langsé,
and there Sheik Ngabdurahkim
stayed to perform asceticism.
He was in the cave for about half a month,

seeking after enlightenment.
The visible world vanished from his sight:
Sheik Ngabdurahkim
only took care for the Life[18] [within him],
and the Life took care for him.
He had returned to the Life
which is such
that it cannot be described.
Let us tell of her whose palace was beneath the sea:

Ratu Kidul[19] appeared
before Sheik Ngabdurahkim.
All was light and clear in the cave,

---

17. A retainer in charge of the upkeep of royal or holy graves.

18. The text reads kang urip, probably the Javanese equivalent of the Arabic al-Hayy (the Living One), one of the attributes of God.

19. Usually called Njai Rara (Loro) Kidul, the queen of the south sea. In the Babad Tanah Djawi she is said to have entered into a sort of union with Sénapati and also with Sultan Agung. See W. Olthof, ed., Poenika Serat Babad Tanah Djawi, Wiwit saking Nabi Adam doemoegi ing Taoen 1647 (The Hague: M. Nijhoff, 1941), p. 78.

but Ratu Kidul knew
that Sheik Ngabdurahkim
was as one dead to the world,
and could not be tempted.
So she spoke to give a promise
that she would return in the future when the time came.

Sheik Ngabdurahkim
heard what she said, though he saw nothing;
then she disappeared.
Now Sheik Ngabdurahkim
released his inner gaze
which returned to the light.[20]
In the morning he went down
to Parangtaritis.
Then he bathed in the sea and slept at Parangkusuma.[21]

He was sunk in meditation, leaning against a stone,
half dozing, when he heard
a voice which spoke thus:
"O Sheik Ngabdurahkim,
change your name.
You are now Ngabdulkamit.[22]
Further, I say,
in three years will come a time
of great disturbances in Jogjakarta

It is the will of God
that the beginning of the disturbances in the land of Java
will be in three years.

p. 5   And it is determined that you[23]
will play the chief part.
I give this sign
to you, Ngabdurahkim,
it is the arrow Sarotama.[24] Wear it.

And again I say
to you, Ngabdulkamit,
take care:
for if in future you fail,
your father will not succeed [to the throne].
But I tell you,
Ngabdulkamit,
you must refuse to be made
the heir-apparent by the Dutch,[25]

---

20. The text reads Bongsa rijahipun, possibly from the Arabic diyā.

21. According to Louw (De Java-oorlog, I, p. 93) Parangtaritis and Parangkusuma are situated close together, to the south of Mantjingan.

22. From the Arabic 'Abdu'l-Ḥamīd.

23. Two lines condensed into one.

24. From the Sanskrit carottama (best of arrows). According to J.F.C. Gericke and T. Roorda, Javaansch-Nederlandsch handwoordenboek, 2 vols. (Amsterdam: J. Müller, 1901) this is the name of an arrow of Ardjuna.

25. This term is misleading; the author means Europeans in general, and in this case it is the English who are involved.

for God has determined that this would be a sin.
But as for your father,
Ngabdulkamit, watch over
his succession to the throne,
for there is nothing else
which can be a means to this but you only.
He will not reign for long,
but will be the ancester [of Sultans].
Ngabdulkamit, you must return home.

Ngabdulkamit woke with a start. He looked around
    but all was clear,
there was no one speaking to him.
Then, high up in the clouds,
something flashed like lightning,
and fell in front of him.
It was Ki Sarotama.
When it had found its mark in the stone,
he took it up at once.
Day broke, and Sheik Ngabdulkamit set out,

carrying Ki Sarotama in his girdle.
He followed the water meadows,
and stopped at the river mouth
for a little while, before setting out again.
He came to Lipura[26]
and on a shining stone
he slept overnight.
In the morning he set out again
until he reached the Setjang[27] cave. Here the Prince stopped,

and slept the night.
In the morning he continued his journey,
back to Tegalredja.
When he arrived there,
he dressed.
Ki Sarotama
he made into a dagger.
Now the subject of the story changes:
in Jogjakarta there was much talk.

* *

[The reign of Sultan Amangkubuwana IV, Dipanagara's younger
  half-brother. The meter is Kinanti.]

p. 79   It was the will of God
that the Sultan should be exceedingly sinful,
though when his elder brother was present
he feared his anger.
The English were replaced by the Dutch:
the [new] Resident's name was Néis [Nahuys].

---

26. Gondanglipura, near Jogjakarta.

27. Dumont, <u>Aardrijkskundig Woordenboek</u>, lists three places with this
    name; one near Kutaradja, one near Purwaredja, and one near
    Tjangkrep (all in Kedu).

His pleasure was in eating and drinking
and making merry in the Dutch fashion.
All the Sultan's relatives
of the younger generation
followed his example,
heedless of the prohibitions of their religion.

Then "Collectors" were appointed,
but without the knowledge
of Prince Dipanagara.
As for their maintenance,
they got money
from all the subjects of the realm.

The Collectors' job
was to help the Patih.
The matter had been discussed
with Nahuys, who had given his approval
and asked that it be authorized
with the Sultan's own seal.

This was given.
Now we tell
that all the Sultan's relatives
of mature years,
and all the Dipati
of the realm of Jogjakarta, were perturbed,

and having discussed the matter, informed
Prince Dipanagara.
The Prince
was greatly surprised,
and set out for Jogjakarta.
He arrived at the kraton

where he met the Sultan's mother.
The Prince asked politely:
"About this matter,
how is it that I have not been told?[28]
It will be a vexation to all the people."

The Ratu Ibu said sweetly:[29]
"I did not know that.
When the matter was discussed,
I asked and was told
that you had already been informed."
The Prince asked politely:

---

28. Two lines condensed into one.

29. It should be noted that words like <u>aris</u> (gently) and <u>arum</u> (sweetly) are frequently used to fill the requirements of the meter and have little semantic force.

"Where is the Sultan?"
p. 80. The Ratu Ibu said:
"He is in the *bangsal panggung*."[30]
The Prince then went to find him.
When he came upon the Sultan,
the Prince said politely:

"Sultan, the reason I have come
is to ask you[31] about something.
I have heard
that you have appointed Collectors.
What is this?"
The Sultan said softly:

"It was on the advice of Danuredja[32]
and Wiranagara,
as there are too few envoys.
As for their task,
it is to collect all the moneys
from the *panjumpleng*[33] tax.

I asked them both
if they had informed you,[34]
and they said that you had already agreed."
The Prince said:
"That is certainly an absolute falsehood.

Sultan, in case you don't know,
in my opinion
this is a piece of absolute villainy
which will certainly lead
to trouble
in the future

for the common people.
And what is the salary
of the Collectors, and how many of them are there?
And for their daily meetings
what buildings do they use?"
The Sovereign said politely:

---

30. A tower of some sort. According to Louw (De Java-oorlog, I, p. 122) it was one of the watchtowers of the kraton, although he was unable to discover if there had ever been such a tower at Jogjakarta.

31. The word used is sira. This is significant because this would be the word used by a ruler to his subject, and not vice versa, which cast some light on the nature of the relationship between the two brothers.

32. Danuredja [III], the Patih.

33. A tax levied either per djung (measure of land) or per door (of house).

34. Two lines condensed into one. Here the word used for "you" is paduka, so that the Sultan addresses his elder half-brother as if the latter were a reigning monarch.

[Change of meter: Sinom

"Their salary comes directly from the tax moneys,
and each of them receives sixty [guilders].
The headmen receive one hundred and fifty.
In number they are forty,
plus two more.
Those two are the headmen.
They gather
at Danuredja's residence
and when the messengers have all gone out, they take over
    their duties.

At the appointed times, it is their duty
to go out to the villages
and collect the panjumpleng tax."
The Prince said politely
with a smile:
"What I said was no lie!
Now another thing, Sultan.
If they don't quite ruin the country,
I shall thank the *gunung*.[35]

In the time of our late father
I asked that all the gunung
should be dismissed,
on account of the burden they are

p. 81   to the common people.
I proposed to substitute
the corvee services and the money
from the tolls in all the ports.
I think this should be more than enough so that there will
    be no shortage of resources.

As for the government of the villages
[I asked] that it should return to the arrangements
existing in the reign of our great-grandfather.[36]
Our revered father agreed to this,
but fixed a future time for its implementation,
that is, after one year had elapsed.
This was to fill [the state coffers]
since the finances were quite depleted.
Before the time had elapsed, our revered father passed away.

And now you
actually intend to increase
the burden on the villagers.
What are you about?"
The Sultan said politely:
"It has already been done.
My seal is on[37]
the letter which will give the instructions to the villages."

---

35. A sort of police official with some judiciary powers (for levying fines, etc.).

36. Sultan Amangkubuwana I.

37. Two lines condensed into one.

"Well, Sultan, you ask for it back
if it has not yet gone out.
Summon Wiranagara."
The Sultan immediately
sent his summons,
and Wiranagara arrived before him.
The Sultan said:
"Major,[38] what is this,
you said before that you had already informed

my beloved elder brother, and that he had consented.
Now I incur his anger!"
Wiranagara bowed his head,
unable to find words.
Then [the Sultan] spoke again:
"Now I want the letter back
and the Collectors will not be appointed."
Wiranagara said:
"I am afraid that the letter has already gone through

and there is the Resident. . . ."
The Sultan was embarrassed
and remained silent.
The Prince became angry
and said to his younger brother:
"Enough, Sultan, you must choose between me,
one man alone,
and these two. What is your choice?
If you choose these two

let the letter go out.
If you choose me,
ask for it back.
As for your Resident,
if he is angry,
have no part in it.

p. 82 If you choose these two
I don't say that I am better,
but I will have nothing to do with it.

Wiranagara said:
"How can it be withdrawn?
The command has already been given,
and according to the book called
Nasihat ul-Muluk[39]
once the king has spoken
it cannot be rescinded."
The Prince listened
to Wiranagara's submission

---

38. Wiranagara bore the hybrid title of Radèn Major. He is also sometimes referred to as Tumenggung, a Javanese title with military connotations.

39. Nasihat ul-Muluk (Advice to Kings) is an eleventh-century Shafiite work. See Carl Brockelmann, <u>Geschichte der Arabischen Litteratur</u> (Leiden: E. J. Brill, 1942-1943), I, p. 483.

and his wrath was aroused.
He pulled both his ears,
and kicked him, shouting:
"Well, Mukidin![40]
You want to give us a lesson.
You are hiding behind your Book,
and you know better than anyone--
the rest of us know nothing,
and you are the only judge of good and evil!"

The Prince [now] spoke
to the Sultan: "I want to know the truth.
You tell me
who thought of this.
If it were you, yourself,
that would be according to the Tables of Destiny;[41]
if it were on the advice of someone else,
then it can certainly be changed,
and as devil's work I will not allow it."

The Sultan said quietly:
"It originated with two people,
Danuredja and Wiranagara.
I asked them,
and they said
that they had already informed you.
So I believed them,
and gave my permission."
Tumenggung Wiranagara bowed his head.

The Prince said:
"It is quite clear
that this is the invention of a devil.
What was said about the Book is so much idle talk."
The Sultan said softly:
"Now tell again,
Major, to my beloved elder brother--
if you still dare--
the matter of this Book. I would like to hear you!"

Major Wiranagara
could find nothing to say.
The Sultan spoke:
"It is decided that I shall ask [for the letter] back,
and the Collectors will be dismissed.
You may leave."
Major Wiranagara
withdrew from the chamber with a *sembah*[42]

p. 83   The Sultan said to his elder brother:

---

40. According to Louw (De Java-oorlog, I, p. 123) this was Wiranagara's name as a child.

41. Lokilmahpul, from the Arabic Lawḥ Mahfuẓ, the table on which everything is written as it is predetermined to happen.

42. To make a sembah is to place the palms of the hands together and hold them before one's face with the thumbs at the level of the nose, while bowing forwards. This is done to signify great respect for the person concerned.

"Let us retire, dear brother,
and take our meal in the kraton."
They went together,
and sat down inside the yellow building.
The Ratu Ibu joined them,
together with Ratu Kantjana.[43]
Then they asked that the meal be brought,
and Njai Rija served them.
The Ratu Ibu asked sweetly:

"What has happned, Sultan,
in the matter of the Collectors?"
The Sultan said:
"It is now settled that we will not continue with it."
The Ratu smiled, and said:
"Sultan, I tell you the truth:
the one who reigns
in Jogjakarta is really
your elder brother Prince Dipanagara.

Indeed, Sultan, this was settled
by your father quite some time ago,
when he was still the heir-apparent.
He said to me:
'Radèn Aju, I tell you,
don't hold high hopes for your son,
for my heart is set upon
his elder brother.'
And I said that I would follow his wishes."

The Sultan seemed embarrassed,
for there were other people present to hear this.
He said:
"There is no need to tell me this.
I already know it,
for my revered father gave the same message
to me, indeed."
The Prince smiled and said gently:
"Ratu Ibu, you are like a child,

with a secret to tell,
so that everyone knows it."
Ratu Kantjana smiled.
When they had finished
the meal, they took their leave.
The Prince retired
to Tegalredja.
After some considerable time has passed
the Ratu Ageng[44] fell seriously ill.

---

43. The Ratu Ibu was, as seen above, the Sultan's mother. Ratu Kantjana was his wife.

44. This title was born at this time by the mother of Amangkubuwana III, that is, by Dipanagara's grandmother.

>   This happened in the fast month,
>   when all the sons and grandsons of the royal family
>   were holding their watch at the kraton.
>   together with the *ulama*.
>   The Penghulu asked [the Ratu Ageng]
>   to break her fast,
>   but she refused to do so.
>   It seemed as if she had decided
>   that when *bakda*[45] came she would find her rest.
>
>   The Sultan said to his elder brother:
>   "What shall we do tomorrow
>   about the Garebeg procession?"
>   The prince said gently:
>   "Do not change the arrangements
>   I myself,
>   together with Ratu Bendara and Ratu Anggèr[46]
>   will keep watch over grandmother.
>   You all go in the Garebeg procession.
>
>   Mangkubumi,[47] you
>   make audience in the morning."
>   The Sultan said gently:
>   "But if it happens that I am not present. . . ?"
>   The Prince said:
>   "God knows of the future,
>   but it seems to me,
>   that our grandmother is waiting
>   until all her sons and grandsons are present."
>
>   Thus it was done.
>   It was God's will
>   that the death of the Ratu Ageng
>   took place after the Garebeg procession.
>   Her sons and grandsons had already come,
>   as well as the Penghulu.
>   All the ulama
>   had gathered there too.
>   She was laid to rest at Djimatan[48] with her son.

p. 84 (before "about the Garebeg procession?")

* *

pp. 85-86   [The ten stanzas omitted here deal briefly with the rebellion of Sinduratmadja and Pangéran Dipasana.]

---

45. The celebrations of the first of Sawal, after the fast month.

46. Ratu Anggèr was Ratu Kantjana's mother. I am not sure who Ratu Bendara was.

47. Dipanagara's uncle (brother of Amangkubuwana III). He took the side of the Dutch in the Java War.

48. The royal burial place at Imagiri.

We tell of the Sultan.
It happened that he had the desire to see
his elder brother again,
and so he sought him at Sélaradja.[49]
It happened that at the time
of the arrival of the Sultan,
who had missed his elder brother greatly,
the Prince himself
was bathing in a pool where the water[50] flowed.

He was amusing himself by watching the goldfish
on the shining stones.
The Sultan arrived
and helped him to choose [the best].
Two other princes
accompanied their brother[51] [the Sultan].
They were the princes Surjabrangta
and Surjawidjaja.
It was the will of God that the Prince [Dipanagara]

should be moved to place complete trust
in his younger brother [the Sultan].
The Prince said:
"Come, Sultan, let us move,
and sit inside."
The Sultan went with him,
accompanied by his brothers
Pangéran Surjabrangta
and Pangéran Surjawidjaja.

The Prince said,
smiling at his younger brother:
"Sultan, I tell you,
all the agreements,
from the English period,
are still with me,
and not in the kraton.
There you will find only the contracts
and the agreement about the state finances.

---

49. From the text it is clear that this was another residence of Dipanagara's, close to Tegalredja. Louw's text reads Batu-ardja throughout.

50. The text actually has tigan but since none of the meanings of this word are at all appropriate, I have supposed it to be a corruption of toja.

51. The text first says that the Sultan was their elder brother, then that he was their younger brother. In fact, according to de Klerck's table (De Java-oorlog, VI, p. 467) Surjawidjaja was older than the Sultan and Surjabrangta younger.

But all the special provisions,[52]
are still here.
Now I am worried
that if you and I should die[53]
it seems certain
that quarrels will spring up
among our sons,
unless God protects them.

So this is my present wish:
I will give the document
to you, Sultan.
But, Sultan, I entrust it to the care
of all your children.
If I should die,
I leave things in your hands, Sultan."
The Sultan
agreed to this, and the Prince said

p. 87
to the Princes Surjabrangta
and Surjawidjaja:
"You both go
and ask for the agreement.
My wife will give it to you."
The two princes withdrew with a sembah
from the presence of their brothers.
They returned immediately,
and gave the document to Prince Dipanagara,

who took it, and said:
"Sultan, you should know
that this document was written
by General Raffles[54] himself.
The Javanese on the other side
was written by [Se]tjadiningrat.[55]
Enough, you take it.
But I must impress upon you
that this is the one thing I am anxious to preserve."

---

52. Neither here nor in any other place does Dipanagara explain what these special provisions were. Louw, however, is of the opinion that they related to the succession of the throne and connects this document with one described by Van Lawick van Pabst, in which Dipanagara was promised that he should succeed to the throne in the event of his half-brother, the Sultan, dying while still a minor or conducted himself improperly. The chief difference between the two accounts is that while Dipanagara says that the document in question was written by Raffles, Van Lawick van Pabst says that it was written by Dipanagara's father (Amangkubuwana III). Both writers, however, agree that the document was burnt by those whose interests conflicted with Dipanagara's. See Louw, De Java-oorlog, I, pp. 115-125.

53. Two lines condensed into one.

54. Raffles was of course not a general. The title probably results from the usage of djéndral to translate the Dutch Gouverneur-Generaal. Djéndral is however also used for military generals, for instance Djéndral Glèspi (General Gillespie).

55. This was the title granted to the Kapitan Tjina, Djing Sing, who had served Dipanagara's father in the negotiations with the British.

The Sultan said that he understood,
and was exceedingly grateful [for this trust].
The document was handed over
to the Sultan, who took it
with a glad heart.
The Sultan afterwards asked leave to return to the capital.
This was granted,
and he left Sélaradja,
carrying the letter on his own person.

We do not describe **his** journey:
he arrived at the kraton.
Now it was the will of God
that before much time had passed
the Sultan fell prey to the schemes,
of devils, who led him astray.
The document he had been given
he now burnt, an evil deed,
[thinking] if this is still in existence who knows what may
    happen?

It seems that it was God's predetermination
that the Sultan easily accepted
evil counsel.
And so the document was burnt.
By God's will,
it happened that only a short time after
his burning of the document [56]
the Sultan died at his appointed time.

The cause of his death, however,
was not an illness which grew from slight [to fatal].
He had been out on a pleasure trip and had come to a stop,
and what did cause his death
was the food offered by
the Patih [Danuredja].
He was drinking *djangan*[57]
when he began to cough and hiccough.
He fell to the ground and died immediately.

His body swelled up all at once.
There was great commotion in Jogjakarta,
and everyone was shocked at the news.
Dipanagara[58] arrived,
but his brother was already dead.
And all the royal relatives,
men and women, gathered there.
There was a noise like thunder from the lamentation,
because of all the women in the palace.

---

56. Two lines condensed into one.

57. A soup-like dish, eaten as an accompaniment to rice.

58. Literally, "his elder brother."

All the officials
gathered there in their full complement.
The Penghulu and his companions
asked that the body should be washed,
but the Secretary, Ibu [D'Abo], did not agree to this,
and asked them to wait,
while he sent a messenger
after the Resident.
The Resident's name was Baron Silwis [de Salis]

and he happened to be away at Sala.
[The Secretary] ordered that the proceedings should wait
while they went after [the Resident].
The Prince looked upon
the body of his brother
and determined
that it must be washed.
This was done,
and afterwards [the body] was laid to rest in the Prabajasa.[59]

A day and a night passed;
Baron de Salis had still not arrived.
The next morning the body was placed in the coffin.[60]
Again the Secretary objected,
but he was overruled again
by the Prince.
Now that the body was in the coffin,
watch was kept over it in the *bangsal*.
At eleven o'clock Baron de Salis arrived.

Then the order was given to carry the coffin [in procession].
The Ratu Ageng[61]
made a strong representation,
but she was told that it was not possible
that her desire should be fulfilled.
Baron de Salis
went arm-in-arm
with Prince Dipanagara.
When they reached the southern *alun-alun* they all returned

to the palace,
all the distant relatives
and the sons of the royal house.
The Resident, de Salis, said politely:

---

59. The entrance hall of the kraton.

60. The text has tinimbalan (summoned), an error for tinabélan.

61. This title had now passed to the mother of the dead Sultan (Amangkubuwana IV). She had formerly been called the Ratu Ibu. We are not told what she so strongly requested, but the implication seems to be that she wanted her own grandson to succeed to the throne and was told that this was not possible since the Resident favored Dipanagara.

"Prince Dipanagara,
do not return home,
but remain and keep watch in the palace."
The Prince replied politely:
"I do not wish to do so. I will return home when you do so.

p. 89 Let the Secretary
and Ditri [Dietré][62] alone
stay and keep watch in the palace
with Kjai Mangkubumi."
Baron de Salis agreed,
and the assembly dispersed.
All the royal relatives
kept watch over the Sultan's coffin,
and the Prince returned to Tegalredja.

All the royal relatives
then went to Djimatan,
where the Sultan was buried.
His tomb was quickly made,
apart from the one where his father lay.
Now we tell
that the Sultan had left
nine children:
but we list only his sons.

[The first] was called Radèn Mas Ménol
and he was three years old.
Nevertheless he had been given
the title of Pangéran Dipati,[63]
although some time later
he had not yet been installed in that position.
His younger brother was Radèn Mas Getot,
and then there were Radèn Mas Mursada,
and Radèn Mas Maw-dan.[64] So there were four boys

and five girls.
Now we tell
of Pangéran Dipanagara.
He was often invited
to the Residency,
but he seldom accepted.
And, moreover, whenever
the Resident visited the palace,
he asked the Prince to come with him. But he rarely did so.

And the Resident often tried to determine
the Prince's exact age.
Whenever he felt the desire to do so
he would ask him to the Residency.
The Resident made every effort

---

62. A translator (See Louw, De Java-oorlog, I, p. 127).

63. The title borne by the Crown Prince. Louw translates that he had only been *promised* this title.

64. Louw's text reads Mangun.

to win his heart,
and often asked [the Prince]
to sit down with him:
the Resident would wait on him himself.

In talking to him, Baron de Salis
asked many questions about[65]
Tegalredja and Sélaradja.
Pangéran Mangkubumi
understood the direction of things,
and set out for Tegalredja.[66]
There he met

p. 90   the Prince,[67] inside the Sélaradja house.

Pangéran [Mangkubumi] said:
"My boy, I do not quite understand
Baron de Salis' intentions.
He is much drawn,
to you, my boy.
I think that in his heart
he is waiting to find out your hopes.
If you will be first
say so." Pangéran [Dipanagara] said:

"That would be quite easy.
[But] I absolutely refuse
to take such a path.
If I had been so inclined, I would already,
before this lapse of time,
have spoken of the promises."
Pangéran [Mangkubumi] said
to his nephew:[68]
"My boy, I am exceedingly worried

that another may be [proposed for the throne].
What should I do?"
Pangéran [Dipanagara] said,
smiling: "Indeed, I am thankful
if they want to depart from
the agreement.
It is better thus:
it will avoid trouble.
I place my trust in God's protection."

Pangéran [Mangkubumi] returned to the capital.
About a week later,
Radén Mas Ménol was raised
to the throne, succeeding
his late father,

---

65. These two lines are reversed in the translation.

66. Two lines condensed into one.

67. Literally, "his son," a confusing usage.

68. Literally, "his son."

though with a regency council.
Those appointed were
Pangéran Mangkubumi
and Pangéran

Arja Dipanagara,
together with Ratu Kantjana
and the Ratu Ageng.
Prince [Dipanagara] was quite unwilling,
but was compelled to accept the position.
Because of this he felt greatly shamed
and was unable to face his fellow men.
Such was his state of mind that when his *kampuh*[69] was torn
as he mounted into the carriage,

he did not see this, and trod on it.
The Secretary was with him,
and he felt as if he had received a mortal blow.
They came to the Residency[70]
and the contract[71] was read.
Radèn Mas Ménol shrieked,
with all his force, saying:

p. 91   "No! I don't want to!"
but the Resident insisted upon his accession

and so did the Ratu Ageng.
When they returned [from the Residency]
[the new Sultan] sat on the *sitinggil*[72] for a moment,
and then they all went in to the kraton,
and sat down in one of the *balé*.[73]
Baron de Salis gave
the contract to Pangéran [Dipanagara],
but he did not want it.
When asked to read it out he was unable to do so.

When his signature was requested
he said that he was unable to write.
Asked for his sign [he said]:
"I do not have my seal with me."
Paku Alam[74]
smiled at this.
Pangéran Dipanagara
was more shamed than ever,
feeling that he had become a laughingstock.

---

69. This is an article of attire formerly worn by male persons of rank at court and also sometimes by bridegrooms. It is a length of cloth draped over trousers.

70. The text has <u>djandji</u>, which I have taken for an error for <u>lodji</u>.

71. The treaty between the new Sultan, represented by the Regency council, and the Dutch government.

72. The name of a square walled terrace with lattice work and door in front outside the entrance to the princely residence. Here the ruler would sit on major festival days to be seen by this subjects.

73. One of the pavilions in the kraton.

74. The ruler of a small principality created out of Jogjakarta by the British in 1812.

So all the business
was taken in hand
by Pangéran Mangkubumi,
with the consent of the Resident.
Afterwards the gathering dispersed.
Now we tell
of Pangéran Dipanagara
who returned to Tegalredja.
After his arrival there he became exceedingly melancholy,

thinking only of his shame,
that he had been so little regarded,
as to be made stand-in for a mere boy.
If he had only been asked!
Now he was put on a level
with an obsequious person
selling his services for a living.
"Was ever anyone in such a situation?
One must have too great a desire for life [to live on so]."

His heart was as if quite broken.
Pangéran Dipanagara
then entered the sleeping apartment,
intending to take his life.
The visible world vanished from his sight,
and only his shame remained with him.
Now Sang Kusuma[75]
was anxious at heart, seeing
her husband,[76] whose innermost feelings she could not fathom.

"What secret does he bear,
that he is so melancholy?"[77]
thus she thought,
with an uneasy mind.
And so Sang Retna followed him
p. 92   into the sleeping apartment.
There she saw that her husband
was about to take his life.
She fell at his feet, and with overflowing tears

said brokenly:
"Dear husband, I cannot bear to remain after you!"
With her head on his breast [she said]:
"Let me die first!
How can I remain after you!"
By the will of God
the Prince's gaze
returned to the light
when he heard the tearful words of Sang Kusuma.

---

75. Sang Kusuma, Sang Retna and Sang Dyah are poetic terms for a lady of rank and beauty.

76. Literally, "her elder brother." "Elder brother" and "younger sister" are forms of address commonly used between husband and wife.

77. These two lines are reversed in the translation.

He looked once more outside himself,
and gently taking hold of his wife,
he set her on his lap,
saying:
"Enough, do not weep, Lady!
Your servant will not take his life."
Sang Dyah said gently:
"What has so deeply affected you
that you wish to take leave of the world, my lord?"

The Prince said:
"My ruby, my mistress, fair one,
light of all Java!
I shall tell you the truth:
I am ashamed to live longer
in this world.
I am a man good for nothing:
I have been made stand-in for a baby.
It seems that I am no longer considered a rational being.

They make merry of me like a man of low repute,
and I am held exceedingly cheap.
Had I wished to be ruler
I would have been so long ago,
and now I am his regent.
I have come so low
that I am greatly shamed:
I have been raised to the office of nursemaid."
Sang Retna smiled and said gently:

"I beg your forgiveness
in the greatest measure for your servant.
It is not possible, my lord, that you have become unmindful
of the best path
to the world which is yet hidden from us.
It is not thus.
In earlier times, my lord,
you spoke of the best path.
I still remember this.

This is my resolve
in case I should be left behind
[by your] going to the eternal world.
I pray that I may go first,
for I could not bear to see
you go, and remain behind.[78]
Truly, I have
prayed to the Lord of All Things.[79]

---

78. Two lines condensed into one.

79. From the Arabic Rabb al-(ālamīn(a).

and implored the blessing
and intercession of the Prophet
Muhammad, the Chosen One,
that when we depart this world for a holier one
I may not be second.
And as for the way thither,
it is excellent and broad,
and it depends upon God's decree.
Between haste and patience we can make but one choice.

Still the best
is patience.
Many indeed are its stories.
And let us increase the number of our works, truly.
If it is allowed,
and with God's help,
it is my purpose
to serve to the end
as your handmaid, my lord.

My lord, you wanted to end things yourself,
not allowing the judgment of the Almighty.
But how can it be otherwise?
What remains to us is most excellent:
in truth, shame in this world,
if we do not swerve from our purpose,
becomes good works, for which we shall be recompensed.
And it is sure that the trials sent by the Almighty
all spring from His love and bounty.

The reason I dare to speak truly[80]
is that it was from you, my lord,
that I learnt this.
I implore your pardon
if I have too far forgotten myself."
When the Prince heard
the words of his wife
he smiled, and it was as if his sorrow were wiped away.

The Prince embraced his wife
and said gently:
"Oh my ruby, my mistress,
who art like a finely chiselled diamond,
and sent down from heaven
out of the bounty of the Lord!
Jewel among the women
of all the land of Java!
I cannot describe my feelings.

Truly, you know right,
and your servant is greatly in error.
Faith is like the sun;
the human heart is like the wind;
and the trials we experience from evil schemes

p. 94 are like unto clouds.
Our corporeal existence
may be likened unto the earth:
if no rain falls

---

80. Two lines condensed into one.

how will they grow,
all the seeds which are in the earth?
Your good deeds
are like a seed,
from which in this corporeal existence
we can grow in faith.
The third part is the human heart.
These together form one whole,
completed by our acceptance [of whatever is God-given].[81]

The significance of acceptance
is that it brings about the growth of the seeds.
If it is not thus
our life is in vain.
Of all men in this world
most favored of all
are those who are greatly tried,
for this is bounty indeed.
If they are able to meet [their trials], this is the proof
    of God's love.

If they are not able to do so,
it is as if all the seeds
are not able to grow;
and so our human life is fruitless.
It would be better to die
as a baby, unknown and unreckoned.
The best things
are four, in one unity:
works, [mystical] knowledge [of God], the knower, and the
    Known.[82]

It has happened that I
have been given God's bounty:
because of you I have been made mindful that this is a trial
    I must undergo,
when I had almost strayed from the right path."
We speak no more of this,
but tell of Jogjakarta.
Prince Mangkubumi was still[83]
being pressed for the seal of his nephew.

---

81. Thus the simile is: The heart is like the earth, the good deed like a seed, and acceptance of whatever God gives is like the rain.

82. The text gives the "four things" as ngamal, ngèlmu, ngamal, maklum, but this seems an error, perhaps for ngamal, ngèlmu, ngalim, maklum. Ngamal (works) and ngèlmu (esoteric knowledge) are often represented as complementary, and we also find the trinity ngèlmu - ngalim - maklum: esoteric knowledge, the knower, and the Known, that is, God.

83. Two lines are condensed into one.

>   Baron de Salis
>   did not accept the three seals[84] that were there,
>   but demanded the full complement,
>   insisting on the fourth.
>   He said:
>   "If that one is not there
>   these three [are useless].
>   The only one that we must have
>   is that of Prince Dipanagara.
>
>   The other three
>   are in the nature of witnesses.
>   If we do not have
>   that single seal
>   then we cannot collect
> p. 95   the moneys[85] from the tolls.
>   I will certainly not allow it."
>   So Pangéran Mangkubumi
>   was pressed by three people of high rank[86]
>
>   because there was no money for the state's expenses.[87]
>   So Pangéran Mangkubumi
>   set out to Tegalredja.
>   Now we tell
>   that it happened that the Prince [Dipanagara]
>   was sitting inside the *balé kentjur*.[88]
>   He had asked for the Ardjuna Widjaja
>   to be read to him,[89]
>   as a way of easing his rended heart.
>
>   He was attended by two retainers.
>   Wirjadikusuma
>   was the name of one,
>   and Sastrawinangun [was the other].
>   Pangéran Mangkubumi
>   on arriving [at Tegalredja] then went straight on
>   to Sélaradja,
>   and when he met [his nephew] they sat down together
>   in the balé kentjur. Pangéran [Mangkubumi] said:

---

84. The three seals would be those of Mangkubumi, Ratu Kantjana, and the Ratu Ageng.

85. The text has duwé, which I have read as an error for duwit.

86. That is, Baron de Salis and the two Ratu.

87. The text has sabab tan saged balaka, which I have read as an error for sabab tan saged balandja.

88. A pendapa situated in a churchyard or near a mosque.

89. The story of the battle between Ardjuna and Dasamuka, taken from the Uttarakanda and put into Javanese poetry by Mpu Tantular (Madjapahit period). See R. M. Ng. Poerbatjaraka, Kapustakan Djawi (Djakarta: Djambatan, 1952), p. 40. These two lines are reversed in the translation.

"My boy, the reason that I have come
is to inform you of the difficulty affecting the state.
The moneys from the tolls
cannot be commanded by myself and the Ratu Ageng[90]
together with
Ratu Kantjana, whose seal makes three;
I must ask for your seal.
What is more, I have incurred the anger
of the Resident. What is your wish now?"

Pangéran Dipanagara
seemed moved to inner wrath.
"It is for this reason that I
did not wish to become a regent.
I am like a hired man,
and am in the position of selling my name.
For the whole time since it was made
I have used this seal
only three times,

and that was in cases of murder.
Pangéran Mangkubumi
said gently:
"What shall they do,
your relatives,
and the soldiery too,
who are all paid from these moneys?
They will certainly be in difficulties
if the money from the tolls does not come in."

Pangéran Dipanagara
was torn two ways in his mind.
Then he bowed before
the shame that had come to him,
though he felt as if his very heart was burnt.

p. 96 He smiled and said politely:
"Kjai,[91] I will do what you ask,
but I take you to witness
that after this is done I cast away my seal,

and so I no longer bear the name
of Dipanagara,
but am to be called Ngabdulkamit."
Pangéran Mangkubumi
said with apparent fear:
"Indeed, whatever you wish:
who would dare to oppose you?"
[The Prince] asked for his seal, and when it was brought
he gave it to his uncle[92]

---

90. Literally, "your elder sister."

91. This title can be used for any older man of some standing and does not necessarily carry any religious connotations.

92. Literally, "his father."

saying:
"Remember this, Kjai,
if it is a matter of money
I will not be brought into it again."
Pangéran Mangkubumi
said softly:
"Well, my boy, I think
that this sign from you [will be sufficient]."
Then he asked leave to return. We say no more of him.

The Prince's heart
was ever more strongly afflicted by burning pain.
To ease it, he went
to the house of his younger brother,
Pangéran Surjabrangta,
whose son was to be circumcised.
When he had supervised the ceremony, the Prince
slept there overnight.
His sleeping place was in the grounds of the house,

together with the women-folk.
Throughout the night he had no desire for sleep,
and played chess.[93]
His partner was
Radén Aju Danukusuma, the elder.[94]
In the morning the Prince returned
to Tegalredja,
and his wife met him on the verandah.

He embraced her, who resembled Supraba,[95]
and brought her into the sleeping apartment.
The Prince then fell asleep,
and slept through the hours of prayer and of food,
all day and into the night.
Sang Retna did not dare to wake him,
but simply kept watch.
Then, in the middle of the night
a sign of the wrath of God descended.

Mount Merapi burst into flames
which seemed to reach to heaven itself.
Jogjakarta seemed full of it;
the sky turned into fire.
The noise was frightful,

p. 97   thundering and roaring.
The fires danced,
and everyone was filled with fear,
and earnestly[96] looked for a place of shelter.

---

93. The text reads *tjatur*, from the Sanskrit *caturangga*.

94. Two lines condensed into one.

95. The name of a particularly beautiful *widadari* (heavenly nymph).

96. The text reads *ting kudandang* (affected by great longing), foreshadowing the next meter, Dandanggula.

[Ḍanḍanggula]

They fled seeking shelter scarcely knowing what they did:
the sky was now completely dark.
Now we tell that it happened
that the Prince did not wake,
but slept sweetly.
Sang Retna did not know what she should do:
she feared to leave him, in case he should be killed [97]
and yet she hardly dared to wake her husband.
So she just kept watch over him.

Sang Kusuma deteremined
to watch over her husband,
in case he should be killed.
Her only thought was to share his fate:
in truth, she did not intend to be left behind.
We say no more of this.
Sang Retna
had a servant
who was very light-headed, and knew no proper respect.
Her name was Bok Buwang.

Looking at the sky, she became very afraid,
and when she heard the noise she lost control of herself
and simply screamed.
The other servants all joined in,
while their master and mistress
still remained inside the sleeping apartment.
Now we tell
that when the Prince heard
the noise of all the servants screaming
he woke with a start.

When he saw his wife
sitting at his feet, the Prince asked:
"What is happening, little one?"
She said gently:
"I don't really know.
I have not been outside."
Then the Prince
went out, hand in hand
with Sang Retna. When they came out into the square in front
    of the house
they looked at the sky

and the burning mountain,
and the shifting earth.
The Prince smiled,
and spoke
to all the servants,
[saying] various things [to calm them].
Afterwards
the Prince took Sang Retna
p. 98   and brought her back to the sleeping apartment,
where he had his wish.

---

97. Two lines condensed into one.

Afterwards the prince asked leave
of Sang Retna, to go to Sélaradja.
Now the scene of the story shifts
to Jogjakarta.
Great was the commotion there.
The Ratu Ageng
was exceedingly distracted
and could only cry for help
to Pangéran Dipanagara.
Every time she heard someone arrive

in haste, she thought
that it was the Prince arriving,
and afterwards she felt much disappointed.
The Secretary, D'Abo,
and Pangéran Mangkubumi,
Dietri, and the Patih [Danuredja],
as well as the Major[98]
and Baron de Salis, were not there:
they had left [on a journey]. Now we relate
that the state of crisis lasted three days.

Let us tell of him whose sorrow was great,
the Prince, at Sélaradja.
His feelings cannot be described,
that in this world
one misfortune had followed upon the other.
What is now related
took place
in the year Dal.[99]
The date was . . .[100] and it was the fast month,
on the twenty-first day.

The Prince was in a cave;
it was the Setjang cave.
Every year during the fast month
it was the Prince's habit[101]
to sit inside this cave,
without leaving it at all.
Now it happened

---

98. Presumably Wiranagara.

99. This is the fifth year of the eight-year windu cycle.

100. Although the number of syllables required for the meter is complete, it seems that the text once contained a date now missing. What remains is the windu year (Dal); the date of the month (the twenty-first of Ramadan, although Louw's text gives the twenty-seventh); and the two words sirah tanggal. Of these sirah (head) could be part of a chronogram (sengkala), with the value "1." Tanggal means "date," unless it is read as tunggal, which would also have the value "1." In any case, at least two more words would be needed for a complete chronogram. Louw's text has a complete date, 1751 (Çaka), (1829 A.D.) and therefore cannot be correct. Louw, De Java-oorlog, I, p. 130.

101. Two lines condensed into one.

that he was sitting on a shining stone
which was called "Ngambar Maja."[102]

Such was his pleasure,
to make this cave his home.
There was a pond containing a spring
which sputtered, like a lake
rising up in a well.
An enclosed widara[103] tree
was of his audience hall
the door. The tree was easy to climb.
The Prince seemed to sleep, his eyes half-closed.
Then there was

a man who came to him,
accompanied by a wind.
He stood before him,
and his clothes
were like those of a hadji.
The Prince was astonished,
and said politely:
"I have not met you before:
where do you come from?" The one asked answered:
"I have no dwelling.

I come here because I have been sent to summon you."
The Prince said:
"What is the name of he who sent you,
and where is his home?"
The man said softly:
"Indeed, he has no home.
All the people of Java
are his dwelling.
He is called the Ratu Adil[104]
and it was he who sent me

to summon you, in truth.
You will find him
on the summit of a mountain.
From where we are
the mountain lies in a southeasterly direction,
and its name is Rasamuni.
But you must meet him alone.[105]
The Prince set out at once, accompanied
by the man who had come to summon him.

---

102. That is, "radiating light."

103. According to F. S. A. de Clercq, Nieuw Plantkundig Woordenboek voor Nederlandsch Indie (Amsterdam: J. H. de Bussy, 1909), p. 347. Widara is a tree with edible fruit, Zizyphus jujuba, the "jujube tree."

104. The Ratu Adil (Just King) is the central figure in Javanese messianism. Here, however, he has been given a strongly Islamic character.

105. Two lines condensed into one.

It was the will of God
that the Prince should follow him without question.
In a short time they came
to the foot of the mountain,
and the messenger disappeared from sight.
Now we tell
that the Ratu Adil
was standing on the summit of the mountain,
and his radiance outrivalled that of the Majestic Sun,[106]
which for long shone but palely.

The Prince could not
look upon the face
of the Ratu Adil, whose radiance
outshone that of the lordly Sun.
The Prince
looked only at his clothes, and saw[107]
that he wore a green turban,
and a silk *djubah*,[108]
silk trousers, and a red sash.[109]
He stood facing northwest,

at the summit of the mountain,
on a shining stone which was quite bald.
He cast no shadow,
and there was no grass:

p. 100   the ground was as clean as if it had been swept.
The Prince below him
looked upwards.
He stood facing southeast.
The Ratu Adil said gently:
"Oh Ngabdulkamit!

The reason I have summoned you
is that you must lead all my soldiers
in the conquest of Java.
If anyone should ask you[110]
for your mandate, it is the Koran.
Let them seek there."
Ngabdulkamit said:
"I ask pardon, I am not able to wage war,
nor can I bear

---

106. The text reads: <u>Sang Hjang Pradongga-pati</u>, <u>Sang Hjang Arka</u>.

107. These two lines are reversed in the translation.

108. A long Arab robe with wide sleeves.

109. The text reads <u>sabi</u>, which may refer to the Malay <u>sebai</u>.

110. Two lines condensed into one.

to see death.[111]
Moreover, once formerly,
I have undertaken such a commission,[112]
and been found wanting
by my fellow men."
The Ratu Adil said:
"It is not possible [for you to refuse],
for it is God's will
that it shall happen thus in Java,
and the one who shall have the chief role is you.

There is no other choice."
When he had finished speaking there was a loud crack
as if a stone had been thrown at a shovel,[113]
and he disappeared.
It is impossible to describe[114]
the Prince's feelings,
as he stood on the mountaintop.

He remained standing as before
facing northwest.
The Prince was exceedingly amazed
and felt a burden in his breast.
Fireflies made points of light,
and he was startled to see
betjak-betjik[115]
and *puṭut* birds, and small bats,
which shrieked. The sea flamed
and there was a thundering noise,

like a rumbling of a volcano.
The Prince descended from the summit
and looked around him.
We say no more of this event:
afterwards the Prince returned directly
to Tegalredja.

p. 101 Now we tell
that many were the disturbances in Jogjakarta,
and the state was set in confusion.
We tell of the Penghulu

---

111. The text actually has aningali ḍumateng papatih (to see Patih), an error for aningali ḍumateng papati.

112. This refers to the time of the English attack on the Jogjakarta kraton when Dipanagara was his father's Sénapati (p. 43 of the printed text).

113. Two lines condensed into one.

114. Three lines condensed into one.

115. I have been unable to locate betjak-betjik in a dictionary. Louw does not translate this passage.

who had come to quarrel with the Patih.
Baron de Salis had been replaced
by Semitsa [Smissaert],
and the Secretary
had also been replaced;
Suwalijé [Chevallier]
was the name of the new incumbent.
To return to the Patih,
and the Penghulu:
their quarrel became worse.

During the fast month, the Penghulu
moved his house to Tegalredja:
he descended upon Sélaradja
with his baggage train.
He arrived at the audience hall
and then occupied the house
of Mas Kartadjaja.
The Prince did not know of this,
for he had gone to the Setjang cave again.
After some time had passed,

the Penghulu was sought out again,
but he did not wish to return.
Then he was replaced
by a Ketib,[116] who was raised to his office.
The Ketib's name was Ketib Anom.
The Prince [Dipanagara] was asked
for his permission but would not give it.[117]
Now we tell of another thing.
It happened that one night the Ratu Ageng had a dream,
and heard a voice [which said]:

"Ratu Ageng, Ratu Kantjana
must marry a Wali Wuḍar[118]
whose dwelling is northwest of this place.
If this is not done,
Java will be devastated
and your life will be forfeit."
It happened thus

---

116. From the Arabic khaṭib. There would be several Ketib to assist the Penghulu in the execution of his duties.

117. According to Louw (De Java-oorlog, I, p. 132) the matter of this appointment is not mentioned in the European sources but figures prominently in the Javanese accounts.

118. In Javanese, the word wali has three main meanings: 1) the guardian of a minor; 2) the person whose consent is necessary for the marriage of a girl or woman (i.e., her father, grandfather, brother, or uncle); and 3) specifically the first preachers of Islam on Java, usually numbered at nine (wali sanga), which include such figures as Sunan Kali-Djaga, Sunan Giri, Sunan Bonang, and Sunan Gunung Djati. These three meanings are derived from the Arabic walī. Wuḍar (uḍar) has the meaning of "loose, open, released." For the possible interpretations of wali wuḍar, see below.

three times,
and the voice spoke always the same words.
The Ratu Ageng was exceedingly afraid.

As the voice had spoken so many times, and was always the
    same,
the Ratu Ageng sent for
Pangéran Mangkubumi.
When he had come to the kraton
and met the Ratu, she said politely:
"Prince, what will you have me do?
I have heard
a voice, when I was sleeping,
and it has happened three times,
and was always the same.

[The voice says] that Ratu Kantjana
must be married
to Pangéran Dipanagara,[119]
and if this is not done
Java will be brought to ruin
and my days in this world will be ended.[120]
What is the right thing for me to do?
I leave it to your judgment."

Pangéran Mangkubumi smiled,
and said gently: "Indeed, it would be most fitting
if he is willing.
If he is not willing
it will be most shameful.
Who would dare to compel him?"
The Ratu said softly:
"What shall I do then, Prince?
I shall certainly die
and Jogjakarta be ruined."

The Prince said gently:
"If you agree,
I will send my wife to him.
If he has no objection, it will be easily done,
and if he objects, there will be no shame in it,
for it will seem as if it were only a joke.[121]
I fear him greatly."
The Ratu Ageng said quietly:
"Indeed, who would dare [to compel him]."

Then Pangéran Mangkubumi
sent for his wife,
Radèn Aju Sepuh,
for Radèn Aju Sepuh
was one person who dared to make jokes

---

119. Two lines condensed into one.

120. Two lines condensed into one.

121. Two lines condensed into one.

with the Prince.
Her husband explained what had happened[122]
and she set out for Tegalredja. When she arrived,
it happened that the Prince

was sitting with his wife.
Radèn Aju Sepuh smiled, and said:
"Let us suppose
that your wife
should be given a pair,
of the same age
and beauty.
They would be like Ratih[123] and Supraba.
How I should like to see it!"
The Prince smiled

p. 103 and immediately embraced the one who had been likened to Ratih,
drawing her close to him.
He said, smiling:
"My ruby, she is talking in her sleep,
for she sleeps sitting up."
Radèn Aju Sepuh, hearing this,
cast him a surly glance,
and said crossly:
"What you say is most annoying!
I sit here [talking to you] and you say I am asleep!"

The Prince said gently:
"Where will you find the like
of my dear mistress,
God's bounty
sent down from heaven,
jewel among the women
of the land of Java,
who has come down to Tegalredja
and been bestowed upon me.
It is a lie to say

that there is any woman her equal!"
Radèn Aju Sepuh said crossly:
"You are making me more and more angry!
I am going home."
Then she returned [to the kraton] and we tell no more of her.
Now we tell
that the Prince happened
to go down to the kraton.
In the company of Pangéran Mangkubumi
he was sitting in the *bangsal kantjana*[124]

---

122. Two lines condensed into one.

123. Ratih is the wife of Kāma.

124. The gold balé. I am not sure what part of the kraton this would have been.

together with the Ratu Ageng.
The Prince asked their leave
to go to the eastern kraton
to see Ratu Emas[125]
who had a slight illness.
When the Prince had gone
the Ratu Ageng
and Pangéran Mangkubumi
discussed the problem of the dream.[126]

"When he returns,
I would like you to tell him
all about the dream.
Perhaps then
he will have pity on the realm.
I have already sent
my wife,
Radèn Aju Sepuh, who went to meet him.
But he only made fun of her."[127]

Not long afterwards the Prince returned,
and the three of them sat down together.
The Ratu Ageng spoke to him
about the dream

p. 104 which had given her an anxious heart.
When it was all told,
the Prince said gently:
"It seems to me, indeed,
that this is only a trial.
If it is truly a warning

and it comes again in the future,
you should say that the voice must come
to me."
The Ratu Ageng said gently:
"So be it: I have told you,
and whether you follow it or not,
I have unburdened the commission placed upon me."[128]
The Prince was inwardly disturbed
about the significance of "Wali Wuḍar;"

he did not show this, but smiled, and asked
his uncle: "Kjai, what is the meaning
of Wali Wuḍar?"
Pangéran Mangkubumi
smiled, and said sweetly:
"The interpretation of 'Wali Wuḍar'
is: one who fails as a Wali."
Pangéran Dipanagara,
hearing this, was increasingly disturbed,
feeling shamed before God.

---

125. The text has "ingkang ibu / Ratu Emas," which is to say that in age and nature of relationship she was like a mother to him.

126. The last four lines of this stanza have been reduced to three.

127. Two lines condensed into one.

128. Two lines condensed into one.

After this they took leave of one another,
and the Prince returned to Tegalredja.
When he arrived there,
he did not even call at the house,
but went on to Sélaradja,
feeling greatly shamed before God.
He entered the building there
and for three days
he did not ask for the Koran to be read nor did he come out
    onto the verandah.
The Penghulu understood [that something had happened]

guessing that the Prince was greatly troubled.
So the Penghulu
sought audience with him. It happened
that the Prince was sitting
in front of the building,
on a shining stone,
which was sheltered by
a *kumuning*[129] tree and ringed by a moat.
He was on an island planted with banyan trees,
and ornamental plants of many kinds.

In front of the house a large pond curved round.
Its water was clear, and it held many fishes
of different kinds.
By the door[130] there was a *sirih* garden.
The Penghulu said sweetly:
"My lord, what is the reason
I see you so sorrowful?

p. 105 Indeed, you have been thus since you returned
from the kraton." The Prince said gently:
"Ki Penghulu, I

am greatly shamed before the Almighty."
He explained the whole matter
of the Ratu Ageng's dream,
and its interpretation
by Pangéran Mangkubumi,
which was the cause of his sorrow.
The Penghulu smiled,
and said:
"The real interpretation of 'Wali Wuḍar' is otherwise:
it means a Wali who has two offices

for God has given to him power to administer justice.
That is its significance.
To give an example:

---

129. According to de Clercq (<u>Nieuw Plantkundig Woordenboek</u>, p. 285) this is <u>Murraya exotica</u>, a tree with beautiful white flowers which are worn by women in their hair. Its yellow wood is used for carving.

130. The text reads <u>kori</u>. Louw's translation reads "<u>aan de linkerzijde</u>" (<u>kèri</u>).

among the 124,000 Nabi[131]
those who may be called 'wuḍar'
are only six.
These give expression to God's will,
and are Nabi Adam, Nabi Nuh, Nabi Ibrahim,
and fourthly Nabi Musa;

then Nabi Ngisa. The sixth and last
is Nabi Muhammad.[132]
To give examples from Java
of 'Wali Wuḍar,'
they are Sunan Giri,[133]
and your ancestor,
Sultan Agung,[134]
for these held a double office,
and were beloved of God. As for you yourself, my lord,
God knows

what He shall will for you in the future."
The Prince recalled
the time when he had met
the Ratu Adil.
He thought to himself:
"So it is already fixed:
I cannot avoid it."
But he did not say this aloud,
but only smiled, and said gently:
"Praise be to God.

In this world, men have nothing to do
but wait till they be given
some great task."
The Penghulu said:
"Indeed, my lord, if we are equal to it,
that is the most excellent thing,
a boon indeed."
The Prince said:
"Let us pray to the Almighty
that it will come to a good conclusion."

---

131. This is an extraordinarily large figure. Surah VI (84-87) of the Koran lists only 18 Nabi and elsewhere the number is given as 20.

132. The English names for these six are: Adam, Noah, Abraham, Moses, Jesus, and Muhammad.

133. In the Babad Tanah Djawi story of the conquest of Madjapahit by Radèn Patah, later Sénapati Djimbun of Demak (Olthof, Poenika Serat Babad Tanah Djawi, p. 29f.), Sunan Giri is said to have reigned for 40 days before Sénapati Djimbun's accession "to remove all traces of an infidel ruler" (the last king of Madjapahit). Thus he had wielded temporal power.

134. Sunan of Mataram (1613-1646). He obtained the title of Sultan from Mecca and introduced the Muslim calendar (in its peculiar Javanese form). He is not, however, usually listed among the Javanese wali, and his reign was after the djaman kawalèn (the age of the apostles of Islam).

p. 106
>We say no more of this:
>The Prince's heart was restored,
>and he prayed with an undivided mind.
>In the morning
>the Prince would come out onto the verandah
>and join the Penghulu
>in reciting the Koran.[135]
>Now it happened
>that during the fast month the Prince went away
>to the Setjang cave.
>
>And to lighten his mood
>he would wander through the gardens
>by the cave.
>Now it happened
>that the Prince was once sitting
>beneath a banyan tree.
>It was after the midday prayer,
>and the garden where he sat was called Modar.[136]
>He heard a voice, distant but clear [which said]:
>"Oh Ngabdulkamit!
>
>Receive now a title
>from the Lord of all things!
>You will be Sultan Ngabdulkamit,
>Érutjakra, Sajidin,
>Panatagama of Java,
>Caliph of the Prophet of God--
>blessing and peace be upon him!"[137]
>Then the voice was heard no more.
>After the sunset prayer, the Prince returned
>to the Setjang cave.
>
>When the *trawèh*[138] prayers were finished, the Prince emerged
>and sat on a shining stone.
>To the right and to the left
>he was attended
>by two retainers:
>Putut Lawa
>and Putut Gurit;
>Botjak-butjik and Suradana.
>Muhjidin and Wirjasemit
>were still in the kitchen.

---

135. The text reads <u>darus Kuran</u>, done in this case as part of the observance of the <u>fast month</u>. These two lines are reversed in the translation.

136. Louw's text has Modang (<u>De Java-oorlog</u>, I, p. 136).

137. Louw gives Brandes' interpretation of Érutjakra as "jewel of the world" (èru being a kawi form of <u>sosotya</u> and <u>tjakra</u> derived from the Sanskrit <u>cakra</u>). <u>Sajidin</u> is from the Arabic <u>Sayyid</u> ("lord," used for the descendants of Muhammad). <u>Panatagama</u> means "regulator of religion." <u>Sajidin</u> and <u>Panatagama</u> were part of the title of Sénapati, founder of Mataram according to the <u>Babad Tanah Djawi</u> account, and are still used in the title of the Sunan of Solo.

138. Prayers held in the fast month after the <u>ngisa</u> prayer in the early part of the night.

It was the twenty-seventh day [of the fast month],
and the year was Bé.¹³⁹ When they had eaten,
the Prince went to sleep
on the shining stone.
The two Puṭut kept watch,
but in a while they both fell asleep
at his feet.
Now the Prince
dreamt that he was not at the cave,
but at Sélaradja,

sitting on the shining stone,
on the island of the banyans.
Then all at once eight men came,

p. 107   wearing turbans with the end hanging behind.
The first of them bore a letter
which he held aloft in both hands.
The Prince looked,
then went to meet them, saluting them,
awestruck, for the radiance of the eight
was like that of the full moon.

The Prince stood before them in respectful greeting,
but they did not heed him,
going straight to the pond.
The Prince followed.
They stood on the edge,
five on the east
and three on the south.
The Prince joined those
on the south, making four.
Then all of them moved towards the north.

Those on the east stood facing westwards.
The one who bore the letter was in front,
and the others on either side.
Then he read out
the letter, and the sound was the same
as the voice of the proclamation.¹⁴⁰
It said: "This is His Highness
Ṣultan Ngabdulkamit
Érutjakra, Sajidin,
Panatagama

Caliph of the Prophet of God
over the land of Java."
[The other seven] answered together:
"On him be peace!"¹⁴¹
The one who had read the letter reprimanded them:

---

139. The sixth year of the windu cycle.

140. The text reads <u>undang</u>. Louw's text has <u>modang</u>, so that the line reads: ". . . as the voice at Modang [Modar]," which makes better sense.

141. The text reads <u>ngalaihisalamu</u> from the Arabic <u>alai-hi's-satam</u> (this is said after the name of a Nabi other than Muhammad).

"That is not the right response!"
Those he had reprimanded asked:
"What is it then, Panembahan?"
and he replied:
"You have created a point of difference

by your response, my young friends!
But let that be:
the only response is the Takbir."[142]
Then all eight of them
recited the Takbir together,
joined by the Prince.[143]
After this the letter
was let fall into the pond. It sank into the water
and disappeared from sight.

The eight men vanished
from where they had been standing,
like smoke, without trace.
The Prince
was left standing alone.
When it was [almost] morning,

p. 108 the Prince was awoken
by Puṭut Lawa,
and they took the *saur* meal[144] and made the dawn
    prayer together.
We say no more of this.

Afterwards [the Prince] returned to Tegalredja.
We tell of what happened
after he arrived at Sélaradja.[145]
The Penghulu had heard
that the Prince
was sought by the Dutch.[146]
The news came from Semarang and was quite clear.
So the Penghulu

sought an audience at Sélaradja
with the Prince, who happened to be sitting
on the shining stone.
The Penghulu said:
"My lord, I have received
news from Semarang
about which there is no doubt.
They want you,

---

142. The recital of the Arabic formula, Allāhu Akbar (God is Great).

143. Two lines condensed into one.

144. The meal during the fast month taken in the last watches of the night before day breaks.

145. These two lines are reversed in the translation.

146. Two lines condensed into one.

and already large numbers of soldiers
have arrived in Semarang.[147]

What will you do
if it happens as I have heard?"
The Prince smiled, and answered:
"What would be the right thing to do?
I have done no wrong.
If what you say is true,
then heaven will be most welcome to me,
and I shall seek a way thither.
Moreover, do you not remember
the dream of the Ratu Ageng?

Perhaps this is the explanation of it--
it was you who interpreted it for me before.
In truth, I have committed no sin,
but if men intend to wrong me
I am not afraid."
The Penghulu said,
with bowed head and overflowing tears:[148]
"You are right, if the revelation is fulfilled.
I believe

that God's will shall be done,
but let it not be by war."
The Prince said:
"What is the right thing to do?"
The Penghulu said gently:
"My lord, if the news is indeed correct[149]
it is best that you suffer
all the ill treatment that the Dutch intend for you,
as did your grandfather,

Sultan[150] Sepuh, in former times,
in order that there should be no devastation.
But should God decree
that you are not free to choose which way you will take

---

147. Here the text is far from explicit. Why should the Dutch have been after Dipanagara? Certainly his conduct had exhibited nothing of the malleability usually expected from their Javanese allies: he had disallowed the appointment of the Collectors, favored by the Resident, and later had strongly objected to putting his seal on a financial document on the grounds that this was merely "selling his name." It is interesting to note that the news of the intentions of the Dutch is said here to have come before the building of the road, usually cited as the immediate cause of the war (see e.g., F.W. Stapel, Geschiedenis van Nederlandsch Indie [Amsterdam: J. M. Meulenhoff, 1930], p. 265; de Klerck, History of the Netherlands East Indies, II, p. 163).

148. Two lines condensed into one.

149. Two lines condensed into one.

150. Amangkubuwana II. The text has Sinuhun Sepuh, but the rulers of Jogjakarta are usually referred to by their title of Sultan.

I should not be deterred
by the fear of suffering or death,
but remain with you.
But if the way is war
I cannot help you, for I am an old man.
Yet how could I leave you alone?"

The Prince smiled, and said quietly:
"I prefer the way of war,
for to die thus gives us good fame."
The Penghulu said:
"If that is your wish, my lord,
I ask your leave to depart,
for I cannot bear to see it.
I will make the pilgrimage to Mecca."
The Prince smiled and said gently:
"That is most fitting,

and I am glad of it. Let us make an agreement:
when you arrive in Mecca,
you must not return [after the pilgrimage],
but remain there the rest of your days.
When I am successful,
tell the news there.
And seek for me
the prayers of all the Iman,
that I may obtain the intercession of the Prophet,
and the favor of Allah[151]

to strengthen me in waging war on the infidels.
And fervent be your prayers
as you bow before the Ka'bah
beseech the Lord
that all may go well, and Java
serve the true religion.
Kjai, if indeed
we are aided by God,
you may speedily return!"
The Penghulu said:

"Be it as you say. I ask your beneficient thoughts
that I may be enabled to reach
the holy Ka'bah."
The Prince said sweetly:
"Indeed, you have all my good wishes
that it may be permitted
of God, who is Great."
We tell no more of this:
Kjai Rahmanudin[152] took his leave
of all those of high rank

---

151. This is one of the few places where the author uses the Arabic word for God. More commonly used are Jang Suksma (the Soul), Jang Widi (The All-Disposer), and Jang Purba (The First).

152. From the Arabic Rahmān ul-Dīn. This is the Penghulu's name.

p. 110 and set out to Semarang.
No more is said of the Penghulu.
At Tegalredja,
the Prince was exceedingly melancholy,[153]
for he had heard news
which was to him as if
the very sky had fallen
But he resolved that he would not flinch,
taking refuge in God alone.

So all his melancholy vanished
and he looked forward to death.
And Sang Retna too
had determined that she would share
her husband's lot, from the beginning to the end.
Now it happened
that the beginning was thus:
the Tegalredja region
was staked out, and [the Prince] not notified.
The intention was to make a highway.

Thus was it God's will
that the devastation of Java
should be caused by this.
Now we tell
that the Prince remained
inside the building at Sélaradja.
It happened one day
that after the midday prayer
the Prince went out
and visited the rice fields

outside Sélaradja.
These fields were called Muntru[154]
and there was a place to sit at the edge,
encircled by a pond.
He sat beneath the shade
of a *soka* tree,[155]
attended by Ki Soban.
At that time
the Prince was forty-two[156] years old.[157]

---

153. Two lines condensed into one.

154. Louw's text has Mantra (De Java-oorlog, I, p. 138).

155. According to de Clercq (p. 261), this is Ixora coccinea, the redflowered "flame tree of the woods."

156. This does not agree with statements of Dipanagara's age given earlier in the text.

157. Two lines condensed into one.

He was startled to see
a crowd of people,
and asked quietly:
"Soban, why is there such a crowd?"[158]
Soban said with a sembah:
"They have all come
to construct a highway,
having been sent by the Patih
three days since.

It seems that Tegalredja is finished, my lord,
for the making of this highway.

p. 111 They are going to divide it into six--
it has already been staked out.
The Prince's anger knew no bounds
when he heard what Ki Soban said,[159]
and he at once sent Brandjang Kawat
to fetch his Patih,
Mas Ngabèi Mangunardja.

Mangunardja arrived shortly afterwards,
and the Prince said:
"Mangunardja,
tell me about this highway,
that it has happened in this manner!"
Mangunardja said with a sembah:
"Your servant dares not say [what has happened],[160]
for he was not informed, my lord.[161]

Indeed, I heard the news
from your peasants,
but I have not been notified,
and so I dare not say."
The Prince spoke again:
"If that is so,
send them away,
and if you cannot, pull up [the stakes]."
Mangunardja said that he would do so and withdrew.
Afterwards he met

the [Jogjakarta] Patih's man,
and told him to withdraw the laborers.
He answered that he dared not, for fear of the Resident,[162]
so then Mangunardja
ordered his men to pull out
all the stakes--
north, south, east, and west,
they were all pulled out.
Then Radèn Brangtakusuma, whom the [Jogjakarta] Patih had sent

---

158. Two lines condensed into one.

159. Two lines condensed into one.

160. Two lines condensed into one.

161. Two lines condensed into one.

162. Two lines condensed into one.

arrived together with some village headmen, and the *gandèk*[163]
   Dutawidjaja,
bringing stakes and rakes.
Their krisses were seized
by the village people
of Timpéjan;[164]
Radèn Brangtakusuma
was not able to escape.
Then they were all chased off,
and they returned to inform the Patih,
who was angered,

and ordered that the road be closed[165]
at Djagalan.
This was the road to Jogjakarta.
When this became known

p. 112 [the Prince] ordered that it be opened again.
When the men left after reopening the road,
it was again blocked off.
This happened three times:
first the road would be opened, and then blocked again.
The Prince was told

that they kept on blocking the road.
[Mangunardja said:] "What shall I do, my lord?
It is at night that they block the road,
during the day they do not dare,
for we keep watch.
But as soon as we go home
it is blocked again."
This angered the Prince:
"If it be so, Mangunardja, it seems there is now
no going back."

---

163. A kraton messenger, usually a person of some rank.

164. Timpéjan and Djagalan are not listed in Dumont's <u>Aardrijkskundig Woordenboek</u>.

165. On the matter of the blocking of the road, Louw (<u>De Java-oorlog</u>, I, p. 139) cites a Chevallier's report that repair work on the Jogjakarta road had proceeded up to the boundary of Dipanagara's estate, and concludes that the road had been closed off while this work was in process. Here, however, it appears as the <u>casus belli</u>; presumably the implication is that the road had been closed by the Dutch in order to trap and take Dipanagara. (Louw comments: "Hoe dikwijls zagen wij niet een voorwendsel aangrijpen om tot een oorlog te geraken, die veel diepere oorzaken had. Alles had Dipanegara tot opstand aangezet, eindelijk gaf hij zich aan zijn noodlot over.") What, above all, distinguishes Dipanagara's <u>opstand</u> from previous ones is that it is not a war of succession. This is clear not only from Dipanagara's own statements (as his speech to the Penghulu) but also from the logistics of the situation; as a Regent he enjoyed as much power as he would have had on the throne, and the limits of his freedom were not set by the six year-old Sultan.

MAHMUD, SULTAN OF RIAU AND LINGGA (1823-1864)

Virginia Matheson[1]

The Text

The life of Sultan Mahmud is described in the *Tuhfat al-Nafis* (The Precious Gift), a Malay text which, according to its author, Raja Hajji Ali, is intended to relate the stories of the Malay and Bugis kings and their descendants. The work opens with a synopsis of the *Sejarah Melayu* and continues in more detail with the history of the kingdom of Johor. The dynamic figures in the *Tuhfat* are the Bugis princes, whose military skill and hard-line diplomacy won them high positions of state in Riau, Selangor, and the Borneo states of Sambas and Matan-Sukadana. A recurring theme in the first half of the *Tuhfat*, which covers the first half of the eighteenth century, is the conflict between the Minangkabau of Siak and the allied Bugis and Malay forces. These clashes occurred both in the Riau area and in Kedah, Selangor, Siak, and Borneo. The second half, which covers the mid-eighteenth century to 1864, portrays the developing hostility between Bugis and Malays on Riau and two major, Bugis-led confrontations with the Dutch at Malacca in 1756 and 1784. This last venture ended when the Dutch made a treaty with Riau in which the Sultan held his kingdom only as a fief of the Dutch East India Company (VOC). After 1818 a Dutch Resident was permanently stationed at Tanjong Pinang.[2]

The religious and cultural life of Riau, especially the island of Penyengat (the seat of the Bugis rulers) and of Lingga (the seat of the Malay rulers) did not seem to be at all influenced by the Dutch. The main area of traditional life which the *Tuhfat* does portray as having been subject to Dutch intervention was piracy. Both diplomatic and financial pressures were exerted by the Dutch to force the rulers to cooperate in its suppression.

The scope of the *Tuhfat*, chronologically, geographically, and politically, is very broad. Its detailed narration of Johor history from the early eighteenth century until 1864 is interwoven with anecdotes from the history of Siak, Kedah, Selangor, Trengganu, Kelantan, and the west coast of Borneo. Where encounters with Europeans--mainly Dutch and British--are described, the accounts tally most strikingly with contemporary European versions of the same events.

---

1. I would like to acknowledge the help and advice I have received from Professor C. Skinner and Drs. L. Brakel. I wish to thank Dr. C. H. H. Wake, Department of History, University of Western Australia, for permission to quote from his "Nineteenth Century Johore: Ruler and Realm in Transition" (Ph.D. thesis, Australian National University, 1966).

2. The Malay spelling of places and titles has been retained in this article.

The Manuscripts

There are four currently known manuscripts of the *Tuhfat al-Nafis*. One of these has only recently been identified as a *Tuhfat* text,[3] and has not been incorporated into the translation which follows. Of the other three manuscripts, one presents a shorter *Tuhfat* text, and two present a longer version. The shorter manuscript is from the Koninklijk Instituut voor Taal-, Land- en Volkenkunde in Leiden.[4] The older of the two longer manuscripts which is catalogued as the "Maxwell 2" manuscript,[5] is from the Royal Asiatic Society in London, and was copied in 1890. The last manuscript is a published Jawi text, which was copied for R. O. Winstedt some time after 1923. It was published in the *Journal of the Malayan Branch Royal Asiatic Society*.[6] The translation from the *Tuhfat* in this article is based on the "Maxwell 2" text. This manuscript was preferred because it presents a better text than Winstedt's. Because the longer version of the *Tuhfat* represents an expansion of the basic Leiden manuscript, the shorter work is preserved within the longer one.

The Author

It is important for an understanding of the *Tuhfat* to know a little of the author's background and milieu. Raja Hajji Ali was descended from the first Bugis princes who established themselves in Riau. The princes had made the office of Yangdipertuan Muda an hereditary Bugis position whereas the offices of Sultan, Bendahara, and Temenggong were left to the Malays. The Yangdipertuan Muda, holders of military power, soon held all commercial and effective political strength as well. Thus, in an effort to maintain their position in the face of the Bugis challenge, the Sultan and the Malays turned to the Dutch, the leading European power in the area. The Dutch found it in their inerests to support the Malays against the Bugis, whose domination of the Peninsula tin trade posed a real threat to Malacca. In the 1784 Dutch treaty with Riau, it was stipulated that there should be no Bugis Yangdipertuan Muda. In the

---

3. This is a manuscript in the library of the Dewan Bahasa dan Pustaka in Kuala Lumpur. It was identified by Moh'd. Khalid Saidin and noted in his article, "Naskhah2 Lama Mengenai Sejarah Negeri Johor," Dewan Bahasa, XV, No. 18 (August 1971), pp. 340-341. From a sample of four pages which he kindly sent me, it seems that this manuucript is very close to the "Maxwell 2" manuscript.

4. Catalogued by Ph. S. van Ronkel, under the title "Sjadjarah Radja2 Riouw," *Bijdragen tot de Taal-, Land- en Volkenkunde*, LX (1908), p. 207. The manuscript was copied in 1896.

5. P. Voorhoeve, "List of Malay Manuscripts in the Library of the Royal Asiatic Society, London," *Journal of the Royal Asiatic Society* (April 1963), p. 68.

6. *Journal of the Malayan Branch Royal Asiatic Society*, X, Part 2 (1932). A romanization of Winstedt's text was undertaken by Inche Munir bin Ali (Singapore: Malaysia Publications, 1965). This text was reviewed by C. Skinner, in the *Journal of Southeast Asian History*, VIII, No. 2 (1967), p. 325.

early nineteenth century, however, a physical withdrawal of the Sultan from Riau to Lingga forced the Dutch to carry out negotiations with the Bugis, who were reinstated as Yangdipertuan Muda at Riau, the center of Dutch activity in the area. During the nineteenth century the traditional pattern of relationships changed. The Yangdipertuan Muda chose, overtly at least, to cooperate with the Residents, while the Sultans, separated and isolated from the center of administration, became less involved in matters of policy and thus did not work closely with the Dutch.

The author of the *Tuhfat* was related to all the Yangdipertuan Muda who are mentioned in the translation. He was a Muslim scholar and was on good terms with the Dutch officials of his time. Some of his other works[7] indicate that he stood strongly for Malay custom in matters of dress, religion, and behavior. It would have been difficult for him to respect a young Sultan like Mahmud, who refused to follow the advice of his elders, involved himself in Christian ritual (Freemasonry), and followed the customs of Europeans rather than the dictates of Islam.

Sultan Mahmud

We know very little about Mahmud before he became Sultan in 1841.[8] It was only then that he began to exert his influence and to become a figure of note in the Riau-Lingga and Singapore world. Of his early life, we know from the *Tuhfat* that he was born in Trengganu. Mahmud's grandfather, Sultan Abd al-Rahman,[9] offended at not being officially installed as Sultan of Lingga, left Lingga in 1821 and sailed to Trengganu with his son, Tengku Besar Muhammad. The Sultan of Trengganu, Ahmad, settled the father and son in their own kampong. Ahmad then married Sultan Abd al-Rahman to his sister and Muhammad to his daughter. Abd al-Rahman's bride died a year later, but in 1823 his son's wife, Tengku Teh, gave birth to Mahmud. Shortly after his grandson's birth, Sultan Abd al-Rahman was brought back from Trengganu to Lingga by a Dutch ship. The regalia was restored to him in a formal installation ceremony in November 1823. Sultan Abd al-Rahman was said to have been interested only in his religious devotions,[10] leaving the administration of his realm to the Yangdipertuan Muda, and to his son Muhammad.

Sultan Abd al-Rahman died in August 1832 at the age of 55 or 56.[11] He was succeeded by Mahmud's father, Sultan Muhammad who

---

7. See, for example, Kitab Pengetahuan Bahasa (Singapore: Al-Ahmadiah Press, 1928), which was intended to be a dictionary, but many of the definitions were used as vehicles for the author's moral percepts.

8. The passage chosen for translation from the Tuhfat begins with Mahmud's succession to the full powers of the Sultanate, after the death of his father.

9. He was the younger brother of Husain, whom Raffles and Farquhar had installed as Sultan of Singapore in 1819.

10. C. van Angelbeek, "Korte Schets van het eiland Lingga en deszelfs Bewoners," Verhandelingen van het Bataviaasch Genootschap, XI, (1826), p. 45.

11. E. Netscher, "Beschrijving van een Gedeelte der Residentie Riouw,"

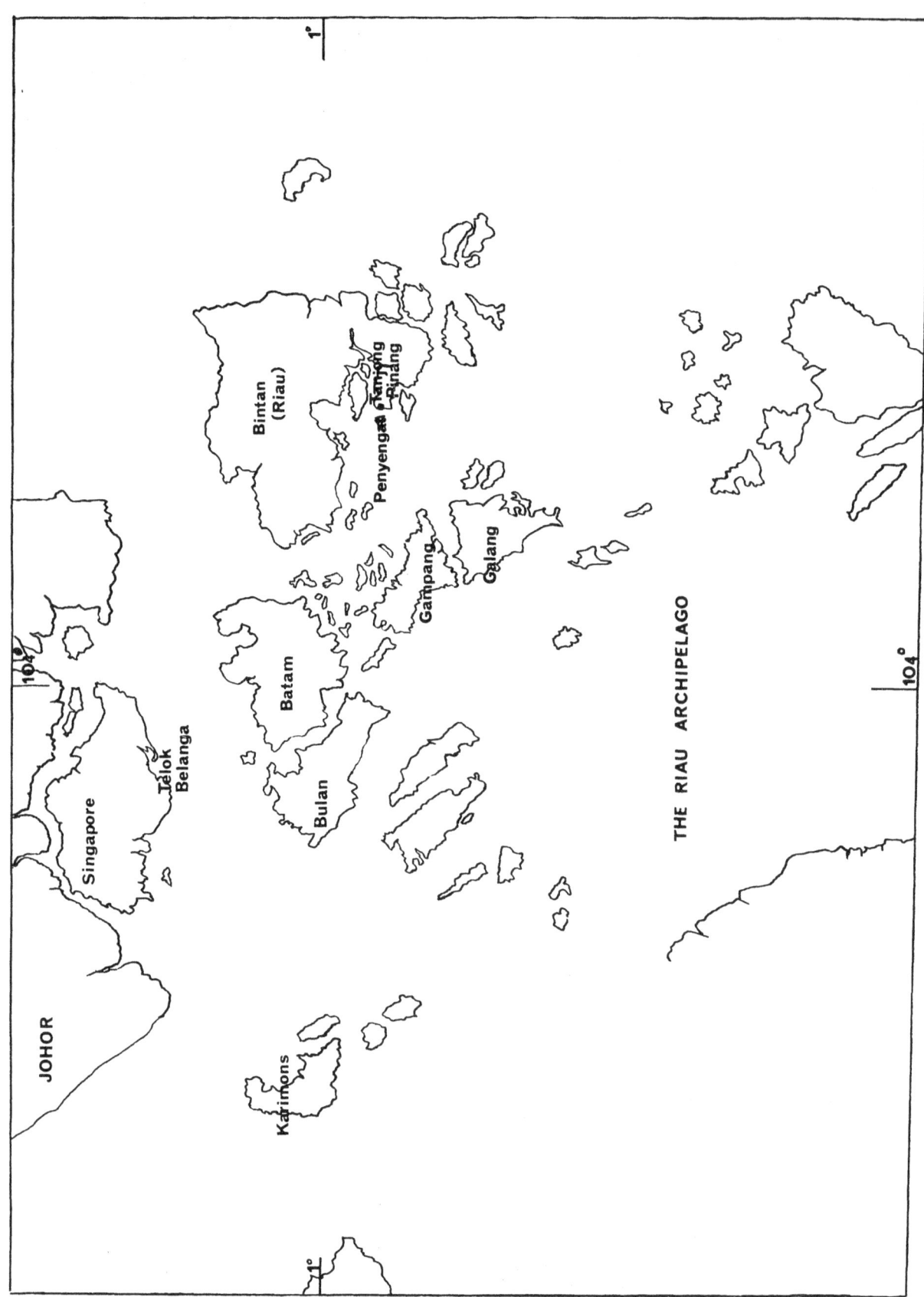

became involved in Trengganu affairs. When his father-in-law died in 1826, there was a disputed succession in Trengganu and the loser, Umar, retired to Lingga, where he stayed with Sultan Muhammad. When a youth succeeded to the Trengganu throne in 1836, Umar returned, ousted him, and became Sultan. Over twenty years later, Sultan Umar was to return the favors he had received at Lingga by sheltering Sultan Muhammad's son, Mahmud, at his court in Trengganu.

In about 1834 Sultan Muhammad had Mahmud circumcized and crowned Sultan. For the rest of his life he acted as a regent to the child. In 1837 Sultan Muhammad went to Singapore and brought back with him Raja Maimunah, the granddaughter of Sultan Husain of Singapore. She was married to her cousin, Mahmud, and received the title Tengku Empuan (Royal Consort). They had one child, Fatimah, who in 1851 married Yangdipertuan Muda Ali's son, Muhammad Yusuf.[12] Sultan Muhammad died on July 20, 1841, at the age of 38, and Mahmud took over the kingdom without a regent.

Before becoming Sultan, Mahmud's experience with the Dutch had been very limited. He appears to have regarded them as clerks, who handled the more trying aspects of the administration without interfering with the internal workings of the Lingga court. In his experience the Dutch were required to show the Sultan all signs of deference. Unlike the Yangdipertuan Muda, he had had little opportunity to gauge the extent of the Dutch Residents' power, which was backed by the Governor-General in Batavia.

When Mahmud became Sultan and tried to act as an independent ruler, he met opposition. Traditionally, opposition had come from the Yangdipertuan Muda, the counterbalance to the Sultan's power. In Mahmud's case, however, this check was not effective. As the translated passage shows, the Yangdipertuan Muda (or his representative) could not persuade the Sultan to stay in Lingga when he insisted on going to Singapore. But Mahmud met stiffer opposition from the Dutch. In 1856 this took the form of a warning from the Dutch Governor-General. The Sultan was not intimidated, and, possibly expecting support from his British friends in Singapore, he ignored the Dutch censure. Having made a threat, the Dutch were forced to execute it and had to resort to deposition. This was a failure for Dutch diplomacy, and foretold the ultimate breakdown of the Malay Sultanate, which within a generation passed to the Bugis.

Summary of the Remainder of Mahmud's Life
(subsequent to the translated extract)

On October 10, 1857 the Dutch installed Mahmud's uncle, Sulaiman, as Sultan of Lingga. Shortly afterwards, Mahmud returned to Lingga, but, on learning he had already been replaced, he went back to

---

Tijdschrift voor Indische Taal-, Land- en Volkenkunde, II (1853), p. 262.

12. E. Netscher ("Beschrijving," p. 153) mentions a second marriage by Mahmud, which is not recorded in the Tuhfat. This marriage was to the daughter of Yangdipertuan Muda Abd al-Rahman. Unlike his father and grandfather who had many children by concubines, Mahmud had only one, to a woman called Sajah.

Singapore, where he stayed with the Temenggong. After six months in Singapore, he moved on to Pahang. In May 1858 he wrote to the Dutch Governor-General seeking pardon but was told this was possible only if he would settle permanently in Java. In Pahang, Mahmud was the guest of the Bendahara, Mutahir; however, he soon left the capital and journeyed to the interior of the state to meet Maharaja Perba of Jelai, the greatest chief in Pahang. During this time, both the British and Bendahara Mutahir heard rumors of a plot to proclaim Mahmud Sultan of Pahang. When Mahmud returned to the Pahang capital, the Bendahara received him coldly, and in October 1858 he left with Maharaja Perba to visit his uncle in Trengganu.

For some reason Mahmud returned to Pahang in 1859,[13] where Mutahir placed at his disposal the revenues of a district. The situation changed, however, when Mutahir abdicated in favor of his son, Koris, who refused to acknowledge Mahmud's status and assumed for himself the position of independent sovereign of Pahang. There had long been a dispute in Pahang over the Bendaharaship in which the claimant to the title was Mutahir's half-brother, Ahmad. Ahmad's previous attempts to gain control of Pahang had been unsuccessful, but when Koris rejected Mahmud, the latter threw his support to Ahmad. Because Ahmad's forays into Pahang had been made from Trengganu, Mahmud returned there in 1860 to seek backing for Ahmad. The British had previously warned Sultan Umar not to further Ahmad's schemes in Pahang, so when his nephew returned, wanting support for Ahmad's intended rebellion, Umar would not respond. This was a blow to Mahmud, who now saw only one alternative source of aid--the Siamese.

The *Dynastic Chronicles Bangkok Era: The Fourth Reign*[14] record many of Mahmud's official dealings with Siam. His first request for assistance was in a letter dated December 18, 1860. The King of Siam (Mongkut) replied that Pahang was a British Protectorate, and, since Siam and Britain were on friendly terms, it would not be in Siam's interests to interfere. The ex-Sultan would, however, be very welcome to visit Bangkok. In June 1861, Mahmud did go to Bangkok[15] in a Siamese ship. Shortly after his departure, Siamese ships reappeared off Trengganu,[16] and rumors reached Singapore that the Siamese had come to depose Sultan Umar and install Mahmud in his stead. The British were afraid that this was the beginning of an extension of Siamese influence over the entire Malay east coast, so the *Hooghly* was hastily sent to Trengganu, and the Siamese ships left. This incident led the British to strengthen their ties with Pahang and Johor. In 1861 they drew up a treaty bringing the foreign relations of those two states under British control; thus, as a result of moves made by Mahmud, the British were forced to become more involved with Pahang and Johor.

---

13. Wake, "Nineteenth Century Johore," p. 140.

14. Chadin (Kanjanavanit) Flood (trans.), The Dynastic Chronicles Bangkok Era: The Fourth Reign (Tokyo: ToyoBunko, Center for East Asian Cultural Studies, 1965).

15. The Dynastic Chronicles, I, p. 242.

16. Wake, "Nineteenth Century Johore," p. 149.

In June 1862 Mahmud returned to Trengganu as Siamese governor of that state and Kelantan.[17] He was now in a strong position to support Ahmad's revolt in Pahang, which began in August 1862. The British reacted strongly to what they regarded as Mahmud's interference, and in November 1862 two gunboats were sent to Trengganu. An ultimatum was delivered, ordering Mahmud to leave. When it had expired, the fort and palace of Trengganu were bombarded for four hours.

A few months afterwards, the Siamese sent a boat to collect Mahmud, and he arrived back in Bangkok in April 1863. He stayed until November, when the *Chronicles* say[18] he received letters from Pahang urging him to leave Siam. Disguised as a sailor, he fled to Singapore and from there secretly entered Pahang. Ahmad's revolt against Koris ended triumphantly in June 1863. Mahmud reached Pahang, sick and exhausted in December of that year, but Ahmad refused to acknowledge him as Sultan. Nevertheless, he stayed there, stateless and powerless, until his death six months later in July 1864 at the age of 41.

The Dutch decision to depose Mahmud in 1857 thus proved to have been short-sighted. Deprived of the Sultanate, he was forced to find a niche for his royal authority elsewhere. Mahmud did not cease to exist as a Sultan merely because the Dutch had withdrawn their recognition of his position. In Malay tradition nothing could rob him of a social status which was his by birth and he remained a powerful figure. Despite extreme Dutch, and later British, opposition, this Sultan of an isolated and dismembered kingdom managed to extend his influence and activities throughout the east coast of Malaya and ultimately to Bangkok.

THE TEXT IN TRANSLATION[1]

Before the seventh day of mourning, Yangdipertuan Muda Raja Abd al-Rahman[2] arrived from Riau, and went to attend the king, Sultan Mahmud Muzaffar Shah. When they met, they both wept. Then the king spoke: "Please see that the state is administered properly." So the Yangdipertuan Muda did what was necessary and continued the administration of [the king's] late father.

Some time later the Yangdipertuan Muda Raja Abd al-Rahman asked leave of the king to return to Riau, to which the king agreed. When he reached Riau he sent Raja Ali, the Engku Kelana,[3] one of his

---

17. *Ibid.*, p. 151.

18. The Dynastic Chronicles, II, p. 307.

1. Some lines of the Tuhfat have occasionally been omitted from the translation, because they are not relevant to the story of Sultan Mahmud. Where omissions occur, they have been indicated by dots, and the content of the passage summarized in a footnote.

2. See the genealogy of Bugis Yangdipertuan Muda on p. 146.

3. The title "Engku Kelana" indicates that he is the Yangdipertuan Muda's successor.

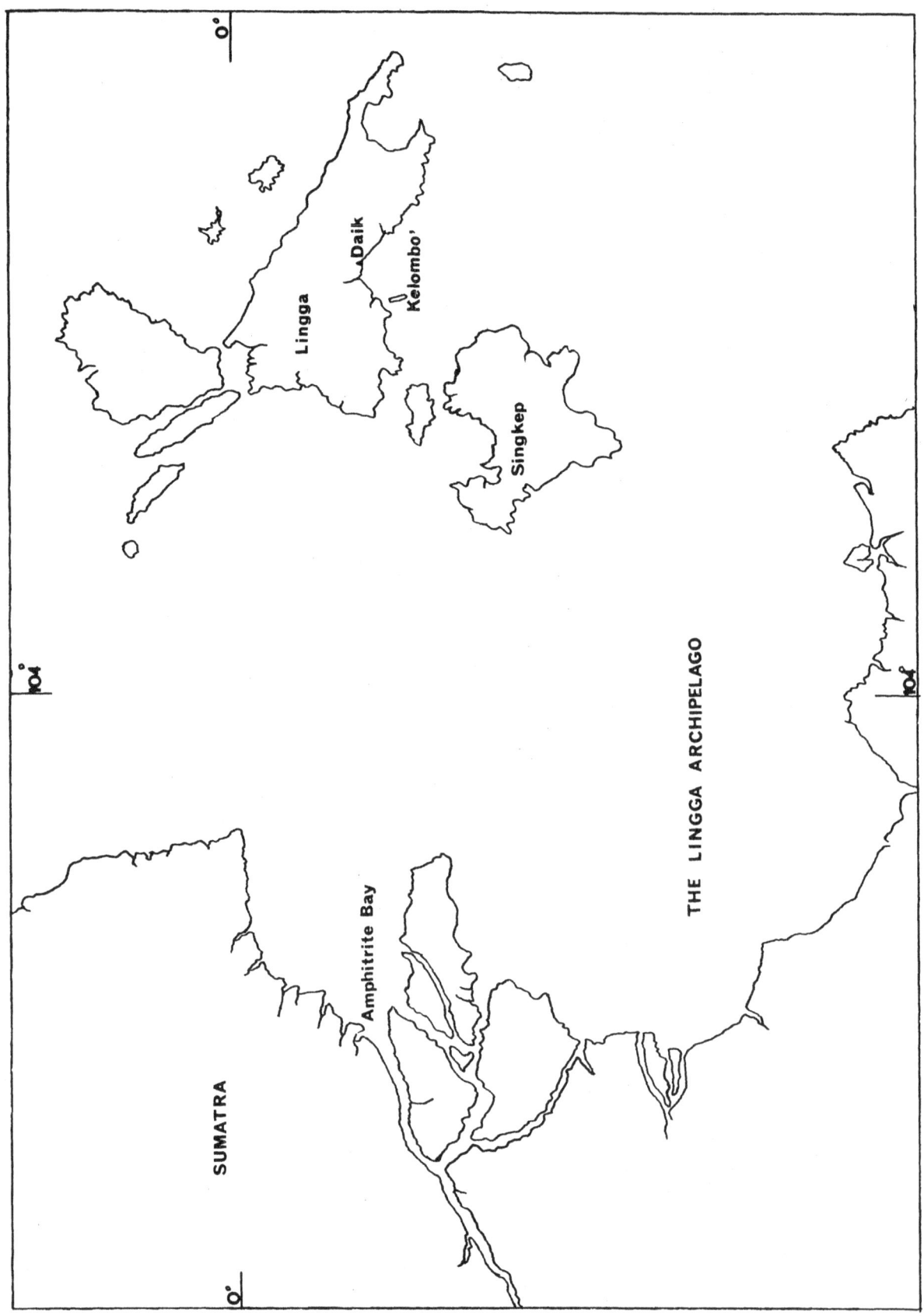

brothers, to Lingga to be his representative there, and one of his cousins, Engku Hajji Ali,[4] went with Raja Ali to assist him in his work. Raja Ali sailed for Lingga, and, when he arrived, he went to attend the king, Sultan Mahmud Muzaffar Shah. Sultan Mahmud handed over all Lingga's internal affairs to Raja Ali. So it was settled, to put it briefly.

Let us now talk of Daheng Rongge', called by some Daheng Kechi'[5] . . . who lived at Telok Belanga.[6] Governor Bonham[7] had consulted the Dato' Bendahara of Pahang, Tun Ali, about appointing Daheng Kechi' as Temenggong. Following the discussion, Daheng Kechi' was appointed Temenggong Seri Maharaja. After that he left for Lingga to attend Sultan Mahmud Muzaffar Shah[8] and to meet Raja Ali, the husband of his sister, Raja Che'. When he arrived in Lingga, he was received with honor by Sultan Mahmud Muzaffar Shah and Raja Ali, and he stayed in Lingga, being entertained and feasted by them, as is the custom among kings when receiving their relatives. Then the Temenggong Seri Maharaja asked leave of Sultan Mahmud and Raja Ali to return to Singapore, and they agreed. When he reached Singapore, he stayed at Telok Belanga.

---

4. Usually known as Raja Hajji Ali or Raja Ali Hajji (see the genealogy). He is the author of the Tuhfat al-Nafis. European writers often confuse him with his cousin Ali, who became Yangdipertuan Muda; however, only the author bears the title "hajji." Raja Hajji Ali served his royal cousins as a scholar and religious adviser.

5. The Tuhfat gives Daheng Rongge's genealogy, which has been omitted from the translation. His distant forbears included one of the first Bugis princes to settle in Riau, Daheng Perani, who married a Malay princess. The title Daheng is Buginese and is reserved for the nobility not of royal descent. Daheng Rongge', properly known as Tun Ibrahim, was born on the island of Bulan, in the Riau archipelago in 1811. He was taken to Singapore at the age of eight, where he became familiar with European customs. In 1825 his father, Temenggong Abd al-Rahman, died and his elder brother Abdullah became chief. Abdullah suffered periodic insanity and was never installed as Temenggong. In 1833-1834 Ibrahim superseded his brother as chief and was formally installed as Temenggong in 1841. His son, Abu Bakar, succeeded him as Temenggong and was later confirmed Sultan of Johor. Ibrahim died in 1862. Wake, "Nineteenth Century Johore," p. 62.

6. The Temenggong's settlement on the central south coast of Singapore, near the present-day Keppel Harbor (see map).

7. Sir Samuel George Bonham, born 1803, joined the government of Fort Marlborough in 1818 and transferred to Singapore in 1823. He was Singapore's Resident Councillor 1834-1836 and Acting Governor for several months in the years 1834-1835. He was Governor of Singapore from December 1836 to January 1843. Wake, "Nineteenth Century Johore," p. 65.

8. Although living at Singapore with a British-installed Sultan, the Temenggong gave his allegiance to his traditional overlord at Lingga.

As for Sultan Mahmud, after the Temenggong Seri Maharaja had returned, he wanted to leave for Singapore too. But this did not seem right to the Yangdipertuan Muda's representative, Raja Ali, who submitted to Sultan Mahmud that to go often across the border to Singapore was not becoming to a king; it was far preferable to improve one's own state and build it up. Sultan Mahmud would not listen to Raja Ali's submission, but left for Singapore with his young attendants.[9] Raja Ali sent a message to his brother, the Yangdipertuan Muda, informing the Temenggong Seri Maharaja and asking him to keep an eye on Sultan Mahmud while he was in Singapore and on what he was doing. The reader will know how it is with young people, and those with him were all young and inexperienced.

When the Yangdipertuan Muda had heard his brother's message, he was worried, and the Resident of Riau[10] was also a little disturbed, because Sultan Mahmud could not be restrained from his ill-considered actions. The Tengku Temenggong of Singapore was continually giving him good advice, persuading him to return to Lingga and to stay in his own country. However, in this case too, the king paid no attention but continued to enjoy himself in Singapore. He travelled about, visiting suitable as well as unsuitable places--places to which no king would properly go.

As a result, a messenger came from Mr. Bonham, the Governor of Singapore, ordering Sultan Mahmud to return immediately to Lingga. Only then did Sultan Mahmud leave. When he arrived in Lingga, he lived as was his custom, spending his day with his young attendants in idle amusements. Later, Sultan Mahmud wanted to return to Singapore for a pleasure trip. Raja Ali did not approve, because he had received many reports about the king; if he went to Singapore [again], there could be a scandal which would damage his name. The reader will understand; Sultan Mahmud was a young man, and those who accompanied him were young servants and attendants, ill-versed in the traditional customs, who could diminish the prestige of the state. Nevertheless, Sultan Mahmud insisted on going, and Raja Ali could restrain him no further, so he sent his relative, Raja Ali Hajji, to inform the Yangdipertuan Muda. When Yangdipertuan Muda Raja Abd al-Rahman and the Resident of Riau heard what Raja Ali Hajji had

---

9. Elisa Netscher, who visited Riau in 1849, 1856, and 1857 and became Resident of Riau in 1861, records his personal impressions of Sultan Mahmud in his monograph, "De Nederlanders in Djohor en Siak, 1602 tot 1865," Verhandelingen van het Bataviaasch Genootschap, XXXV (1870), p. 299. He had had official contact with the Sultan several times and considered him intelligent but without sufficient experience to look after his own interests and those of his kingdom. In Singapore he fell prey to a group of unscrupulous Europeans and the Parsee Cursetjee, who pandered to his vanity and love of pleasure. They encouraged him to spend his money on expensive trifles and gained for themselves monopoly rights and exclusive privileges. Netscher blames these "friends" for urging him to buy a steamship, whose engine was in such disrepair that it had to be rowed to Lingga. These Europeans were also responsible for persuading him to build his European-style residence on Lingga, to fill it with costly furnishings, and to keep horses and carriages.

10. A. L. Andriesse, Resident of Riau, 1839-1848.

to say, they discussed it together. Then the Yangdipertuan Muda left for Lingga.

When he arrived, he attended the king, Sultan Mahmud, and his mother, Tengku Teh.[11] He told her about her son always wanting to go to Singapore without good cause; it was not proper for great kings to act thus. On several occasions the Yangdipertuan Muda and the Resident issued counsel and advice to his mother and to Sultan Mahmud himself, with the result that he abandoned the idea of going to Singapore.

The Yangdipertuan Muda stayed in Lingga and administered the state. At that time Sultan Mahmud had many disagreements with the Yangdipertuan Muda Raja Abd al-Rahman and the Resident of Riau concerning administration, ideas, aims, and policies. The reader will understand that the ideas of the young are opposed to the ideas of their elders who are used to ruling, while the young are not yet used to it. They do not welcome the advice and counsel of their elders but follow their own inclinations with their young attendants.[12] This was the reason then, that disagreements arose. . . .[13]

The Yangdipertuan Muda Raja Abd al-Rahman had been in Lingga for two or three months and had experienced many differences of opinion with Sultan Mahmud. The Yangdipertuan Muda found difficulty considering [the matter before him] and continually sent news to the Resident and kept him informed [of the situation], seeking counsel as to how to reform Sultan Mahmud so that he would remain in his kingdom. The Resident of Riau, too, was constantly advising Sultan Mahmud to stay in his kingdom and govern it well. Notwithstanding this, Sultan Mahmud still had disagreements with Yangdipertuan Muda Raja Abd al-Rahman. Then, at about this time, rumors were started by the servants and attendants that Sultan Mahmud was going to attack the Yangdipertuan Muda's house at night, and words were used to malign the Yangdipertuan Muda's good name. The Yangdipertuan Muda was furious and would have ordered that the attack on his house by servants and attendants be resisted by force. But he accepted the reasoning of one of his relatives, Raja Ali Hajji, and one of the elders from the upper class, Enche Jawa, that there should be no conflict, and he avoided creating a disturbance. The following day the Yangdipertuan Muda sailed back to Riau, as though he had taken offence at their behavior.

When he reached Riau, the Resident was aware that Sultan Mahmud had treated the Yangdipertuan Muda improperly. The Yangdipertuan

---

11. Sister of Sultan Umar of Trengganu.

12. This is the first indication that Sultan Mahmud interested himself in the administration of the kingdom. The author of the Tuhfat ascribes Mahmud's clashes with the Yangdipertuan Muda and the Resident to his youth and unwillingness to conform to the traditional pattern of following the advice of his seniors.

13. The passage omitted describes the return of the Yangdipertuan Muda's brother, Abdullah, from a year's visit to Mecca. He brought two Muslim scholars to teach Islam in Riau. When he heard that his brother was in Lingga with the Sultan, he sailed there to meet him.

Muda conferred with his family and with the Resident and reached the decision to invite Sultan Mahmud to renew the pledge of loyalty,[14] which had existed of old between Bugis and Malays, i.e., between the Yangdipertuan Muda and the Yangdipertuan Besar.

Following this, the Yangdipertuan Muda left with his family and about thirty naval vessels, accompanied by the Resident of Riau in his warship, which was commanded by Mr. Ferdokh.[15] When they arrived, the Yangdipertuan Muda's flotilla dropped anchor at Kuala Daik.[16] In the evening Sultan Mahmud came out to the estuary to welcome Yangdipertuan Muda Raja Abd al-Rahman, as though he regretted his past actions. When he met the Yangdipertuan Muda, he invited him to sail up the river. The Yangdipertuan Muda asked leave to wait, and Sultan Mahmud waited with him so that they might sail up together in daylight. The following day the Yangdipertuan Muda sailed upstream with Sultan Mahmud. When they arrived, the Yangdipertuan Muda's vessel berthed at Pangkalan Dalam[17] with the rest of the fleet and the warship. Later, Ferdokh took a sea berth at Kelombo'.[18]

The Yangdipertuan Muda stayed in Lingga, governing Sultan Mahmud' kingdom. Not long afterwards he invited Sultan Mahmud to renew the traditional pledge of loyalty between the Yangdipertuan Muda and the Yangdipertuan Besar--in other words, the pledge of the Bugis rulers with the Malay rulers. So they both gave their pledge in the *balai-rong*,[19] beneath the fringed umbrellas of state, both holding the glorious Koran, as is the tradition when making a pledge. Immediately afterwards, a cannon was fired to mark the safe conclusion of the pledge.

---

14. This pledge was the legal basis for the existence of the Bugis Yangdipertuan Muda. It was regarded as a pact between not only the Sultan and the Yangdipertuan Muda but also between Malays and Bugis. The first contract was made in 1722 and was renewed by each new Sultan and Yangdipertuan Muda. The contract was binding on the rulers' descendants in perpetuity and states that the Buginese rulers and the Sultan of Johor shall regard each other as brothers and regard the interests of their respective lands as one. The history of the renewal of this pledge is preserved in von de Wall manuscript 621, Djakarta Museum.

15. P-r-d-w-kh. He has not yet been identified.

16. G. F. de Bruyn Kops gives a contemporary description of Daik in "Sketch of the Rhio-Lingga Archipelago," Journal of the Indian Archipelago, IX (1855), pp. 99-100.

17. The landing stage for the Sultan's kampong.

18. The Eastern Archipelago Pilot (London: British Admiralty, 1953), IV, pp. 217-218, says that Kelombo' is a hilly islet in the roadstead of Lingga, surrounded by a reef. To its north, anchorage can be obtained in a depth of about five fathoms (see map).

19. A pavilion, with different levels for various state officials, the Sultan being at the top. It was used an audience hall and for state ceremonies. The penghulu balai was responsible for the preparation of the balai for ceremonial occasions when it was hung with curtains and drapes. Hadji Ibrahim's Tjakap2 Rampai2 Bahasa Malajoe Djohor (Batavia: Government Printer, 1868), I, p. 241. Netscher ("De Nederlanders in Djohor en Siak," p. 299) says the pledge was made June 17, 1844.

The Yangdipertuan Muda stayed in Lingga and discussed measures to wipe out piracy.[20] As for the Dutch warship, it returned to Riau when the Yangdipertuan Muda had concluded his pledge of loyalty with Sultan Mahmud. After that, the Yangdipertuan Muda also went back to Riau. On his return he built a residence and a mosque. . . .[21]

Not long after this, Sultan Mahmud came to Riau and asked that a boat[22] be purchased, worth 36,000 silver *rupia*, so the Yangdipertuan Muda purchased it. Soon afterwards the Yangdipertuan Muda became ill, and by the decree of Almighty God, after a few days he died, on Wednesday, June 19, 1844,[23] at 10:00 p.m., returning to the mercy of Almighty God. Verily we belong to God and to Him we return. There was a commotion at Penyengat and Riau with the princes, the people of the palace, and the populace weeping and wailing. He was buried by Sultan Mahmud and his family, according to the ritual followed when great rulers die. About one month later, Engku Puteri[24] also died, on Monday, August 5, 1855,[25] at 3:00 p.m. She was buried by her brother, Engku Hajji Ahmad, and his family in her own *kota*,[26] and Ahmad had a vault made.

---

20. Piracy had been a serious problem in the Riau-Lingga archipelago, especially throughout the 1830's, when Dutch and British authorities had combined in an effort to destroy some pirate hideouts. See N. Tarling's Piracy and Politics in the Malay World (Melbourne: Cheshire, 1963).

21. The passage omitted describes Yangdipertuan Muda Abd al-Rahman's religious studies and his encouragement of foreign Muslim scholars to visit Riau.

22. The vessel was probably the schooner Young Queen, which is mentioned in C. B. Buckley's An Anecdotal History of Old Times in Singapore (Kuala Lumpur and Singapore: University of Malaya Press, 1969), pp. 520-521. The Sultan used his boat to transport some Masons to the Raffles Lighthouse for the laying of the foundation stone in 1854.

23. The Muslim date is 2 Jumad al-akhir, malam senen, 1260. All conversions of dates have followed the Wustenfeld-Mahler'sche, Vergleichungs-Tabellen (Wiesbaden: Franz Steiner Verlag GMBH, 1961). However, the "Wednesday" of the converted date does not correspond with the Tuhfat's eve of Monday, i.e., Sunday night. Netscher ("De Nederlanders in Djohor en Siak," p. 299) dates the Yangdipertuan Muda's death as June 17, which would be a Monday. The Tuhfat probably gave the correct day but the incorrect date.

24. Engku (or Tengku) Puteri, wife of an earlier Sultan Mahmud, who gave her the island of Penyengat as a home for herself and her family (see the genealogy). She became an international figure in the early 1820's, when she refused to surrender the Johor regalia.

25. The Muslim date is 20 Rajab, malam senen, 1260.

26. Kota usually indicates a fortified area but can also mean a settlement. Tengku Puteri's residence was known as Kota Ranteng.

As for Sultan Mahmud, after the death of the Yangdipertuan Muda Raja Abd al-Rahman, the representative of the Dutch government, the Resident of Riau, asked who would succeed the late Yangdipertuan Muda.[27] Sultan Mahmud requested time to consider[28] and to confer with the princes of Penyengat, but he could not reach an agreement with the princes and the elders of Penyengat. Meanwhile the Resident was pressing for the appointment of a successor to Yangdipertuan Muda Raja Abd al-Rahman, but Sultan Mahmud did not want to make the appointment.

Finally, Sultan Mahmud proposed three candiates to await [his] decision as to which was to become the Yangdipertuan Muda: first, the brother of the late Yangdipertuan Muda, Raja Ali; second, his brother, Raja Hajji Abdullah; and third, Raja Idris, son of the deceased. After having appointed his representatives, Sultan Mahmud departed for Singapore.

When the Resident learned what Sultan Madmud had done, he was far from pleased, because he had nothing definite to inform the Governor-General in Batavia.[29] The Resident then consulted the princes and the elders on Penyengat as to whether Sultan Mahmud's actions had any precedent. The princes, high officials, and elders replied that nothing like that had ever happened before. Then the Resident indicated that he wished the princes to come to an agreement as to who was fit to become the Raja Muda.[30] The majority of the princes suggested Engku Hajji Raja Abdullah, brother of the late Yangdipertuan Muda. Then Raja Hajji Abdullah spoke to his kinsmen: "The Resident of Riau is asking for our collective opinion about who should become Raja Muda. I, myself, am out of it, so long as my elder brother Ali is here. I do not wish to take precedence over him." Raja Juma'at, also a brother of the late Raja Abd al-Rahman and the eldest of Raja Ja'afar's sons but of a different mother to the late Yangdipertuan Muda Raja Abd al-Rahman, replied: "As far as

---

27. The contract which the Dutch Residents refer to throughout the translation is that of October 29, 1830. Netscher gives the text in full ("De Nederlanders in Djohor en Siak," pp. 290-291). The contract replaced all earlier ones between the Dutch government and Riau-Lingga. Under article 7, the Sultan was required to nominate Yangdipertuan Muda who met with the approval of the Dutch and who were descended from the line of Raja Ja'afar (see the genealogy).

28. Netscher ("De Nederlanders in Djohor en Siak," p. 299) gives a slightly different interpretation of the Sultan's behavior. He says that the Sultan delayed naming a successor because he wished to take the opportunity to abolish the Bugis Yangdipertuan Mudaship and draw their share of the revenues for himself. Netscher says that Resident Andriesse had considerable difficulty trying to make the Sultan understand that this would be contradictory to the 1830 contract and would be impossible to realize.

29. Either Pieter Merkus (1841-1844) or Joan C. Reijnst (1844-1845).

30. In nineteenth-century Riau, a synonym for Yangdipertuan Muda. The heir to the Sultan (or Yangdipertuan Besar) bore the title Tengku Besar.

I am concerned, it doesn't seem right that it should be anyone else
but my younger brother, Ali." Then all his relatives and the princes
answered: "We all feel the same way; if it were anyone else but
Raja Ali, it would seem less than proper." Raja Ali Hajji then
spoke: "If you are really speaking sincerely, you should each put
your signature on paper to our agreement." All the princes replied:
"So be it." Then Raja Ali Hajji took ink and paper, and each of
the princes signed. So the matter was agreed, at 9:00, Wednesday,
June 26, 1844,[31] in the balai-rong of the late Yangdipertuan Muda
Raja Abd al-Rahman.

When the deliberations had concluded, Engku Hajji Abdullah sent
Hajji Ibrahim,[32] son of Dato' Shahbandar Abdullah, to the Resident
with the letter [containing] the decision of the princes. When the
Resident of Riau received the letter, he was pleased and said:
"Hajji Ibrahim, the princes' decision is in accord with my own and
with that of the Dutch government." Then he continued:

> Of the Sultan's three candidates the only one I could
> accept was Raja Ali; but Raja Abdullah must not feel
> slighted because of this incident with the Sultan.
> There were two matters which were not at all according
> to our statues.[33] [First] we requested that only one
> [person] be chosen to become Yangdipertuan Muda; the
> Sultan proposed three as if to ridicule the govern-
> ment. Second, the Sultan selected three candidates
> who were all worthy of becoming Yangdipertuan [Muda],
> and all three were left with the authority of Raja
> Muda, the Sultan deliberately seeing to it that the
> Riau princes would quarrel and that there would be
> dissension within the state. It was as well that the
> princes of Penyengat had the good sense to come to an
> agreement, because if they had not the Sultan would
> certainly have [succeeded in] creating contention.
> One further matter, when the late Yangdipertuan Muda
> Raja Abd al-Rahman was still alive, he had already
> appointed his brother Raja Ali as Kelana[34] in his
> administration. It is only proper that he should
> succeed him in the realm. Why wasn't the Sultan con-
> tent to follow the principles and ways of his for-
> bears?

---

31. The Muslim date is 9 Jumad al-akhir, Rabu, 1260.

32. Ibrahim appears in the Tuhfat as confidant, courier, and special
    agent of the Yangdipertuan Muda; e.g. in the 1830's he was sent
    on several diplomatic missions.

33. Probably refers to the treaty of 1830.

34. Hadji Ibrahim (Tjakap2 Rampai2 Bahasa Malajoe Djohor, I, pp. 319-
    321) stated that whoever was going to succeed the Yangdipertuan
    Muda bore the title Engku Kelana. His duties were to participate
    in discussions, to execute the orders of the Yangdipertuan Muda,
    and to punish those who disobey the Yangdipertuan Muda's com-
    mands, even to the point of waging war on them.

Hajji Ibrahim replied: "That is something about which I dare not speak because Your Excellency knows best."

Then Hajji Ibrahim returned and reported the Resident's words to Engku Hajji Raja Abdullah and to all the princes. So it was definitely settled that Raja Ali should be appointed Yangdipertuan Muda of Riau because he was the choice of the princes as well as pleasing to the Dutch government.

While Sultan Mahmud was having a holiday in Singapore, he met the Temenggong, Tun Ibrahim, Yangdipertuan Muda Raja Ali's brother-in-law. Sultan Mahmud told him how he had nominated three candidates for the Yangdipertuan Mudaship, because he wished for [time] to consider [the matter]. Temenggong Ibrahim replied: "In my opinion, if the way is still open for it,[35] Raja Ali should succeed the late Yangdipertuan Muda. Indeed, there is no one else suitable or even willing." After hearing Dato' Temenggong Ibrahim's opinion, Sultan Mahmud was silent. He later returned to Lingga escorted by the Temenggong.

Not long after his arrival in Lingga, [the Temenggong] asked leave to return to Singapore, wishing also to stop at Riau to meet Raja Ali. Sultan Mahmud then composed a letter, inviting Raja Ali to Lingga for the presentation of his regalia, making him Yangdipertuan Muda of Riau. He gave the letter to Dato' Temenggong Ibrahim and further requested him to urge Raja Ali to come to Lingga within the month. So the Temenggong left Lingga for Riau, and, when he arrived, went ashore to meet Raja Ali. He gave him Sultan Mahmud's letter and said: "Sultan Mahmud commanded me to ask you to hasten to Lingga within the month." Raja Ali replied: "I will obey his command, but I wish to assemble my relatives, wherever they are, because I am going to be appointed [their] leader.[36] If I can't ask my own family, whom can I invite to participate in my coronation?" The Temenggong replied that this was so. When he had finished his conversation with Raja Ali, the Temenggong asked leave to return. So he went back to Singapore, where he stayed at Telok Belanga.

As for Raja Ali, after Temenggong Ibrahim had returned to Singapore, he assembled all his relatives from among the princes and then conferred with them about travelling to Lingga to attend Sultan Mahmud. After consulting with them, Raja Ali sailed for Lingga. When he arrived there, he attended Sultan Mahmud and concluded a document of loyalty. Afterwards Sultan Mahmud installed Raja Ali and bestowed the regalia on him, making him Yangdipertuan Muda of Riau-Lingga and dependencies and following the time honored ritual for the installation. The ceremonies began on July 22 and continued until Wednesday, August 27, 1845,[37] and thus his title was ratified.

---

35. The Malay is: *jika lain daripada itu*. The Temenggong is saying that he knows the Sultan had given his decision, but if the way is still open for an alternative, Raja Ali should be nominated.

36. The Malay is: *tua*, probably an abbreviation for *ketua* (elder or leader).

37. The Muslim dates are 17 Rajab and 23 Sha'aban, 1261. Netscher ("De Nederlanders in Djohor en Siak," p. 299) says that the two rulers sealed the pledge of loyalty on July 19, 1845. Further

When Yangdipertuan Muda Raja Ali had completed his business, he asked leave of Sultan Mahmud to return to Riau. The Sultan granted it, and the Yangdipertuan Muda set sail. When he arrived, he was respectfully received by the Resident of Riau with a cannon salute from the Hill[38] and with salvoes from Penyengat. All the Chinese put to sea in scores of fishing boats with gongs and cymbals to welcome the Yangdipertuan Muda. Then he came ashore to pay his respects to his uncle, Engku Hajji Ahmad, and to his mother, Raja Lebar.[39] Afterwards he returned to his residence to entertain all his relatives.

In the course of his reign, Yangdipertuan Muda Raja Ali instituted some important things which brought glory to the name of the realm and strengthened the religion.[40] His brother, Engku Hajji Raja Abdullah, generally called Engku Hajji Muda, was the one who implemented them for him. It began with the organization and arrangement of food for his relatives from the Riau revenues,[41] wherever the late Yangdipertuan Muda Raja Abd al-Rahman had not been able to do it. Where it was appropriate and possible, he updated their allowances. He did the same with the regulations concerning the tenure of all official state positions held by his relatives, and he held frequent consultations before delegating responsibility [to those] who did not seem unsuitable or unworthy in the estimation of the elders and in the eyes of people of intelligence and discernment. Moreover, he delighted in close discussions on matters of state, and he liked asking the elders and high officials for their ideas and opinions and personally sought out in their homes people like Shahbandar Abdullah and Ponggawa[42] Ahmad, not to mention his senior relatives.

---

information about the installation date is given at the end of a manuscript of the Hikayat Negeri Johor (Kuala Lumpur, 24. A), which says that Sultan Mahmud gave Raja Ali the Yangdipertuan Muda's seal and pledge of loyalty on July 20, 1845.

38. This refers to the Dutch garrison, Fort Kroonprins, at Tanjong Pinang. G. F. de Bruyn Kops ("Sketch," p. 73) describes this fort.

39. They were the Yangdipertuan Muda's last surviving forbears.

40. By eulogizing the Yangdipertuan Muda, the author of the Tuhfat is tacitly censuring the Sultan. It is interesting that his praise is centered on those policies in which he had a personal interest, e.g. the promotion of Islam and the welfare of relatives.

41. Netscher ("Beschrijving," p. 158) lists Yangdipertuan Muda Ali's revenues. He stresses that the minimum total was f. 105,000. The bulk of the income came from f. 72,000 paid to him by the Dutch as compensation for cessation of the revenues of Riau. It was probably this sum that the Sultan later felt was his.

42. Hadji Ibrahim, (Tjakap2 Rampai2 Bahasa Malajoe Djohor, I, p. 237) says the ponggawa is the laksamana's equivalent on land, i.e. he is the chief of the army. If a Malay, his title is panglima perang besar, if a Bugis, ponggawa. Ibrahim (p. 339) says that in Sanskrit the title means lembu jantan (bull).

Before he had become Raja the late Raja Muda Abd al-Rahman had had him made Kelana to improve the outer territories.[43] He went alike to the houses of the elders and the high officials to ask their advice and guidance, only then setting out on his travels. Furthermore, he was fond [of the company] of learned men, both respecting and honoring them; when he was the [Yangdipertuan Muda's] representative in Lingga, there was a learned Bandjarese, Hajji Hamin, whom, on the advice of his cousin Raja Ali Hajji, he brought back with him, and paid him an allowance. He revered the learned hajji and would not walk before him. He never missed the Friday service, being humble before Muslim scholars, and so it was with his uncles, like Raja Ismail and Raja Ja'afar [to whom] he was very polite and courteous. In the same spirit he was not comfortable sitting in a chair if his seniors were on the ground or if tuan *sayyid*[44] were present.

It was his custom to enjoy entertaining those relatives who would come to him on a certain day, and likewise he too would visit them in their houses. During his reign he upheld the Islamic faith, attending the mosque on Fridays and ordering women to be veiled. He completed the construction of the mosque,[45] which the late Yangdipertuan Muda Raja Abd al-Rahman had left unfinished because of his death. He later had a bridge constructed of wood and stone, so that the faithful could comfortably get about when the tide was down.[46]

In the time of Yangdipertuan Muda Raja Ali, many religious scholars came. After consultation with his relative, Raja Ali Hajji, he paid their expenses and ordered all state officials to study religion, recite religious works, and to improve their recitation of the glorious Koran. He himself loved the quest for knowledge. His relative, Raja Ali Hajji, selected several learned men, like Sayyid Abdullah Bahrain and others, to settle and teach in Penyengat for a year. When they left they were given 400 to 500 *ringgit*.[47]

Yangdipertuan Muda Raja Ali prohibited the wearing of gold and silk. He exiled all malefactors and forbad [recreations] like

---

43. The outer territories were considered to be the smaller islands of the Riau-Lingga archipelago and the settlements on the adjacent Sumatran coast, especially those around Amphitrite Bay.

44. Traditionally sayyid are the descendants of the Prophet through his grandson Husain. In the Malay world, however, the term is also applied to Arabs who were not descended from the Prophet but were nevertheless accorded great respect.

45. G. F. de Bruyn Kops ("Sketch," p. 98) describes the mosque.

46. De Bruyn Kops ("Sketch," p. 98) talks of "a capital stone jetty, with a landing place built on piles," which was built 1848-1849, and so would have been constructed on Yangdipertuan Muda Ali's orders. But other bridges were necessary, because the people of the archipelago used boats as the main means of transport. When the tide was down and they could not use their boats, they either had to walk in the mud or to cross by bridges.

47. A ringgit is a dollar. Spanish dollars were in currency in Riau and Lingga, at this time valued at approximately 5/-sterling.

gambling and cockfighting; these pastimes were no longer tolerated. If a Muslim was discovered gambling or cockfighting he was punished accordingly. Even when celebrating his own son's wedding, he would not allow any gambling or cockfighting. Pirates were punished, sometimes with exile and sometimes with death by beheading. This was done several times and acted as a deterrent to others. Furthermore Yangdipertuan Muda Raja Ali abhorred those who indulged in pleasures which lead to loose behavior between men and women and those who sang and crooned *pantun*[48] with veiled invitations to adultery. Sometimes he ordered the instruments of those who serenaded near the houses of decent people to be confiscated, so that their young girls would not be corrupted and so that there was nothing unseemly in the state.

He was like this because he enjoyed the company of learned men, liked to hear their moral instruction and advice, and enjoyed having religious works recited to him. It was Yangdipertuan Muda Raja Ali who received a gift from the government of about 40,000 rupia because of his wise counsel and cooperation with the Resident. From the Governor-General[49] in Batavia he received a valuable silver tea and coffee set, and he received as a gift from the King of Prussia[50] a clock, which chimed automatically and was ornamented with a mechanical golden singing bird. He also received a beautiful crown and some gold and silver cloth. He wore the crown in the mosque at Penyengat. Yangdipertuan Muda Raja Ali also received a gift from a Dutch prince called Hertokh[51] a pistol chased with silver (the pistol had been given to Hertokh by a Pasha). Yangdipertuan Muda Raja Ali received an increase [in his share] of the Riau revenues from the government, bringing the total to 6,000 rupia, in recognition of the good counsel and courtesy which the Resident had received from him and his family....[52]

---

48. Pantun are quatrains, which traditionally have two parts. The first couplet has a hidden meaning, and the second couplet explains the first.

49. Jacob Rochussen, 1845-1851.

50. The reigning king of Prussia was Frederick William IV, ruling 1840-1861. There is no record, however, that he visited or was even interested in Southeast Asia.

51. H-r-t-w-kh. Since the Tuhfat specifies that this was a Dutch prince, it is unlikely that this is the surname "Hartog" but rather the Dutch hertog (duke). The only Dutch prince who visited Indonesia in the nineteenth century was Prins Hendrik, "de Zeevaarder," who was in Java for eight months in 1837. Although he returned to Holland via Riau, on chronological grounds it is unlikely that this is the "Hertog" of the Tuhfat. I am indebted to Drs. Brakel for bringing to my attention a more likely candidate, Hertog Bernhard of Saxe-Weimar (1792-1862). From 1847 until some time after 1850, he was Commander of the Netherlands-Indies army in Java, and it would therefore be appropriate for him to send a gift of a pistol to the Yangdipertuan Muda of Riau.

52. The passage omitted tells how Sultan Mahmud had his daughter, Fatimah, married to the Yangdipertuan Muda's son, Muhammad Yusuf, in 1851. The Nakshabandiyyah tarekat (mystical group) was introduced to Penyengat, and the Yangdipertuan Muda became a member. He also visited Singapore with the Resident of Riau, possibly

Let us talk now of Sultan Mahmud in Lingga, who conceived the idea of wanting to go to Trengganu with his mother. When the time was propitious he sailed for Trengganu. On his arrival the Yangdipertuan of Trengganu[53] honored both his sister, Tengku Teh, and his nephew, Yangdipertuan Besar Sultan Mahmud Muzaffar Shah, so he stayed in Trengganu, being regaled and entertained as is customary among royalty newly reunited with their relatives.

After some time in Trengganu, he returned to Lingga, stopping at Riau for a short time before going on to Lingga. Later he set out again for a pleasure trip to Singapore. He joined a Christian

---

to consult the British authorities about Sultan Mahmud. In 1851 and 1852, Tengku Ali, would-be Sultan of Singapore and Johor, had visited Lingga and offered to transfer his Peninsula inheritance to Sultan Mahmud. The Dutch had informed the British of this offer, and Ali was ordered to return. In 1852 Mahmud had visited Singapore, ostensibly to discuss the development of coal desposits on Lingga. Wake, "Nineteenth Century Johore," p. 127. In 1853, Wake says (p. 129) that Mahmud was in communication with W. H. Read, Tengku Ali's adviser. Read did not become Dutch consul in Singapore until 1857, so the Sultan would hardly have consulted him about domestic affairs. Read was a Mason of high standing in Singapore, and it was probably through him that Mahmud became involved with the Brethren of Lodge Zetland in Singapore. It is likely that the Sultan was trying to persuade Read to use his influence over Tengku Ali to prevent him from transferring his rights over Johor to the Temenggong. Wake says (pp. 125 and 127) that Mahmud and Ali were probably trying to retain their authority "in the face of the upstart pretensions of the Bendahara and the Temenggong, who being of royal descent, appeared now to aspire to royal pretensions."

53. This was Sultan Umar, whose sister, Tengku Teh, was Sultan Mahmud's mother. In 1853, Mahmud had strengthened his family ties with Trengganu by marrying one of his sisters to Sultan Umar's son (Wake, "Nineteenth Century Johore," p. 127). On this visit to Trengganu in 1854 which the Tuhfat describes, both Wake (p. 128), and Netscher ("De Nederlanders in Djohor en Siak," p. 301), say that Mahmud was encouraging his uncle to extend his influence over his neighbors. Umar even wrote officially to the Governor of the Straits Settlements, saying that he recognized the Sultan of Lingga as the rightful sovereign of Johor and Pahang. The British became fearful that Mahmud would start hostilities which could jeopardize their trade on the east coast. Butterworth, the Governor, informed the Dutch of Mahmud's actions, saying that he was a bad influence on Tengku Ali and that he was fostering misunderstandings between the Sultan of Trengganu and the rulers of Pahang and Kelantan. The Dutch Governor-General responded by sending Mahmud a letter (dated April 2, 1854), exhorting him to give up his visits to Singapore and to the Peninsula and to return to Lingga as quickly as possible. Mahmud did return, but made demands of the Dutch Government--an advance of f. 70,000 and a Dutch civil servant at Lingga whom he could treat as a subordinate. The Dutch gave nothing despite the Sultan's threat that he could get a European for the job from Singapore.

religious society called Freemasons,[54] and became friends with a Parsee called Cursetjee.[55]

When he returned to Lingga he built a residence in European style,[56] which was spacious and beautifully constructed. Never had the Riau-Lingga kings had such a residence built, complete with fine and beautiful furnishings and stocked with various European foods and drinks, and with paintings on the walls. When Europeans came, like the Resident of Riau and others, they were received and entertained in this residence. He also kept some large dogs and cared for them as would a European. There is nothing wrong with having a European house as long as this does not entail a change in religion. . . .[57]

Raja Abdullah, Engku Hajji Muda, conferred with his relatives on Penyengat and with worthy elders; then he sent a letter to Sultan Mahmud on Lingga with keepsakes,[58] and he also sent keepsakes to Singapore with a letter. The messengers set sail. When the Lingga messenger arrived, there was a commotion when it was learned that the Yangdipertuan Muda Raja Ali had died. His wife wept with all those who were in his Lingga residence, and they held a funeral feast as is customary on the death of a great king. When Sultan Mahmud received the letter from Riau, he wanted to go there. A *perahu* was sent from Riau to fetch him, and he set sail.

---

54. He was a member of the Brethren of Lodge Zetland in the East, from C. B. Buckley, An Anecdotal History of Old Times in Singapore (Kuala Lumpur and Singapore: University of Malaya Press, 1965), pp. 520-521.

55. Buckley (An Anecdotal History, p. 350) mentions Cursetjee. He was a Singapore merchant who took over the business of John Martin Little in 1845. "Cursetjee was the son of Frommurzjee Sorabjee, a Parsee merchant, who established his firm in Singapore in 1840 and died on February 17, 1849. Cursetjee afterwards did business on his own account and was very popular in Singapore. He had an English wife. He died here in 1881."

56. G. F. de Bruyn Kops ("Sketch," p. 100) describes this house. A contemporary Malay account of the construction of this residence is to be found in sha'ir form in Sha'ir Sultan Mahmud di Lingga (Ms. in Djakarta Museum, von de Wall 274).

57. The passage omitted describes the death of Yangdipertuan Muda Raja Ali at the age of about 47 in June 1857. His illness and death are described in a manuscript (Djakarta Museum, Bataviaasch Genootschap 159) which is wrongly entitled Sha'ir Sultan Mahmud Raja Muda. His brother, Raja Abdullah, the Engku Hajji Muda, took his place as senior Bugis on Penyengat.

58. These could have been small personal belongings of the deceased, but there is a more specific kind of keepsake in this context. W. W. Skeat, Malay Magic (New York: Dover Publications, 1967), p. 406, says that just before burial the bands tying the shroud are removed. They are then handed to the next of kin, who tear them up and plait the strips into a rough kind of bracelet, which they wear as long as it lasts in memory of the deceased.

On his arrival, the Engku Muda, Raja Hajji Abdullah, and Engku Hajji were in attendance and invited him to come ashore to the palace at Kampong Bulang. There all the princes on Penyengat came to attend him and awaited his announcement as to who would succeed the late [ruler]. But no announcement of a decision was forthcoming, and the princes were disappointed because their leader had not yet been determined. The person whom Sultan Mahmud had decided was to succeed the late Raja Ali was his [Raja Ali's] son, Raja Muhammad Yusuf, who was his [own] son-in-law. But Raja Muhammad Yusuf was unwilling to succeed his father as long as his uncle, the Engku Hajji Muda [was alive]. He was even willing to be estranged from Sultan Mahmud and risk his displeasure rather than be alienated from his uncle, the Engku Hajji Muda. This had the effect of frustrating Sultan Mahmud's wishes and prevented his deciding on a successor to the Yangdipertuan Muda. The Resident, too, was pressing for a decision on a successor.

Sultan Mahmud had no desire to settle it because the princes and elders on Penyengat had already decided for several reasons that the only fitting successor to the late Raja Ali could be the Engku Hajji Muda. Firstly, the Engku Hajji Muda was already acquainted with the ways of government. Secondly, he was versed in both religious and traditional law.[59] Thirdly, as long as he was present, there was no one from among the princes, young or old, who wished to become Yangdipertuan Muda, providing that the person favored by Sultan Mahmud did not wish to be so. Fourthly, the government representative approved the decision of the people of Riau, and he upheld article 7 of the contract, which dealt with the conditions for the appointment of the Raja Muda: if the Dutch government did not approve of the Sultan of Riau and Lingga's choice, there could be no appointment, unless Sultan Mahmud followed the government's directions. For these four reasons, the Resident held Engku Hajji Muda Raja Abdullah as a suitable successor to his brother, the late Raja Ali, and requested that Sultan Mahmud appoint him forthwith, lest affairs of state be further impeded. But Sultan Mahmud paid no attention to the advice of the Resident and the people but still wanted his own way. This was the root of the conflict between Sultan Mahmud and the Resident of Riau, and all the princes, high officials, and elders on Penyengat.

In the meantime, there was much he said and did which neither met with the approval of the Dutch government nor the people. Sultan Mahmud wished to go to Singapore and leave the matter undecided. The Resident tried to persuade him not to go[60] before settling such a

---

59. The Malay is: hukum shari'at dan adat istiadat. Al-shari'at is the revealed or canonical law of Islam. H. Wehr, A Dictionary of Modern Written Arabic (Wiesbaden: Otto Harrassowitz, 1966).

60. Although after his 1854 trip, Mahmud had been warned not to return to Trengganu, in August 1856 the Sultan informed the Resident that he was going to Singapore to begin a journey to Trengganu. This was ostensibly to collect his mother. Netscher ("De Nederlanders in Djohor en Siak," p. 302) says Mahmud had the guile not to inform the Singapore authorities of his intended destination. However, after his departure Cursetjee informed the British Resident, who sent a ship to collect Mahmud and returned him to Lingga in October 1856. The Dutch had to pacify the British with assurance that stronger measures would be taken against the Sultan. Resident Nieuwenhuijzen and A. A. de Vries went to Lingga with a letter from the Governor-General dated December 14, 1856.

grave matter which was weighing heavily on the state of Riau-Lingga.
Sultan Mahmud, however, paid no heed to the Resident's advice but
still strongly insisted on going to Singapore. All this caused much
concern to the Engku Hajji Muda, Raja Abdullah, lest there be a
breach between Sultan Mahmud and the Dutch government. So he ventured to offer a letter of advice which read:

> About the matter of the Raja Mudaship; we are [now] completely at your disposal to do as you wish, as if indeed
> we have not already done your will for generations past.
> I beg you, do not quarrel with the Dutch government and
> do not break the contract which your forbears entered
> into and which you [yourself] have ratified.

But Sultan Mahmud paid no heed to the Engku Hajji Muda's request and
still wanted to leave for Singapore the next day. Engku Hajji Muda
was silent, being at his wits end.

Meanwhile Sultan Mahmud had sent a messenger to the Resident of
Riau asking for the Riau revenue money. The Resident replied: "The
Riau revenues had already been pledged in the contract; under
article 16,[61] the money belongs to the Raja Muda. So now, quickly
appoint a Raja Muda, so that we may hand the money over to him as
[stipulated] in the contract." When Sultan Mahmud heard the
Resident's reply, his fury increased, and there were many improper
words which I will not record in this history. Suffice it for those
with intelligence to imagine the words of two people disagreeing.

The Riau revenues were withheld for about two months, and the
princes and elders of Penyengat suffered hardship because they were
all accustomed to receiving their monthly allowance regularly. Now
it was withheld because of Sultan Mahmud's behavior in not appointing
a successor to the Yangdipertuan Muda. The result was that many who
were penniless came to pester the Engku Hajji Muda, who distributed
about 1,700 ringgit to his distressed relatives. Where he was short
he borrowed a sum of about 1,000 ringgit from the Chinese.

> The Sultan was told he had violated article 3 of the 1830 contract
> (the Sultan owed allegiance to the Governor-General, and they
> shared common enemies), and that it was only as a great favor
> that the Governor-General was not exercising his right (article 6
> of the contract) to deny him government protection. The Sultan
> was now forbidden to move outside his territory without the
> Governor-General's permission. If he was disobedient or disrespectful to the government again, he would lose his kingdom.
> A letter was also sent to the Yangdipertuan Muda warning him not
> to provide the Sultan with vessels for his travels. Apparently
> the Yangdipertuan Muda had complained to Batavia about Resident
> Nieuwenhuijzen because in the letter the Governor-General expressed his complete confidence in his Resident and said he
> would not be replaced. This suggests that in Riau Nieuwenhuijzen
> was not very diplomatic, and it is possible that his attidue and
> actions aggravated the Dutch position with Sultan Mahmud. However,
> here he is obviously reminding the Sultan of the Governor-General's
> ultimatum that he was not to leave Riau-Lingga without permission.

61. Actually the article concerning the Yangdipertuan Muda's revenues
    is number 17. It deals with the compensation of the Yangdipertuan
    Muda for the loss of the revenues of Riau.

Sultan Mahmud wished to leave for Singapore the next day. The Resident detained him, asking who was to be appointed because the people on Penyengat were in difficulties, especially the Engku Hajji Muda, Raja Abdullah. He was at the mercy of his relatives because he had been nominated in the late Raja Ali's will [to care for] all his family. Sultan Mahmud took no notice of the Resident's restraints but sailed to Singapore in his schooner.[62] The Engku Hajji Muda sent for his son, Raja Muhammad Yusuf. He said: "Try to follow Sultan Mahmud; I'll send you a small perahu and as much money as I can for expenses." So Raja Muhammad Yusuf set out to follow the Sultan as envoy from his father, the Engku Hajji Muda.

When Sultan Mahmud set sail, the Resident of Riau felt humiliated because [his orders for] Sultan Mahmud to stay had been disregarded and so the code of the high officials had been dishonored. If the Resident was dishonored, this reflected onto the Dutch government. Moreover, the Dutch government had had a plan for Sultan Mahmud--a certain government decree[63] which would not have harmed his kingship. But even this, Sultan Mahmud did not want to accept, and this also offended and caused embarrassment to the Dutch government. This matter and Sultan Mahmud's actions were to have far-reaching consequences.

When Sultan Mahmud reached Singapore, he stayed with his non-Muslim friend Cursetjee, the Parsee, who was a Zoroastrian. Several times Cursetjee tried to coax Raja Muhammad Yusuf into wanting to succeed his late father, Raja Ali, but at this he became angry and said: "Don't speak to me like this again. My uncle in Riau will succeed my late father. I have no wish to succeed my father as long as my uncle is alive." Cursetjee was silent.

Meanwhile the Resident had also sent a message to Singapore inviting Sultan Mahmud to return to Riau and requesting him to appoint his representative, the future Raja Muda. But still Sultan Mahmud did not wish to appoint a representative from the Riau princes. In actual fact he was conferring with a prince called Raja Ahmad. . . .[64] This was the Raja Ahmad who had been put forward as a candidate by Sultan Mahmud when discussing the matter of the Raja Muda. The Resident's messenger returned to Riau without a directive.

---

62. Netscher ("De Nederlanders in Djohor en Siak," p. 303) dates his departure as August 30, 1857.

63. Netscher makes no mention of a special government decree other than the Governor-General's warning of 1856.

64. The passage omitted describes Raja Ahmad's forbears. He was a descendant of a Bugis Raja Tua, who betrayed the Bugis in one of the periods of Malay-Bugis conflict on Riau in the early 1760's. Yangdipertuan Muda Kamboja exiled the Raja Tua to Palembang. Obviously the Bugis on Penyengat would never support such a candidate. The choice of Raja Ahmad also violated article 7 of the 1830 contract.

On Monday, October 5,⁶⁵ a steam warship called the *Celebes* came from Batavia to Riau and berthed at Tanjong Pinang, bringing a commissary, Tuan Mejor.⁶⁶ He conferred with the Resident of Riau about Sultan Mahmud. On Tuesday, October 6,⁶⁷ a boat which Sultan Mahmud had borrowed from his friend Cursetjee came from Singapore, bringing Raja Ahmad Tengku Long to Riau to be his representative there. Raja Ahmad was competent to be his representative because he would stand up to the Resident. Even if the dispute went as far as Batavia, he would handle it; Sultan Mahmud was not to worry.

When he reached Riau he went ashore to Tanjong Pinang to meet the Resident. Raja Ahmad announced that he was Sultan Mahmud's representative for Riau affairs and gave him a letter from the Sultan. When the Resident had read it, he understood its purport. Then Raja Ahmad Tengku Long returned to his vessel to await the Resident's reply to the letter.

After Raja Ahmad had gone, the Resident sent for Raja Abdullah Engku Hajji Muda. When he came, the Resident said: "Have you met Raja Ahmad Tengku Long?" Raja Abdullah said, "No." So [the Resident] said: "Perhaps you should come and meet him." Then he showed him the letter from Sultan Mahmud which Raja Ahmad had brought. Raja Abdullah read as follows:

> We wish to inform our honorable friend that when we were in Lingga, you called us to Riau to discuss a successor to the Raja Muda. When we arrived in Riau, you broached the matter of the government decree. This came at a time when the late Yangdipertuan Muda Raja Ali was no longer capable of receiving it, let alone ourselves. Furthermore you have requested [that we name] our representative in Riau, so we have sent Raja Ahmad Tengku Long to be our representative there. We desire that you hand over the Riau revenues and the [taxes of the] *orang laut*⁶⁸ to him.

---

65. The Muslim date is Ahad, (Sunday) 15 Safar. As the 15 Safar fell on a Monday, either the day or the date in the Tuhfat is incorrect. Evidence from Netscher ("De Nederlanders in Djohor en Siak," p. 305) suggests that the Tuhfat's day is correct, but that the date is incorrect. All further dates in the translation have been adjusted in view of this discrepancy.

66. He has not yet been identified. It appears that "Mejor" is a title and not a surname. Netscher ("De Nederlanders in Djohor en Siak," pp. 305-306) gives a full account of Dutch proceedings at this time, and only mentions that Resident Nieuwenhuijzen and Assistant Resident von de Wall were concerned with the action taken against Sultan Mahmud.

67. The Muslim date is thalatha, 17 Safar.

68. G. F. de Bruyn Kops ("Sketch," p. 108) describes the orang laut: "There are two distinct classes to be distinguished amongst the Malays, the orang darat and the orang laut. . . . The first named reside on land, are traders, agriculturalists, handicraftsmen and the like. The second class have their residence in prahus, in which they constantly live with their families." Netscher ("Beschrijving," p. 127) estimates their number as

These were the words of Sultan Mahmud's letter to the Resident of Riau. It is approximately the text, but I could not vouch for it, because I had it from Raja Abdullah, the Engku Hajji Muda, by word of mouth; I did not copy it from the document.

Then the Resident said to Raja Abdullah: "This is our commissary, sent by the government to divest the Sultan of his realm because of his misdeeds. There are nine matters which implied disrespect for the government and its representative. Tomorrow the proclamation will go out." Raja Abdullah was shocked when he heard this and fell silent. Then he asked the Resident's leave to return to Penyengat.

When he arrived he assembled his relatives and told them that Sultan Mahmud was going to be deposed by the Dutch government. This plunged them all into thought because nothing like it had ever happened before. Then they discussed it and [decided to] send a letter containing three points to the Resident of Riau. Firstly, "that our good name and institutions should never be allowed to disappear; secondly, that the government support Raja Abdullah and his successors in any future difficulty; thirdly, that our names be expunged from what is an affair of the Dutch government so that we cannot be accused of treason." The Resident accepted all their requests. The letter was written amidst extreme turmoil on Tuesday, October 6, at 3:00 p.m.

The following day, Wednesday, at 7:00 a.m., the commissary set sail with one other European called von de Wall,[69] who was an expert in the Malay language. They sailed to Singapore[70] in the steamship *Celebes*, and, when they arrived, they both called on the Govenor of Singapore.[71] Then they set out to find Sultan Mahmud, going everywhere, even to the Temenggong's house, but without success. Finally they found him in Cursetjee's house on the hill. The commissary then read the proclamation deposing Sultan Mahmud from his kingdom.[72] The

---

15,000, but this figure probably includes the orang laut around the eastern coast of Sumatra as well as in the Riau-Lingga archipelago. Netscher (p. 155) says the Sultan kept his revenues from lands and subjects confidential, but that he estimates the amount to be 40,000 Spanish dollars per annum.

69. Hermann von de Wall was sent to Riau in 1855 as Assistant Resident to compile a Malay-Dutch Dictionary. He was later made Resident of Riau, where he died in 1873.

70. Netscher ("De Nederlanders in Djohor en Siak," p. 305) says they arrived in Singapore on October 7, 1857. It is quite possible to make a return journey from Riau to Singapore in one day by steamship.

71. Edmund A. Blundell, Governor of Singapore, 1855-1859.

72. Netscher ("De Nederlanders in Djohor en Siak," pp. 304-305) gives the full text of the manifesto, which was dated September 23, 1857 and signed by Governor-General Pahud. The reasons for the deposition were that: 1) the Sultan had repeatedly overlooked his obligations as a vassal of the government; 2) despite the exhortations of the Resident and Governor-General, he had meddled in the affairs of rulers on the Malay Peninsula, who were under British protection; 3) he had even gone to Trengganu with an armed

Sultan's expression altered only slightly[73] when he heard it. Then the commissary returned to Riau, leaving a copy of the proclamation with Sultan Mahmud. They reached Riau that night.

The following day, Thurday, at 8:00, the Resident and the commissary invited Raja Abdullah, the Engku Hajji Muda, to come to Tanjong Pinang, and the Resident honored him as befitted a Yangdipertuan Muda. Then he said: "The Sultan had already been deposed, and now Lingga and Riau are without both a Yangdipertuan Besar and a Yangdipertuan Muda. So the government now appoints you as the Yangdipertuan Muda to rule the realm of Riau-Lingga and dependencies according to custom." Then the letter of his appointment was read so that all might hear it, and the cannon in the fort was fired.

GENEALOGIES

1. Nineteenth Century Riau-Lingga Sultans

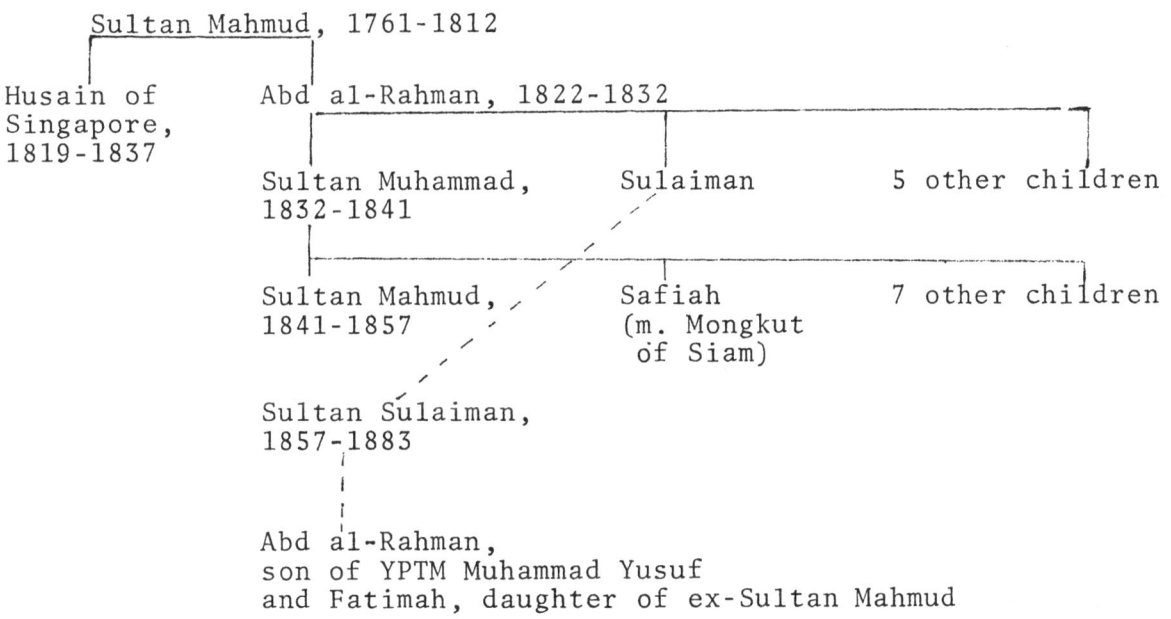

---

    force and hostile intentions, misleading the British authorities in Singapore about the object of his journey.

73. Netscher ("De Nederlanders in Djohor en Siak," p. 305) confirms this: the Sultan received the news "zonder de minste blijkbare aandoening." In this respect, at least, the Sultan conformed to the behavior that tradition demanded.

2. Bugis Yangdipertuan Muda and Author of Tuhfat

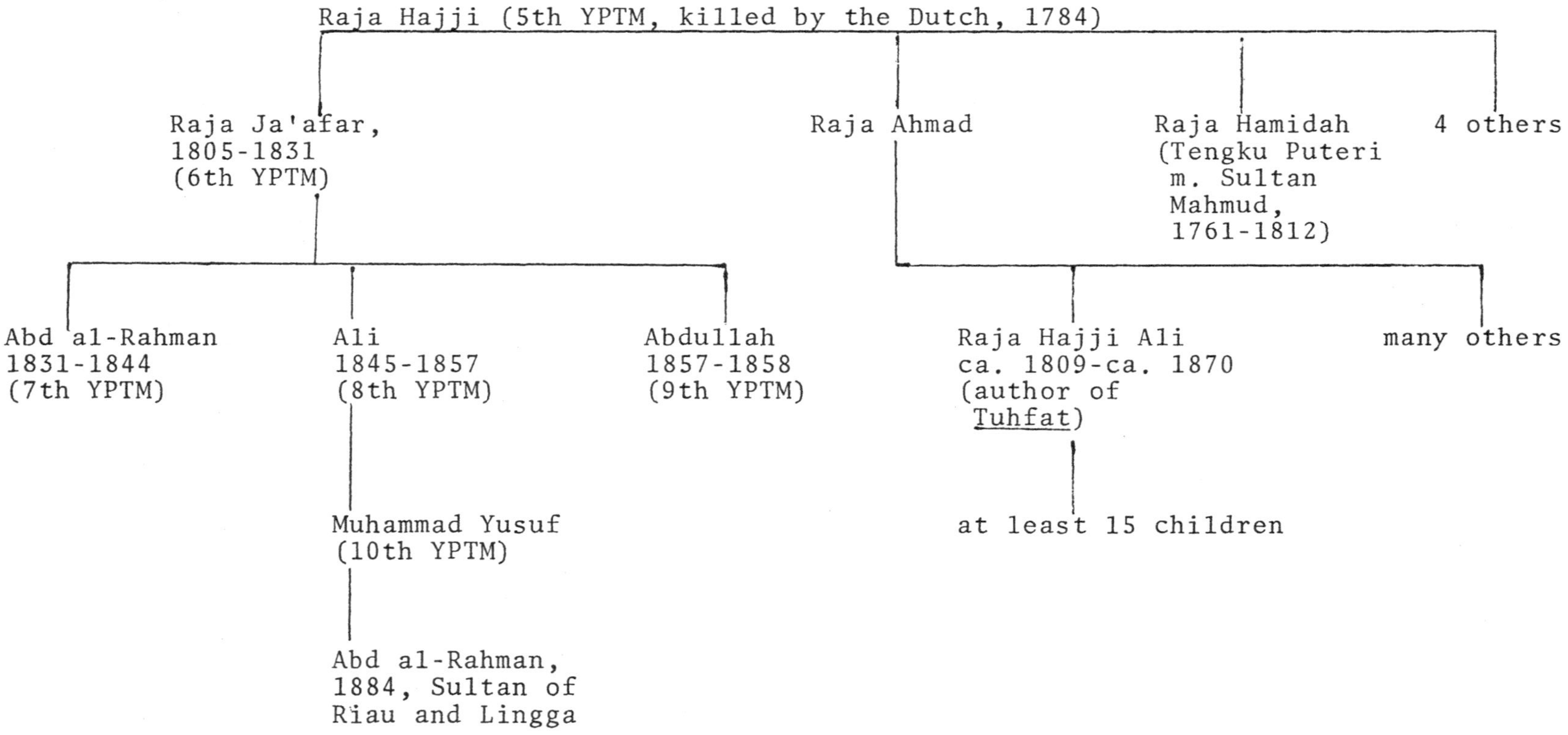

```
Raja Hajji (5th YPTM, killed by the Dutch, 1784)
    │
    ├─────────────────────────┬──────────────────────────────┐
    │                         │                              │
Raja Ja'afar,            Raja Ahmad                   Raja Hamidah        4 others
1805-1831                    │                        (Tengku Puteri
(6th YPTM)                   │                        m. Sultan
    │                        │                        Mahmud,
    │                        │                        1761-1812)
    │                  Raja Hajji Ali
    │                  ca. 1809-ca. 1870
    │                  (author of
    │                  Tuhfat)
    │                        │
    │                  at least 15 children    many others
    │
    ├──────────────┬──────────────┐
    │              │              │
Abd al-Rahman    Ali          Abdullah
1831-1844    1845-1857        1857-1858
(7th YPTM)   (8th YPTM)       (9th YPTM)

Muhammad Yusuf
(10th YPTM)

Abd al-Rahman,
1884, Sultan of
Riau and Lingga
```

THE POST-REVOLUTIONARY TRANSFORMATION OF THE INDONESIAN ARMY

Part II*

Ruth McVey

The rebellion of 1958 marked a turning point in the development of the Indonesian army, for it provided the central military leadership with the means to establish its ascendancy over the officer corps. Had there been a compromise in the settlement of the insurrection, General Nasution might have continued for some time to inch his way toward control, in the manner in which we saw him progress during 1955-1956,[1] and the relations between the army center and the powerful territorial commanders would have continued for some time to be roughly equal. But the central military command moved with great success against the rebel forces, whose failure was apparent within six months of their revolt. This victory both eliminated Nasution's principal rivals for army leadership and gave him great military prestige, with which he consolidated his personal position and reshaped the army's structure.

Of even greater significance for the army's ultimate role in Indonesia, the rebellion--or, to be more exact, the State of Emergency proclaimed in April 1957 in response to the regional crisis--allowed the military to expand its activities into the economic and political spheres. This expansion provided the army leadership with vital sources of finance and patronage, strengthening its position over the officer corps and enhancing the army's status in the society as a whole. The proliferation of the army's functions and of its members' contacts with civilian elements that resulted from this development increased the chances for extra-military alliances and civilian influence over individual officers, but in another and ultimately more important sense, it diminished army disunity. The military now clearly had elite status within the society. Under the Guided Democracy system of 1959-1965, territorialy officers participated down to the local level in political decision making; with civilian forces increasingly at loggerheads and government administration declining in efficiency and authority, the military representatives assumed an ever more influential role.

Increasingly, the military functioned in a socially conservative manner. The direct role assumed by the army in the economy, and particularly the control over Dutch-owned enterprises which it assumed in late 1957, gave it a stake in the economic status quo and an

---

* This is the second part of a two-part article. The first part appeared in the April 1971 issue.

1. See "The Post-Revolutionary Transformation of the Indonesian Army," Part I, <u>Indonesia</u>, No. 11 (April 1971), pp. 157-176.

appreciation of the problems of management confronted by labor's demands. Its position in territorial government put army officers in a close working and social relationship with civilian elites, and it also enhanced their professional military tendency to value order imposed from above rather than effervescence from below. Moreover, Sukarno's use of the Communist Party to provide a mass backing for his efforts to prevent the army's political advance underlined the rivalry between the PKI and the military as the country's two great sources of organized initiative--two structures whose ideological differences were strengthened by the tendency for civilian interests to seek their patronage and protection. This polarization, in which the army assumed the post of the Right, strained the sympathies of officers who looked to the revolutionary tradition, and it created an acute problem of military loyalty to Sukarno, who was seen as a national father-figure by officers who were by no means otherwise leftist. At the same time, however, powerful civilian opposition to the army enhanced its corporate sense, for in the post-rebellion period the army leaders' principal rivals were without rather than within the military, and they could therefore portray the contest in terms of preserving mililtary solidarity against civilian subversion.

More concretely, army officers who, under Guided Democracy, had acquired (or aspired to) posts and perquisites far beyond those they could have imagined in the earlier period were concerned to preserve the army's expanded role, and they were correspondingly alarmed at the advance of the PKI, which threatened ultimately to put its own hierarchy in the favored position which the army now occupied. Nor does it seem probable that this concern to preserve existing privileges was limited to members of the officer corps. As we shall see, the economic decline of Guided Democracy straitened the circumstances of the soldiery in spite of the army's acquisition of new resources. Nonetheless, army men had that very important possession--a relatively secure job. They received relatively advantageous allotments and housing, and even after retirement they could be far more certain than the mass of the population that their voice would be heard.[2] They

---

2. Official retirement ages were 42 for non-commissioned officers, 45 for junior officers (lieutenants and captains), 48 for middle-grade officers, and 55 for officers of general rank. Angkatan Bersendjata, September 9, 1968. However, these limits were not closely observed, for there was strong resistance to demobilization, which usually meant a significant loss of income, prestige, and security. This even proved the case with conscripts: a 1958 scheme for rejuvenating the army through the institution of a two-year draft was dropped when it proved difficult to demobilize them when their time was up. Nusantara, November 10, 1960, statement of Brigadier General Sajidiman; and see Pedoman, May 21, 1958, for the conscription plan. Demobilization and the classification and organization of veterans had been problems since the end of the revolution, the more so since it was generally expected that the army would find sources of employment for those who were sent back to civilian life. See the statement by Brigadier General Sajidiman above, and also Pikiran Rakjat, February 18, 1963, statement of Colonel Djohari; and Berita Yudha, August 14, 1965, statement of General Yani.

Because of the danger posed by discontented men with a knowledge of weapons, the army was, within its means, generous in the treatment of ex-servicemen; indeed, of 800,000 claimants to veteran

were, moreover, men who possessed the means of violence in a time when order was gradually breaking down. Particularly in the defeated rebel areas of the Outer Islands, where the army behaved like a force of occupation, soldiers experienced the psychological and material satisfactions of mastery; but everywhere common soldiers found their status to be greater than that of their civilian equivalents, the *rakjat* of which Guided Democracy spoke so much and for which it did so little.

Because of the army leadership's greater stability after 1958, the consolidation of central military authority proceeded more through reforms of the army's institutions than through the personal struggles for power characteristic of the parliamentary period. Consequently, I shall turn my discussion of the post-revolutionary military transformation from a chronological approach to a topical consideration of the changes in the army's structure and practices that took place in

---

status only 5,860 went unrecognized (Pikiran Rakjat, March 21, 1963, statement of General Sambas, Minister for Veterans' Affairs), although many of these would have been at best intermitten members of the revolutionary lasjkar. Aside from the attention paid them in recognition of their potential for trouble-making, the veterans could express themselves in the early 1950's through the division-based solidarity groups and the officers' league (IPRI), as those included both active and non-active military men. They also had their own veterans' associations, and, reflecting the restiveness of the demobilized soldiers, the largest of these was the Communist-oriented All-Indonesia Union of Former Armed Fighters (Perbepbsi), which was founded in 1951 and claimed 300,000 members in 1957. See Dokumentasi Konggres ke-VI Serikat Buruh Kereta Api (Djakarta: Pimpinan Pusat SBKA, 1957), p. 96. It enjoyed its greatest influence in the post-1952 period of army weakness, when it pressed for the creation of People's Security Troops, composed of its members, who would supplement the army's counter-insurgency efforts. For the debate see Antara Warta Berita, July 23, August 22, September 4, 5, 8, and 16, 1953.

Perbepbsi's importance can be assessed from the fact that high army officers, including Colonels Nasution and Gatot Subroto, attended its executive session of November 1955 in order to present their views on veterans' affairs (Pikiran Rakjat, November 15, 1955). A year later, however, Nasution's position had improved to the point where he could seek to impose a single, army-controlled veterans' organization. This was formally instituted in January 1957 (Harian Rakjat, January 4, 1957), but it did not actually succeed in supplanting the independent organizations until the end of the decade. Its commandant and chairman was the Minister of Veterans' Affairs, and it served less as a veterans' lobby than as a supplement to the ministerial organization. In 1960 it joined the World Veterans Federation (PIA news bulletin, July 6, 1960). In addition, the divisional associations that began to develop in the late Guided Democracy period, beginning with the 1963 formation of the Body for the Fostering of the Siliwangi Corps (BPC Siliwangi), attempted to involve veterans and prevent their forming undesirable civilian ties (Pikiran Rakjat, June 25, 1963, statement by General Ibrahim Adjie). Nonetheless, the veterans appear to have remained a politically disaffected group; it was estimated that 80 percent of the Central Java veterans sided with the September 30th Movement in 1965 (Berita Yudha, May 31, 1966, statement of Lieutenant Colonel Sumitro, head of the Central Java Veterans' Administration).

the late 1950's and early 1960's in the fields of leadership, promotion and patronage, training, and organization. In these areas we can see the working out of longstanding ideas regarding the kind of army Indonesia ought to have as well as more general efforts to enhance the authority of the high command. This period saw the first substantial decline of some of the major problems of discipline and structure inherited from the revolution as well as the emergence of questions created by organizational proliferation, technological specialization, and social participation that were to affect the army's development in the post-Sukarno period.

Reconstituting the Army Leadership

With the defeat of the 1958 rebellion the army's top leadership, for the first time in Indonesia's post-revolutionary history, no longer consisted of broadly equal rivals quick to band together to sabotage the claims of any one of them to power. Gradually, during the course of Guided Democracy, General Nasution lost some of his claims to primacy, as his apparent inability to resist Sukarno and to formulate a successful response to the PKI irritated his anti-Communist supporters, while his tacit opposition to the President disturbed officers strongly loyal to that leader. In the period with which we are concerned, however--1858 to about 1963--Nasution was able to use his stature as the military's unquestioned leader to secure a relatively free hand in determining army placement and policy, and one of his principal efforts was naturally directed toward preventing the emergence of any rivals. He did not completely succeed in this effort, but he did acquire a high command whose members were far more congenial, homogeneous, and obedient than the army had possessed before. The members of the general staff were clearly his subordinates and not his equals, as were the *panglima* (territorial commanders at division level), the ensuring of whose obedience we shall consider later.

Nasution's dominance did not mean that his word automatically became army policy, especially in matters concerning the military's more delicate internal and external relations. Leadership remained collegiate in the sense that important matters required the acquiescence of the major portion of the panglima and heads of central army institutions as well as the decision of the general staff; a good deal of negotiation took place in order to achieve the necessary unity, and often enough the interests and attitudes of the senior generals were so diverse as to prevent any firm decision. Nonetheless, there was general acknowledgment as to who had the right to make the less critical decisions on army policy and to gather consensus on the more weighty ones. Moreover, the top army leaders strove to increase their overall control by making the general staff, rather than broader conferences of senior generals, into the acknowledged forum of discussion on important matters of policy. They did not wholly succeed, but the overall result of their endeavor was to produce a military hierarchy whose visible decision-making process was much more like the textbook image than before.

Nasution's position as leader of the army was greatly enhanced by his accession to the post of Minister of Defense in 1959.[3] The

---

3. This took place in July 1959 with the formation of the Kabinet Kerdja, the first cabinet following the return to the 1945

vesting of this ministerial post in military hands did not receive much attention amidst the more dramatic events surrounding the formal introduction of Guided Democracy, but it was of great importance, for it marked the army leadership's establishment of a principle for which it had struggled from the very beginning of the revolution and which had hitherto been denied by Indonesia's civilian governments.[4] The ministry was not, henceforth, to go out of army hands, in which it remained the instrument of the paramount military chief.[5]

In addition to the Ministry of Defense, Nasution occupied the office of Supreme War Administrator (Peperti), which was established under the State of Emergency which existed from 1957 to 1963. It headed an army hierarchy which paralleled civilian territorial administration down to the local level and which administered the martial law under which the country lay.[6] It provided a regular means for military intervention in civilian affairs at all levels, and particularly in the early years of Guided Democracy, the decisions taken by the Supreme War Administration were often more important than the deliberations of the cabinet. The acquisition of this office not only enhanced Nasution's personal prestige and political influence but, like his possession of the Defense Ministry, it gave him a hold on the army outside that provided by his position as Army Chief of Staff. This was important for the one great defeat which Nasution suffered in his efforts to secure undisputed claim to military leadership was his removal from that post in 1962. This blow to his power was struck in the reshuffle of general staff posts that followed the death of Deputy Chief of Staff Gatot Subroto. At that time, Nasution was promoted to a newly created post, Chief of Staff of the Armed Forces; his old office of Army Chief of Staff became that of Commander of the Army and was given to his erstwhile Operations deputy, General Ahmad Yani.

This transformation, the effect of which was to remove Nasution from immediate command of the army and to supply an alternative focus for military loyalties, appears to have been arranged by President Sukarno, who desired to weaken Nasution's grip on post-rebellion army loyalties, which now formed a threat to his own power. The President could not have made this move stick without the army leaders'

Constitution. Initially, Sukarno tried to persuade Nasution to give up the post of Army Chief of Staff in return for the cabinet position; but Nasution, being well aware that the dual function was a vital key to power, refused to go along with this. See Daniel S. Lev, The Transition to Guided Democracy (Ithaca: Cornell Modern Indonesia Project, 1966), p. 279.

4. See "The Post-Revolutionary Transformation," Part I, pp. 136-137.

5. Under the New Order, General Suharto has also held the posts of Minister of Defense and Commander of the Armed Forces (in addition to the Presidency), though he has relinquished the office of Commander of the Army. See below, pp. 179-180.

6. Normally the head of the war administration was the chief of staff of the territorial army command at the appropriate level. For a discussion of the powers and effect of the martial law administration, see Lev, The Transition to Guided Democracy, pp. 59-74.

acquiescence, but there were reasons why it was attractive to them as well. In reviving the office of Armed Forces Chief of Staff, which had been abolished following the October 17, 1952 Affair in the interests of promoting inter-service rivalry, it allowed the army to reassert its hegemony over the other services, a dominance that was becoming increasingly important to possess as the air force and navy expanded and grew in confidence with the aid of their new foreign equipment. It also reinsured Nasution's position as Minister of Defense, which he continued to occupy in his new capacity as armed forces head.

As Yani received his post in preference to several more senior generals, Sukarno could hope that he might be weak enough in his new office to remain dependent on Presidential support. This calculation proved only partially correct, for Yani, who had already acquired a considerable military reputation for his direction of operations in the regional rebellion, proved sufficiently adept at army politics to overcome much of the resentment at his premature promotion. In spite of the best efforts of Sukarno and the civilian left, he maintained a lively appreciation that he would have less room for maneuver if he broke with Nasution than if he maintained a position in the middle. Thus, although he assumed a more cooperative public stance than Nasution did vis-a-vis the civilian leadership of Guided Democracy, he remained essentially a leader of the army and opposed to Sukarno's camp.[7]

Though Nasution and Yani had different ethnic and divisional backgrounds[8] and possessed separate personal clienteles, their military and social outlooks were sufficiently alike for them to represent roughly the same style of officer. They belonged to the "metropolitan superculture"[9] which developed in Indonesia's great cities towards the end of the colonial period, a mestizo mingling

---

7. Towards 1965, with the army increasingly on the defensive in capital politics, there was growing talk that Nasution would be removed to an exalted but powerless post, that he would be replaced as Armed Forces Chief of Staff by Yani, and that the latter would turn over his old job to a more malleable army commander. Nasution's position was by that time sufficiently weak that he probably could have been replaced had Yani agreed to cooperate with Sukarno in the effort, but in the ensuing months there was little sign that the Commander of the Army had lost his awareness that what was done to Nasution now might later also be done to him. It was General Suharto, relying on the great prestige he had won for his role in the October 1965 coup and on the demoralization of his opponents, who succeeded in kicking Nasution upstairs; having used Nasution's dismissal as Defense Minister by Sukarno following the coup as a reason to seize the Presidential powers for himself, he then did not restore Nasution but made him head of the Temporary People's Consultative Assembly (MPRS), effectively removing him from active military politics.

8. Nasution was of Mandailing Batak origin and a Siliwangi man; Yani was Javanese and of the Diponegoro Division.

9. I have taken the concept from Hildred Geertz, "Indonesian Cultures and Communities," in McVey, ed., *Indonesia* (New Haven: HRAF Press, 1964).

of Western and Indonesian styles of life characteristic of the modern-educated, urban elite. Officers from this group were men of high education for the Indonesian army, of relatively distinguished birth, people who possessed good access to the upper levels of the civilian elite. Dutch was often their common language of informal discourse.[10] They were the type of officer who had dominated the central leadership of the army in the early postcolonial period;[11] most of their post-revolutionary military experience was in the capital rather than in a divisional context, and in staff rather than line duties. Yani's accession thus did not greatly alter the style of the army leadership; nor did it change the direction of military reform, for, as we shall later see, he had a principal hand in shaping this reform even before he became army commander.

As Yani's appointment showed, the army's acquisition of the Defense Ministry did not mean the final liberation of the military from civilian supervision. Sukarno, acting in his capacity as Supreme Commander of the Armed Forces and relying on his increasing political stature to secure the loyalty of officers, continued to exert some of the influence which previously civilian governments had wielded on the armed forces. But he was the only civilian element that could interfere at the top level. Political parties and interest groups might endeavor to infiltrate and manipulate, but they could only affect the behavior of individual officers, usually in a local context; they were not capable of influencing army policy as a whole. Moreover, even at the height of Sukarno's influence, it was not possible for him to achieve the measure of *control* over the military leadership which the parliamentary governments had enjoyed a decade before. The civilian politicians had made a fatal step in deciding to recall Nasution to power in 1955 and to grant him full backing in order to prevent regional disintegration, for, when the rebellion was over they found themselves faced with a military leadership too strong and too deeply entrenched for them to be able to reassert their prerogatives. Sukarno found himself engaged instead in a struggle for power with the army chiefs, a contest in which he, though nominally dominant, had in fact the weaker hand, for time and the possession of force were on their side. They needed only to preserve their unity and authority over their troops to succeed, while he needed to attack, to divide their forces, and to set them to quarrelling . This was no longer so easy to do.

---

10. For the social connotations of language usage in Indonesia, see Benedict R. O'G. Anderson, "The Languages of Indonesian Politics," Indonesia, No. 1 (April 1966), pp. 89-116.

11. It is perhaps not surprising that, of the seven military leaders who were targets of the coup group on October 1, 1965, three had played major roles in the October 17, 1952 coup attempt. These were Generals Nasution, Suprapto, and S. Parman. It should be noted, however, that this did not mean that they were faithful followers of Nasution on all issues. We have seen earlier that Parman, for example, engaged in conflict with Nasution at the time of the Zulkifli Lubis Affair in his capacity as IPRI secretary.

Promotions and Patronage

As we have seen in the discussion of the early efforts to impose central authority on the post-revolutionary army, the absence of adequate means to satisfy the material requirements of officers and units was a major factor in internal disaffection. In amending this condition on his return to office as Army Chief of Staff in 1955, General Nasution turned to an increase in the rate of promotions as the most immediately efficacious salve. Nasution had had little luck in handling the promotions issue earlier, for it had been his group's efforts at channeling assignments and promotions that had largely been responsible for uniting his military opponents in 1952.[12] In the three years that had followed his downfall, discontent over ranks and placements had festered, and it was apparent that he had to take immediate and generous steps if he wished to secure cooperation and prevent the further dispersal of the high command's control in the direction of civilian and regional interests. At the same time, he was comforted by the fact that promotions were easy to make, needing only central fiat; and they were relatively cheap--a major consideration for an army leadership which disposed of very few ways of satisfying the material demands made on it.

The first major reform which Nasution undertook on his return was, therefore, that of bringing order into the arrangements for promotions. To give army men a sense of regularity and structure in their careers and to bind them to the ideas of discipline and objective bureaucratic routine, it was necessary to introduce the appearance of impersonal and earned reward into the matter of advancement, for so long as promotion was thought an affair of patronage, alliance, and the power play at the top it was not likely that officers would abandon a personalistic approach to their pursuit of their ambitions. Accordingly, at the beginning of 1956 a commission was installed to review army ranks and assignments and to advise the Chief of Staff on their revision. It was headed by the Deputy Chief of Staff, Colonel Gatot Subroto. That officer had been a Nasution ally in both the October 17 and Lubis Affairs, but he commanded independent respect both through his own strong claims to army leadership and the contrast between his flamboyant personality and the gray bureaucratic image of his chief. In addition, the Commission included Nasution's erstwhile enemy Colonel Bambang Supeno, evidently as evidence of Nasution's intention not to repeat the policies that had brought charges of favoritism in 1952. This time, too, the Nasution leadership did not repeat the mistake of coupling reorganization with the threat of unemployment. Instead, the Gatot Commission's deliberations were accompanied by assurances that the army would expand in size and that, since it appeared that Indonesian ranks were lower than those of military men doing equivalent jobs in other countries, massive promotions would take place.[13]

---

12. See "The Post-Revolutionary Transformation," Part I, pp. 143-148.

13. Madjalah Angkatan Darat, I (January 1956), announcing the formation of the Gatot Commission. See also Waspada, August 9, 1956, for a communiqué by the Army Information Service on the progress of the Commission's work. The Commission consisted at that time of Colonels Gatot Subroto, Bambang Supeno, Suwondho, and S. Parman. It is interesting to note that these officers were all of East and Central Java divisional background; there was no Siliwangi or Outer Island representation. It was probably reckoned that

At the same time, the high command stressed that these pleasant prospects were tied to sacrifice. It forbade army men and veterans henceforth to have associations of their own, for too often, it declared, such groups had interfered in military matters and tried to establish "shadow hierarchies" in rivalry with the official chain of command. Once the Gatot Commission had completed its deliberations and a central system of education and training had been established, there must be no more regional efforts to establish training units and schools or otherwise interfere with central prerogatives in placement and instruction. All matters of the officer corps must go through the officers' union, the IPRI. Even this organization was reminded that it was an unofficial association which might not make public pronouncements concerning internal army affairs, but only make proposals aimed at improving the army's organization and methods of work.[14] Coming as this proclamation did in a time of regional defiance, it was not much more than a declaration of intent; but it described an intention firmly held, and the high command applied it with an increasingly strong hand in the areas which it controlled.

The Gatot Commission's task of sorting out the multitudinous claims of officers after six years of retrenchment, confusion, and favoritism was clearly very difficult, but it was aided in its efforts both by the policy of rank increase and by the fact that the 1958 rebellion removed a great many claimants from consideration. Moreover, in the 1957-1959 period the army leadership moved rapidly from rags to relative riches: The declaration of a State of War and Siege in early 1957, the seizure of Dutch enterprises later that year, the turn from parliamentary rule to Guided Democracy, and the acquisition of substantial amounts of foreign military aid, all opened new vistas for promotion, advantageous assignment, and power. However, as the question of promotion and placement was not one that vanished with the first major sorting-out, it was decided to make the commission permanent as the Central Advisory Council on Offices and Ranks.[15]

Nasution's presence as Chief of Staff would ensure attendance to Siliwangi interests.

It is not clear why Indonesian ranks were held at a relatively low level through the early 1950's. A possible explanation is that the general reduction of ranks that accompanied the rationalization effort was intended to be succeeded by the selective promotion of the type of officers desired by the Nasution-Simatupang leadership, but that neither this group nor succeeding leaders were strong enough to promote their clients above other claimants. The first post-revolutionary general, following Simatupang's retirement, was Nasution, who advanced from colonel to major general on his return to office in 1955.

14. _Waspada_, March 8, 1957 (Army Information Service Communiqué) announcing the opinion of the high command. The reference to IPRI pronouncements on internal army matters was no doubt related to that association's hapless intervention in the Zulkifli Lubis Affair (see "The Post-Revolutionary Transformation," Part I, pp. 172-173).

15. Dewan Pertimbangan Djabatan dan Kepangkatan Pusat. It consisted of Gatot Subroto and six other officers. _Kedaulatan Rakjat_, October 1, 1958.

In 1960, in response to the rapidly increasing complexity of the officer corps, it was split into the Council on Assignments and Ranks for Senior Officers (WANDJABTI) and the Advisory Council on Assignments and Ranks (DEPDJABKA), which dealt with the middle grades. The WANDJABTI, known as the Generals' Council, was to play an increasingly important role in the 1960's because it gave a say to some of the army's most senior and powerful officers who would otherwise have been unable to present to the general staff recommendations for promotions and assignments outside their official spheres of responsibility.[16]

Side by side with the effort to regularize promotions, the high command endeavored to secure acceptance of a two-year tour of duty as the norm for army assignments. This policy, of course, ran directly counter to the territorial commanders' interest in entrenching themselves, and indeed it was aimed particularly at destroying their independence. The principle was necessary for other reasons as well, particularly to ensure the smooth flow of promotions and assignments, which, after the early 1960's, again showed signs of becoming blocked. In the pre-1965 period the high command could never really overcome resistance to a standard length of assignment, try as it would, for it was still too weak and divided to be able to impose its will on senior officers (including its own members) who had no intention of losing advantageous positions or weakening their subordinates' support by the untimely movement of themselves or their favorites. The roughly equal age of the officer corps inherited from the revolution was incompatible with the highly pyramided hierarchy of posts, and it was only after 1965, with the massive post-coup purges of the army and the arrival of the revolutionary generation at an age indisputably close to retirement, that this major obstacle to the regularization of promotions and assignments was removed.[17]

Promotion and placement were important for pacifying individual officers, but to keep troop commanders loyal to the center and in control of their men, the high command had to provide supplies, equipment, and amenities on a far greater scale than it had done in the early post-revolutionary years. In the late 1950's, the high command proceeded to acquire substantial resources of its own, in a transfer to control over resources that entailed a major reorganization of the Indonesian governmental and economic system.

The first step in the direction of securing greater control over patronage sources had already been taken with the reappointment of

---

16. At the time of the October 1965 coup the chairman of the council was General Sudirman, head of the Army Staff and Command School, and its vice-chairman was General Suharto, head of the Army Strategic Command. The term "Generals' Council" (Dewan Djenderal) was used to refer to this group from an early date (see, for example, Kedaulatan Rakjat, June 8, 1962).

17. In the post-1965 period the tour-of-duty principle was also extended to the posts of chief of staff of the various services. Suharto declared on the installation of Soewoto Soekendar as head of the air force in January 1970 that the government intended to limit the service chiefs to a three or four-year assignment. Merdeka, January 8, 1970, reporting Suharto's speech.

Nasution as Army Chief of Staff, for, as we have seen, it reflected a decision on the part of Sukarno and the Djakarta political leadership to subordinate their desire to divide and rule the military to the cause of preventing regional rebellion. Consequently, Nasution received full governmental backing in his appointment policies and in his handling of the Zulkifli Lubis Affair. He also seems to have received assurances of considerably greater allocations of funds than the army had obtained since the October 17 Affair, and he placed much stress on this in soliciting support from within the army.[18] Nasution also secured government acquiescence in major arms purchases abroad, and at an early date a mission was dispatched to Indonesia's previous suppliers to discover what new arrangements could be made. Unfortunately, the initial enquiries yielded little of promise: Indonesia's supply of hard cash was very low, and the major country likely to supply arms for credit, the United States, was uncertain of Djakarta's political reliability and more than a little attracted by its regionalist opponents.

With foreign assistance temporarily unavailable and Indonesia's own resources drained by economic decline and smuggling, it is very doubtful that the army leadership could have acquired the sort of patronage it needed short of a coup that would have placed civilian posts and perquisites at military disposal or a radical reorganization which would have enlarged the government's portion in the society as a whole. There was, indeed, much talk of an impending army takeover during 1957 and 1958, and Nasution hinted that this was the alternative if, by one means or another, the military's requirements were not met.[19]

This crisis was resolved by two means: the utilization of Cold War competition to provide Indonesia with substantial sources of foreign backing, and the progressive extension of governmental authority over available domestic resources, with the army getting a major share of the new public domain. The first of these moves involved the decision to seek aid from the Soviet Union as well as from the Western sources to which Indonesia had previously looked. This decision, in spite of the officially neutralist postiion of the army and governmental leaders, was not an easy one for them to take. However, when they did make the move they found an excellent reception on the Soviet side, for the Khrushchev regime, in the ebullient beginnings of its effort to win Asian and African friends, was more than pleased to acquire the largest Southeast Asian country as a potential client. The Americans, for their part, rapidly reversed their position once it became evident that Djakarta would win out over the regional rebels; and as relations between Indonesian and American military representatives had never deteriorated as those between the civilian leaderships had done, it was possible to make swift amends. For some time, Indonesia was in the pleasant position of being able to bid its two great suitors against each other, though in the end it was the Soviets who supplied by far the greatest amount of aid through their large-scale provision of heavy equipment, particularly modern ships and airplanes.

---

18. See "The Post-Revolutionary Transformation," Part I, p. 152, ftn. 26; and also Pesat, XV, No. 41 (October 11, 1958), pp. 5-6 (Nasution's Armed Forces Day speech of October 5, 1958).

19. See Lev, The Transition to Guided Democracy, pp. 182-190.

This aid provided the Indonesian military with the naval and air capability it needed to enforce Djakarta's authority throughout the archipelago, for the central command's lack of means to move troops massively and rapidly from Java had been a major factor in the regional defiance of the 1950's. More generally, the acquisition of this advanced equipment was a move in the direction of the sophisticated and highly mobile cadre army to which Nasution and his military colleagues aspired.[20] They could also reckon that regional commanders would be impressed by the possibility of acquiring advanced equipment and, insofar as they gained access to it, would bind themselves further to the center through its heavy logistical requirements. In turn, however, the central army leadership found itself bound to its foreign suppliers by the advanced nature of its new armament, particularly since the country had virtually none of the industrial base and few of the specialized maintenance skills needed to support a large, sophisticated armed force.[21]

Although foreign aid was an important source of central patronage for the army, its scope and significance were far inferior to those of the domestic political and economic resources made available to the high command. The initial promises made by a government ready to give the army leadership whatever backing it could in return for support in the regional crisis were soon transformed into real power through the proclamation in March 1957 of a State of Emergency. This meant the introduction of martial law and a hierarchy of "war administrator" offices which, in effect, placed the supervision of civilian government in the hands of the military command of that territorial level. This not only gave great political power to the army at all levels but, because of the war administrators' influence on licenses, permissions, and means of communication, it provided important possibilities for economic gain as well. The State of Emergency was

---

20. See "The Post-Revolutionary Transformation," Part I, pp. 143-146.

21. Much of the military aid solicited by the Indonesians in connection with the rebellion arrived instead in time for the Irian campaign of 1960-1962, and it played an important role in a reorganization and upgrading of army combat units which was initiated at that time. The Soviets were quite willing to have their arms used for the seizure of West Irian, as they proved by providing further supplies. But the next major operation, the confrontation of Malaysia, was a different affair so far as Indonesia's foreign creditors were concerned. By this time the Soviets and Americans no longer responded automatically to attempts to play the one against the other, and neither of them saw much attraction in financing an Indonesian political course that seemed likely to benefit not their interests but China's. The Americans urged economic stabilization and the regularization of relations with the West; the Russians also looked for Indonesian retrenchment, for it seemed otherwise unlikely that their huge loans would be repaid. When Indonesia abandoned its economic stabilization effort of 1963 in favor of Confrontation and moved significantly closer to China in its stand on international issues, the Americans and Russians rapidly lost interest in providing substantial military aid. The effects of this decrease in aid were soon felt by the Indonesian armed forces, for the demands of Confrontation operations and the stringencies of a rapidly declining economy rapidly reduced their available materiel. By 1965, military leaders were discussing the necessity of "standing on their own feet" in the matter of maintenance and spare parts.

important for the legitimation which it gave to the massive penetration of the civilian world by the army in the first years of Guided Democracy. No one could challenge the military physically in its new role, but the army leadership was still sufficiently unsure of its further amibitons and still legalistically minded enough to find this provision for its presence a very important one. We can see the weight that this was accorded in the fact that the lifting of the Emergency in 1963 gave the army a marked if temporary diffidence in its intervention in the civilian political world.

During Guided Democracy, the army presence grew steadily in all fields. In some areas older ideas of social hierarchy and proper government were sufficiently strong to guarantee the dominance of the head of the civil administration but more and more local military representatives were acknowledged to possess the greatest weight by virtue of the physical resources at their command. Indeed, military men were increasingly appointed to posts in the civil service, and thus both the heads of local military and civil administrations might be army men. This began in the areas that had been under the control of regionalist rebels and in localities where the Darul Islam revolt had destroyed the regular governmental structure, but during the 1960's it spread until most governorships and a great many other civilian administrative posts were in army hands.

This extension of the army role was most valuable as a source of patronage. In the first place it gave the high command--which controlled all appointments of army officers to civilian posts--access to political and economic power at all levels of the society. In the second place, it provided an opportunity for removing officers judged too incapable or unreliable for further advancement in the mainstream of army promotion. The emoluments of the new posts would, it was hoped, preserve the loyalty of the officers concerned, and they would represent the interests of the army in the civilian world while lacking the military base that would allow them to interfere effectively in intra-army politics. In addition, the army extended its political activities by sponsoring a series of mass organizations, beginning with the National Front for the Liberation of West Irian in 1958 and continuing through the "functional organizations" of Guided Democracy.[22] These organizations, too, had the dual purpose of controlling civilians and providing an opportunity for employing unwanted members of the armed forces.

But by far the greatest source of patronage to come into the hands of the high command in the pre-coup period was the control over enterprises seized from the Dutch late in 1957. The takeover occurred in the context of the West Irian dispute, but its domestic effect was perhaps even more important than its impact on Indonesia's foreign affairs. It brought under Indonesian control a critical area of the economy which had hitherto remained in foreign hands, and it transferred that control to a particular segment of the Indonesian state, its army.

---

22. For a discussion of the army's efforts at mass organization, see Lev, The Transition to Guided Democracy, pp. 65-67, 223-228; Herbert Feith, "The Dynamics of Guided Democracy," in R. McVey, ed., Indonesia (New Haven: HRAF Press, 1963), esp. pp. 335-336.

This was the beginning of a major military presence in the economic life of the country, a presence which gave great power to the central command and to the army as a whole but which also served to settle the social role of the military in a particular fashion--to ensure that it became a conservative force.[23]

The extension of army activity into the economy meant, among other things, that military leaders were provided with substantial sources of funding outside the regular government budget, which itself expanded the defense allotment greatly.[24] The direct tapping of the resources of the state enterprises was not simply a matter of providing luxuries for well-placed officers, for the Indonesian armed forces, though not large in relation to the problems of security which the country's geography and social divisions presented, were expensive in relation to the funds available to the government. Attempts at retrenchment--such as the government's stabilization effort of 1963--involved a real sacrifice of military supplies; they were felt by army members in the form of reduced rations and benefits, and this reduction in turn created a problem of internal military instability.[25] Not surprisingly, the army leaders sought to forestall this, by opposing effective reductions of the army's share of government funds or by tapping moneys before they reached the government.

This independent system of funding had considerable advantages for the central army command. For one thing, it made it even freer of civilian control than before. For another, it provided great patronage powers, not only because the appointment and removal of officers placed in charge of government enterprises or otherwise

---

23. For a general discussion of the army's role in the takeovers, see Lev, The Transition to Guided Democracy, pp. 69-70; J. A. C. Mackie, "Indonesia's Government Estates and Their Masters," Pacific Affairs, XXXIV, No. 4 (Winter 1961-62).

24. The high point of military utilization of the government budget was in the final stages of the Irian campaign, when about three quarters of the budget was devoted to defense. In 1966, the armed forces were still consuming 70 percent of the budget, according to Colonel Sajidiman Surjohadiprodjo. Of this, he said one quarter was used to maintain the organization and the rest for operations; even if all operations ceased, the minimum necessary to keep the military would be 25 or 30 percent. Berita Yudha, May 30, 1966. The government's subsequent ability to reduce this percentage drastically has been aided by the practice of informal financing discussed below and by the devotion of sizeable funds earmarked for "special projects" to military purposes. The direct role of the army in enterprise management has been greatly reduced, however.

25. Thus in 1963 the Central Java panglima, General Sarbini, urged army members to understand the necessity of budget cuts which had meant the reduction of that year's standard ration and the discontinuation of refined sugar, butter, and cigarette allowances for soldiers. Kedaulatan Rakjat, June 19, 1963, speech to the Jogjakarta garrison. No doubt the common soldiers were the first to suffer under such cutbacks, but, particularly as inflationary pressures increased, a lack of funds was felt as well in the officer corps.

inserted into the economy lay in the hands of the high command, but also because the informal system of financing created a "slush fund" of sizeable proportions which the military leaders could use largely as they wished to enhance the army's and their personal power. However, the system also contained substantial drawbacks, which made themselves most evident in the general decline of the economy and which also acted to reduce the power of the army leadership.

The most visible of these disadvantages was the conflict of purpose which arose as a result of the high command's utilization of economic appointments as a means of buying off recalcitrant or incompetent officers as well as a means of obtaining funds. Aside from the fact that the officer appointed to manage or supervise a government enterprise very rarely had any relevant experience, he was also, because of this policy, unlikely to be very competent or eager in the matter of learning. Especially in the first years of Guided Democracy, many army estate supervisors used their position essentially to divest the enterprise assigned them of whatever sources of income it possessed, with the result that productivity declined disastrously and considerable reinvestment was required in order to make the concern at all viable again. In the seized export-import concerns, where the military supervisors' lack of experience quickly led to crisis, the frequent resolution was that the official administration became a front for the actual backroom running of the enterprise by businessmen from the Chinese minority, whose position as Indonesia's main commercial force was enhanced by the removal of the great Dutch firms that had hitherto dominated the country's international trade.[26]

These developments placed the military in a parasitical role which was not conducive to high morale and incorruptibility. The question of military corruption first became acute in 1958, as it became apparent to the army leaders that their entrance into economic and political life was not leading, as they had hoped, to efficiency and the ousting of rascals but to the bewilderment and corruption of military men faced with many temptations and armed with small sense of purpose. The army heads endeavored then and later to combat corruption in their forces, but their efforts were foiled by the ready possibilities of temptation, the pressures of inflation, and the army leaders own visible reliance on extraordinary sources of finance.

The army's direct utilization of the economy as a major source of income, and the widespread appointment of army officers as managers of already established enterprises gave the military a very considerable stake in the existing economic structure. Strikes were banned in important enterprises soon after their seizure from the Dutch and were not again allowed; military units and civil defense groups under army supervision saw to it that labor discipline was preserved and that squatters were driven off estate land. This was a principal reason why, in spite of the populist rhetoric of Sukarno and the public

---

26. See Robert Curtis, "Indonesia and Malaysia," New Left Review (November-December 1964); J. Panglay Kim, "Some Notes on the Administrative Aspects of Indonesian State Trading Corporations," Maandschrift Economie, 18 (October 1964); Lance Castles, "The Fate of the Private Entrepreneur," in T. K. Tan, ed., Sukarno's Guided Indonesia (Brisbane: Jacaranda Press, 1967).

expansion of the PKI, the position of the Indonesian labor organizations declined precipitously in terms of being able to launch effective actions for wages or other improvements in their members' standard of living. The sources of social conservatism already present in the Indonesian officer corps[27] were thus reinforced by a concrete and substantial identification with the economic status quo.

Although the army high command claimed the right to appoint army managers of enterprises and appointees to political positions, its use of these sources of patronage resulted in another sense in the weakening of its grip. The expansion of military activity into the civilian sphere led to the growth of alliances and entanglements there between individual officers and their civilian counterparts. It opened up new, local sources of patronage and support; and, because the high command itself indulged in highly informal fund raising, officers easily felt justified in making arrangements of their own. Nor, given the great power which an army officer represented, were civilians likely to refuse the chance to obtain the friendship of one that was strategically placed; on the contrary, both as individuals or representatives of parties and interest groups, civilians made considerable efforts to obtain military patrons and to take advantage of whatever army factionalism might be bent to their interests. Finally, the continued stringency of army finances meant that local commanders often felt obliged to make informal arrangements for the support of their troops; moonlighting and the commercial use of army vehicles were common, and local sources of income were tapped by officers and men. Thus, a rather sprawling system of army financing emerged, partly distributed from the center and partly locally derived or acquired from patrons elsewhere in the military structure. It was difficult for the army leaders to oversee this development, and it acted as a brake on their efforts to create an obedient and efficient military machine.

Education as a Source of Central Control

One of the principal projects which General Nasution promoted after his return to power in 1955 was upgrading the army's instruction and training system and transforming it into a means of enhancing the army's ideological unity and hierarchical discipline. The early moves in this direction, which began about 1956, went largely unnoticed amidst the more dramatic events of the Lubis coup and the subsequent regional rebellion; but when the dust of these conflicts had settled, it was apparent that the new policies were already well on the way toward creating a military force of quite different character from that of the 1950's.

We might have expected, given the orientation towards expertise which we observed in Nasution's earlier leadership of the army, that he would place considerable emphasis on instruction and training, but recognition of the key role of education did not stem from the ideas of his kind of officer alone. It flowed as well from the "red"

---

27. See "The Post-Revolutionary Transformation," Part I, pp. 133-134.

tradition[28] of the revolution and the earlier experience of the Peta during the Japanese occupation, in which military and ideological training were seen as equally vital to the creation of the fighting man. This consideration indeed continued to be important during Nasution's term of office. In the first place, his emphasis on expertise over indoctrination was only relative, for he was of the revolutionary generation himself; moreover, the army's great role in civilian affairs in post-parliamentary Indonesia made the military leaders feel strongly the need for a doctrine which would provide them with a broader national purpose and prevent army members from being drawn toward civilian political movements. Consequently, they saw education as including not only technical training and the principles of soldierly obedience but also the shaping of a broader ideology. In the end, however, while the technical side of their program flourished, the doctrinal effort did not. It was a victim not of lack of emphasis--for it received a great deal of that--but of the army leaders' own puzzlement as to their ultimate political goals and of their inability to compete with the ideas put forward by Sukarno and other major civilian political forces.

The acute shortage of trained personnel for the revolutionary armed forces and the desire to acquire the accoutrements of full nationhood inspired Indonesia's leaders to create a system of military instruction soon after the declaration of independence. In October 1945 a National Military Academy (Akademi Militer Nasional, AMN) was formed in Jogjakarta.[29] In Malang, an Army School (Sekolah Tentara) emerged to provide instruction and upgrading, particularly for the forces fighting in East Java. In July 1948 the Malang school was formally incorporated into its Jogja counterpart, which continued until 1950. At that point the Academy found itself stranded by the removal of the capital to Djakarta, the lack of educated young men attracted to a peacetime army career, and factional rivalries for control over military institutions. Only ten candidates presented themselves for admission, and these, given the chance, chose training with the Corps of Engineers in Bandung or at the Royal Netherlands Military Academy in Breda instead.[30] As a result, the AMN was ordered to close its doors.

The primary focus of military instruction now shifted to Bandung, where the Chandradimuka Academy had been established to provide courses

---

28. Ibid., p. 134.

29. The Academy opened on October 28, 1945, with five hundred students; in November 1948 it graduated its first class, 196 second lieutenants. Forty-five of the original group were listed as killed in action before graduating. The second and last revolutionary class was much smaller, some two hundred students. Kedaulatan Rakjat, November 21, 1957. According to Benedict Anderson, the Jogjakarta academy was preceded by a school set up in Tanggerang by Peta-trained officers including Sukanda Bratamenggala and Daan Mogot; it was dissolved when the Republican forces abandoned Djakarta. (Private communication to the author.)

30. Kedaulatan Rakjat, November 21, 1957. Military scholarships to Holland were offered as part of the Round Table Conference agreement and ceased with the 1953 expulsion of the Netherlands Military Mission; they never became an important source of post-revolutionary Indonesian military training or clique formation.

to upgrade military officers and in particular to create for them a common ideological base. Unfortunately for its survival, this institution was headed by Colonel Bambang Supeno, who, as we will remember, fell afoul of the Nasution-Simatupang army leadership.[31] In the course of the quarrel the high command eliminated the school as a source of Supeno's support by abolishing it.[32] Thereafter the Staff and Command School (SSKAD, later SESKOAD) was developed as the prime center of military instruction and ideological formulation. It drew its clientele, for varying periods of assignment, from officers on active duty, whom it was supposed to provide with the highest level of instruction in the military educational establishment. It did not, in other words, do what the National Military Academy was supposed to have done, that is to provide university-level instruction for young men who wished to embark on a professional army career. Nothing did so for five years: evidently Nasution and his allies lacked sufficient support to establish an academy to their liking but had enough backing after their 1952 fall from power to keep their opponents from doing so themselves.[33]

---

31. "The Post-Revolutionary Transformation," Part I, pp. 145ff. The name of the academy fit well with Bambang Supeno's ideological leanings, for Chandradimuka is the name of the boiling crater into which the wajang hero Gatotkatja is dipped to make his body like steel. I am grateful to Benedict Anderson for pointing this out to me.

32. Herbert Feith, The Decline of Constitutional Democracy in Indonesia (Ithaca: Cornell University Press, 1962), p. 250; Pelopor, May 17, 1955. The Academy accepted officers from the rank of major up, and as the highest officer was then colonel, it thus accepted the army's most senior members. Feith emphasized the close identification of the Chandradimuka leadership with President Sukarno. The academy's ideological endeavors were oriented toward the inculcation of the principles of the army oath of loyalty, Sapta Marga, which Bambang Supeno had drawn up and which was to continue as the army's fundamental pledge. The instruction was designed to contain something for the group of officers of fundamentally revolutionary bent, something for the technocrats, and something for those who wished to see the army play a more active role as an instrument of state power. Pelopor, May 17, 1955.

33. The Defense Ministry had urged reopening the National Military Academy in 1952 but had not been able to push the project far before the October 17 Affair. Subsequently army committees and commissions studied the problem of reopening the academy, but nothing was decided until 1956. The school reopened its doors in October 1957. In December 1965 it was renamed Armed Forces Academy of the Republic of Indonesia (AKABRI) and given charge over the education of cadets from all services. Sapta Marga, December 3, 1965.

  General Nasution noted that candidates for the AMN, who were required to have senior high school (SMA) certificates, experienced great difficulty passing the psychological test required for entrance: on average, only 23 percent got through. Their main failings were a low state of general knowledge, insecurity and timidity, inability to distinguish real from false problems and solutions, lack of judgment and character, and lack of leadership talents. See A. H. Nasution, Menudju Tentara Rakjat (Djakarta:

With no other high-level educational or planning institutions in existence, the Staff and Command School emerged as the army's intellectual center; in later years, when challengers did exist, it was still able to maintain its primacy as the source of military doctrine and thought.[34] Moreover, owing to the fact that the officers who attended its courses were drawn from all over the country, it afforded an opportunity for acquaintances to be made and bonds to be formed among officers of varied divisional background. For many officers in the 1950's it provided their first chance to meet colleagues outside their home territory, and the school tie soon acquired importance, especially for young and ambitious officers who saw their schooling as a key to appointment in the capital or as a means of pressing claims against uneducated superiors at home. The placement of an officer who underwent a course at the school was normally made by Djakarta; a promising student might well find himself assigned to the staff of a difficult panglima from which delicate perch he might, if he acted successfully in the interests of the high command, aspire to promotion and perhaps the panglimaship itself.

But as we have seen from the SSKAD's part in the Lubis Affair of 1956,[35] the political role of the Staff and Command School (and for that matter of any other major military educational institution) could work against the central command as well as for it. In cutting across regional ties, it also created loyalties of its own, in which army headquarters had no necessary share. It could and did foster notions of elitism and of collective representation for the officer corps, and the school's leaders felt this opinion provided sufficient legitimation for political action so that they used it on occasion to challenge Djakarta. The army leadership could not feel this threat was over once the crisis of the Lubis Affair was past, for it recognized that the SSKAD intervention was a reflection of the broader problem created by the army leaders' effort to increase central control over a diffuse and diverse military force. Under such gathering

---

    Jajasan Penerbit Minang, 1963), pp. 194-198. The psychological test appears to have been as much an I.Q. test as anything else, and its results may have reflected in part the declining standards of Indonesian secondary school education; in addition, it was probably very difficult for students of provincial background to respond adequately to what appears to have been a rather westernized personality test.

34. The principal one of these was the National Defense Institute (Lemhanas), which was established in 1965 as a "think tank" to study matters of defense policy in a more thorough manner than was possible at the Staff and Command School. Pikiran Rakjat, July 26, 1963, statement of Major General Sudirman, commander of the SESKOAD, concerning plans for the new institution. Its location in Djakarta placed it closer to the center of power than the Bandung-based SESKOAD and made it easier for military and civilian leaders stationed in the capital to participate in its activities, but it has remained less important than the SESKOAD as a center of army thought.

35. See "The Post-Revolutionary Transformation," Part I, pp. 171-172.

central pressure, army institutions which possessed prestige and which brought together officers of widely different background were almost bound to become sources of criticism, whether or not this was encouraged by those in charge. And yet, if the high command wished to possess a militarily qualified and doctrinally unified army, it would have to bring officers together and grant prestige to the centers of their instruction. The question in the mid-1950's was whether to put aside the development of a central educational and training structure for the short run, in the interests of economy and the preservation of diffuse opinion--much as the Military Academy had been put aside earlier--or whether to grasp the nettle firmly and strive to pass as quickly as possible to the stage where the central command possessed a reliable and effective instrument for shaping the Indonesian army man.

A prime factor in the decision to move massively in the direction of developing the educational system was the return of Colonel Ahmad Yani from the United States in 1956 and his assumption of the role of Deputy in charge of Operations on Nasution's staff. Yani had spent a year at the American army's staff and command school at Fort Leavenworth, Kansas, and while there he had been greatly impressed by the ability of that institution to mold effective and ideologically compatible officers in a brief period of time. In the American system of military instruction he and his colleagues on the army general staff saw a model which was modern without being Dutch, one which, moreover, had fashioned the world's paramount military force, a wealthy potential patron with a rising interest in Southeast Asia. It seemed possible, following the American example, to construct a training and instruction system that would expose army men at all levels to new ideas, skills, and central control and which would have a transforming role in the creation of a unified army. But this could not be a matter of half-measures: a great deal of the army's resources would have to go into the enterprise, so that the schools would impress their attenders instead of adding to their discontent; and the officers assigned to teach in them must be of high caliber and not, as too often in the past, those without the ability or connections to obtain posts closer to the seat of power.

The immediate ideological goal sought was, with gestures to the Indonesian revolutionary heritage, the Western ideal of the professional soldier: a nationalism deemed to be above partisan politics, a stress on hierarchy and discipline, and a sense of pride at being part of a vital and highly trained organization. By intensive indoctrination and the development of military skills, it was hoped, army men would adopt a more "modern" and professional way of looking at their role and would cease to be distracted by the anti-hierarchical ideals of the revolution, by patron-client ties, and by regional and religious loyalties.[36]

---

36. The Western ideals of professionalism, while overtly nonpartisan, do contain powerful incentives for military intervention in public affairs, as has been demonstrated by S. E. Finer, The Man on Horseback (New York: Praeger, 1962), pp. 25-32. However, in the Indonesian situation, where the army had both a revolutionary tradition and an immediate political role, the short-run effect was to confuse officers as to the extent of their proper participation in nonmilitary affairs.

Before July 1956 army instruction had been the theoretical prerogative of the central inspectorates and offices, which provided training in their respective fields of specialization. Much of the military's basic education in practice was not supervised from the center at all, for territorial commanders wishing to upgrade their units and to improve their cohesion and local loyalty had provided instruction and indoctrination quite independently. In mid-1956, in line with the decision to stress education as an instrument of the center, all instruction and training was placed under a single authority, from whose control only the Staff and Command School and the about-to-be-revived National Military Academy were exempted.[37] This move was accompanied by a general upgrading and ideological weeding-out of the training institutions' teaching personnel. Greater emphasis was now placed on securing politically reliable instructors, in order to provide soldiers with the uniform outlook that would ensure their loyalty and efficient response to orders.

At first, all teaching was channeled through a general instruction center (Pusat Pendidikan), but this extreme concentration soon proved impractical and the major corps were given qualified control over their own centers of training. For the infantry, a special infantry center (Pusat Kesendjataan Infanteri) was placed in charge of both actual instruction and of planning the broader development of infantry combat capabilities. Logistically and administratively this body was directly under the office of the Army Chief of Staff, while operationally (that is, in actually giving instruction) it came under the Instruction and Training Command.[38] Within each division-level regional command, cadre regiments (*Resimen Induk*) played an equivalent role. They were in charge of the instruction and training of the infantry units in their territories and were linked administratively and logistically to the office of the divisional commander and operationally to the Instruction and Training Command. These regiments had charge of the infantry cadre school (SKI) which existed in each military region, and of the one or more instruction depots (Dodik) which offered refresher courses and basic infantry training. The idea behind the whole system was that army men would periodically undergo instruction, the successful completion of which would be the stepping-stone to promotion and favorable reassignment. The educational structure was highly pyramided and culminated, for the most successful graduates of earlier phases, in courses for field-grade officers at the Staff and Command School.

As it existed in theory, this system not only fitted ideas of modern military organization and bureaucratic procedure, but it offered immediate practical advantages to the army leadership. Education was highly valued in postcolonial Indonesia, and while the officer with

---

37. This body was first called the General Instruction and Training Inspectorate (I. Djen. P.L.), but after a few years it assumed the title of Instruction and Training Command (KOPLAT).

38. Pikiran Rakjat, January 17, 1963, speech by the commander of the Infantry Center. From 1960 to 1962, he declared, the center had trained some 5,700 commissioned, noncommissioned, and candidate officers and specialists. When in 1962 the office of Army Chief of Staff was replaced by that of Commander of the Army, organic (administrative and logistical) control of the center was assumed by the office of the army commander.

a revolutionary reputation but few educational qualifications might do his best to deny the need for formal learning, he could not feel completely comfortable with his lack of it, and therefore could not effectively resist the demand to attend a course. Officers called to do a training course might suspect their summons was part of an effort to remove them from the local scene, but as long as the principle of universal retraining had been laid down and the possibility existed that successful study would lead to a desirable new assignment, it more often than not made sense for them to cooperate. Once an officer was at a central installation, cut off from his divisional base and dependent on the high command for his next post, army headquarters could shunt him aside with less chance of resistance from himself and his associates than if the blow fell at home.[39] Ultimately, the army leadership could hope that periodic instruction at central training institutions would orient ambitious officers away from the cultivation of a local power base and towards the pursuit of expertise and the favor of the center--would create, in other words, the attitudes essential to firm hierarchical control.

Needless to say, this system did not become actuality overnight. There was a good deal of trouble securing reliable and competent staff, and even when the army's income had begun to increase there were severe material shortages.[40] Moreover, once the new program was under way it became evident that the highly centralized system originally envisioned would have to be greatly modified. The rapid upgrading of army units, the expansion of highly specialized services, and increasing sophistication of equipment--all worked for a return of authority over instruction to the inspectorates, directorates, and offices in charge of specialized functions. Moreover, it became evident that extreme vertical organization of military institutions made for lack of coordination between local units, and at times engendered a rivalry between them that hindered the effort to present a solid army front in dealing with local civilian affairs.

As a result, another reorganization of the educational system took place in mid-1963. This time the Instruction and Training Command relinquished its control of actual teaching, though it retained general supervision and policy-making powers vis-a-vis the training institutions.[41] At the same time, full authority over the cadre

---

39. See "The Post-Revolutionary Transformation," Part I, pp. 172-173.

40. Thus Colonel Suharto, then commander of the Diponegoro Division, announced in 1958 the temporary closing of the region's Infantry Cadre School because there was no money to run it. Kedaulatan Rakjat, July 12, 1958.

41. These training institutions were divided into three groups: Kesendjataan (infantry, cavalry, and field and anti-aircraft artillery); Kedinasan (adjutant general's office, finance, transport, physical education, health, psychology, and justice); and Korps (military police, quartermaster corps, engineers, signal corps, and women's auxiliary). Nearly all the national-level training centers were in Java, and a great many of them were in West Java. The Bandung area, where the majority were concentrated, boasted twenty instruction centers capable of handling fifty to sixty thousand noncommissioned and commissioned officers a year. Pikiran Rakjat, June 25, 1963, announcement of the Instruction and Training Command.

regiments was returned to the divisional commanders; furthermore, these regiments were placed in charge of all army instruction provided in their territories at the divisional level and below, thus extending their scope considerably beyond their original infantry sphere.[42] One reason for this appears to have been the great expansion in local-level army activity in the course of Guided Democracy, which meant that lower training institutions evolved new courses and included non-army members in their activities.[43]

Not all the army's instruction and training took place in Indonesia itself. A significant portion of the officer corps received training abroad, most notably in the United States, where over four thousand Indonesian officers were trained before 1965.[44] Lesser centers for overseas instruction were the Philippines, Pakistan, India, and Yugoslavia. Very few Indonesian army officers were trained in the USSR in spite of that country's role as Indonesia's chief arms supplier in the 1960's, although naval and air force personnel went there in rather greater quantity to learn to use Soviet-supplied equipment. Russia's absence from the list of Indonesia's military instructors appears to have been due in the first place to the army leadership's fear of the possible ideological consequences of Soviet indoctrination.[45] In addition, the Soviets trained Indonesians (and other foreigners) in separate courses in order, they claimed, to minimize the language problem and provide instruction more suitable to the circumstances a tropical army would face; this division had its merits, but the Indonesians suspected they were getting second-class instruction. Even more important, the Soviets neglected, in the Indonesian

---

42. For an illustration, see Kedaulatan Rakjat, June 30, 1964, which provides a description of the competence of the Diponegoro cadre regiment.

43. The instruction depots, at least on Java, seem to have handled a great variety of training projects. The Fifth Instruction Depot Battalion in Klaten had, for example, trained the following by 1964: officers undergoing refresher courses, paramilitary "volunteers" for Irian and Malaysia, people doing compulsory military training, the "Garuda I" battalion which did UN duty in the first Suez crisis, a company of Papuans receiving training in connection with the Irian campaign, army-sponsored militia (OPR), and civil servants required to undergo part-time military training. Kedaulatan Rakjat, April 28, 1964, statement by Major Sudibjo, the depot battalion commander.

44. The great majority of these trained after the end of the regional rebellion, for between 1952 and mid-1958 only about 250 officers had received instruction in the United States. PIA news bulletin, May 15, 1958.

45. Interestingly, this stricture did not apply to Yugoslavia. The Indonesian military leadership under Nasution had excellent relations with the Yugoslav regime, which was seen as nonaligned, acceptable to respected Western opinion, and opposed by the Indonesian Communists. In the pre-coup period there does not seem to have been much alteration in the Indonesian army's attitude to Soviet Communism as a source of disruptive ideas in the light of the Sino-Soviet dispute.

participants' opinion, certain of the patronage aspects expected of such tours, and so an assignment to study in the USSR was not highly valued.

From the viewpoint of the high command, training assignments abroad were a most useful form of patronage; there was a very clear order of prestige, with a tour at Fort Leavenworth most highly valued.[46] Foreign training was also held to increase the ideological self-confidence of officers. Particularly in the Guided Democracy period, it removed them from the Sukarno-dominated Indonesian scene and showed them that the ideals held up by their own military leaders were the international norm. The host countries were, of course, interested in winning friends and influencing opinion among the foreign students, and particularly the American programs pursued these aims effectively. It did not always work, but its general result was to temper suspicion of cooperation with the West and to reduce the impact of Guided Democracy exhortations.

In spite of their use of foreign examples and training, the Indonesian army leaders did not employ a permanent staff of foreign advisers to guide them in the construction of a modern military force following the removal of the Netherlands Military Mission in 1953. In this respect, Indonesia's experience was quite unlike that of most postcolonial states. Nonetheless, an effective military machine was created, and if the process was accompanied by many expensive mistakes it resulted in an army that was probably more capable of handling the situation at home than it would have been had its evolution been guided by outsiders. Moreover, consciousness that the army was shaping its own character counted a great deal for its internal morale and the prestige of its leaders.

This self-consciousness was not translated into a clear sense of the army's larger purpose, however. There was emphasis enough on indoctrination and ideology, for Indonesian military leaders of the Generation of '45 were too conscious of the importance of these elements in their own experience to neglect them after the revolution.

---

46. An attempt was made in 1958 to standardize Indonesian levels of military training with the educational opportunities available abroad: The AMN in Magelang was, according to this plan, to conform to the standard of the Royal Netherlands Military Academy; the advanced officer course was to be equated with the company grade and basic officer training in the US and with the junior officer course in India; the second level advanced officer course was to conform to the US advanced officer courses and the Indian senior officer course. The second grade of the SSKAD was to meet the standard of the Command and General Staff College at Fort Leavenworth, the Higher War College in the Netherlands, and the Defense Services Staff College in Pakistan. *Kedaulatan Rakjat*, April 26, 1958, statement by General Nasution.

The normal progress of a Military Academy graduate in the infantry was supposed to be via training periods at the Basic Infantry Development School (Sarbangif), the first and second Intermediate Officers' Course and the Advanced Course (all held at the Infantry Instruction Center in Tjimahi) to instruction as a middle-rank or senior officer in the Staff and Command School. This progression was not always adhered to in practice, however.

Moreover, Indonesia's later circumstances emphasized the importance of possessing a coherent world view--first the confusion and demoralization of the parliamentary years and then the intense ideologizing of Guided Democracy. But the army's leaders found it hard to reconcile Western ideas of professionalism with a larger social role; they found it impossible to resist Sukarno's ideological presence; and above all they possessed no sure vision of Indonesia's goals themselves. They continued to think of themselves and the army as revolutionary in spite of the military's increasingly conservative social role. They saw the great hold of Sukarno's ideas on their own forces as well as on the civilians, and they saw the Communists' ability to maintain discipline and mobilize popular support in the face of adversity. They feared and envied these rivals, for though they knew they possessed the ultimate physical power, they could not--before October 1965--see how this could be employed in a way which even a substantial part of their own forces would hold to be legitimate.

As a result, the military's indoctrination efforts had a curiously hollow character, a circling about a center that was not there. They appeared as a search for a formula that would somehow provide a single social meaning for the disparate traditions, experiences, and interests that went into the Indonesian army's being. Nasution argued that the army should pursue a "middle way," neither accepting direct leadership of and responsibility for the country's course nor yet abandoning its claims to participate in political and economic life,[47] but though this allowed the army to act in its interests without being bound by formal government responsibility, it did not provide the clarity of purpose essential to give meaning to the army's broader role. This meaning had to be total and dynamic, the first in order to seal soldiers off from unwanted outside influence and the second to provide a vision through which the army could engage the society as a whole. The line was never found, and the army's doctrine was always in the process of coming into being, its formulation debated in the SESKOAD, discussed in commissions, and weighed in seminars.

Reorganizing the Army Structure

We have already noted that Djakarta's victory in the regional rebellion eliminated Nasution's most prestigious rivals among the panglima and allowed him to emerge as the army's acknowledged head. But this was not enough to secure the continued dominance of the army center over the territorial commanders, whose strong local roots could supply a new threat should Nasution's prestige begin to fade. The

---

47. This formulation was developed by Nasution in defining the army's role in the emergent Guided Democracy system; he declared that the Indonesian army should neither be a political football like those of Latin America nor yet a dead instrument like those of Western Europe. See his address to the first anniversary celebration of the National Military Academy, in Pos Indonesia, November 13-14, 1958. For a general discussion of the army's political behavior in that period, see Lev, The Transition to Guided Democracy; and Lev, "The Political Role of the Army in Indonesia," Pacific Affairs, XXXVI, No. 4 (Winter 1963-64), pp. 349-364.

army leadership therefore endeavored to ensure its continuing authority by three major changes in the army's structure and distribution of power--garrisoning the Outer Islands with forces from Java, reducing the authority of the regional military commanders, and creating a strike force under direct central control. These moves did indeed limit the panglima's autonomy, but they also created other pressures and sources of challenge which were eventually to prove fatal to the Nasution leadership.

The army's most public response to the defeat of its regionalist opponents, aside from the relatively mild reprisals taken against those who participated on the rebel side, was its transfer of large numbers of officers and men from the three Java divisions to the Outer Islands. In effect, the areas outside Java came under military occupation by the central island's forces. The Outer Islands were parcelled among the Siliwangi, Diponegoro, and Brawidjaja divisions; in these dependencies, they supplied the panglima, most of the key officers, and a good proportion of the combat troops. The army leadership reckoned that the infusion of Java forces would prevent the identification of military units outside Java with local civilian interests, and that in an emergency the Java troops could be relied upon to side with their home island.

The military leaders' calculation was almost certainly correct, but there were also considerations which helped to limit the extent to which the forces from Java identified with the center and against their new environment. Economic interests and a desire to preserve their freedom of action against Djakarta impelled officers who came from Java to make arrangements with regional civilian elites in spite of their initial lack of local ties. Locally popular parties and political leaders were often unable to act after the rebellion, and in any case they were allowed little influence by the occupying military authorities. Local pressure groups in the post-rebellion Outer Outer Islands therefore tended to seek the backing of officers as much as that of civilian political leaders, with the result that civil and military factionalism often became intertwined.

A second method by which the army leaders sought to reduce regional power vis-a-vis the center was greatly to increase the number of the regional commands, a move which satisfied localist demands and created new positions for patronage as well. From an initial seven military territories, the number of divisional-level regions was raised to seventeen.[48] The number of Java panglima was not increased (except involuntarily, by the creation of the Djaya Division in Djakarta), but their relative strength in army councils

---

48. These are: I, Iskandarmuda (Atjeh); II, Bukit Barisan (North Sumatra); III, 17 Agustus (West Sumatra); IV, Sriwidjaja (South Sumatra); V, Djaya (Djakarta); VI, Siliwangi (West Java); VII, Diponegoro (Central Java); VIII, Brawidjaja (East Java); IX, Mulawarman (East Kalimantan); X, Lambung Mangkurat (South Kalimantan): XI, Tambun Bungai (Central Kalimantan); XII, Tandjungpura (West Kalimantan); XIII, Merdeka (North and Central Sulawesi); XIV, Hasanuddin (South and Southeast Sulawesi); XV, Pattimura (Maluku); XVI, Udayana (Lesser Sundas); XVII, Tjendrawasih (West Irian).

was improved rather than diminished, for as the older, better manned and equipped, more stable, and more prestigious divisions, they had the weightiest voice; moreover, the fact that most of the Outer Island commanders were alumni of one or the other of the Java divisions extended Java's influence to other commands as well.

Another structural alteration undertaken by the central command in order to increase its power was the establishment of Inter-Regional Commands (KOANDA), which were introduced at the time of divisional expansion in order to link the several regional commands of Sumatra, Kalimantan, and East Indonesia.[49] At first these were little more than liaison offices between the territorial panglima and the center. However, both the Mandala and Mandala Siaga operations--the Irian and Malaysia campaigns--were used to strengthen them, as they were to secure other structural changes desired by the center. Instead of the army leadership establishing a separate chain of command for these campaigns or working directly with the panglima, the KOANDA commanders were placed in charge in their respective areas. This gave a KOANDA head operational claims over a good portion of the best troops located in his territory, with the result that his position vis-a-vis his panglima was greatly strengthened. They were also granted the title of Deputy to the Army Chief of Staff (later Commander), which enhanced their status and emphasized their roles as representatives of the center.

In theory, it was possible for a KOANDA commander to establish himself as a sort of super-panglima challenging the central command. In practice, however, he had little possibility for doing this.[50] Insofar as a KOANDA commander could succeed in establishing his paramount authority over an entire island he could achieve an appreciable independence of the center, but regional rivalries within any one KOANDA grouping were so great, and the existing divisional bonds so strong that Djakarta could reckon on being able to check unacceptable aggrandizement with the cooperation of the regional commands. The KOANDA commander, therefore, could act as a counterweight to the panglima without being easily able to play the same role against the center.

---

49. It was not considered necessary to establish this new level of command in Java, possibly because it was thought it would be unwise to unite the four Java commands in this fashion. However, under the Suharto reorganization of 1969, this was done with the creation of a KOWILHAN with jurisdiction over the central island (see below). It is possible that the development of cooperation among the Java commanders in the form of the Panglima se-Djawa faction, which had expressed itself strongly in favor of a more radical New Order stance in 1967 (see Nusantara, July 10, 1967, for its Jogja declaration of principles), Suharto concluded that it would be better after all to establish an office that would serve as a counterweight to the Java commanders.

50. The nearest approach to it appears to have been the aggrandizement of General Mokoginta, whose accumulation of power against the local panglima seems to have been one of the irritants leading to support for the September 30th Movement in that area, and whose subsequent assertions of autonomy led to his removal by Suharto.

The final major structural change which was begun by the pre-coup army leadership centered about the creation of a strike force that was under its direct control. As we have seen, one of the major problems faced by the army high command, which was reflected in its inability to deal with the regional coups in the October 17 Affair and in its later difficulties with recalcitrant panglima, was the lack of direct control over troops who would be moved quickly into an area of resistance. Expeditionary forces were sent to quell disturbances outside Java, and troops were transferred across divisional boundaries on the central island to deal with security problems beyond the control of local forces; but these troops consisted of soldiers from the Java divisions, whose participation had to be procured by negotiation with the territorial commanders. The panglima were not often eager to commit their forces to actions whose outcome was uncertain; moreover, the use of troops particularly identified with Java was bound to rouse Outer Island tempers more rapidly than those which represented the center alone. At an early date, therefore, the high command sought to obtain a substantial force under its own direction.

The first step towards this was the creation of the Army Paracommando Regiment (RPKAD). This force had originated as an elite unit within the Siliwangi Division, where it was founded as the Third Territorial Commando Force by Colonel Alex Kawilarang in 1952.[51] When, soon after, it came under central control, it dropped all formal regional identification, though during the 1950's its personnel continued to be drawn largely from the Siliwangi Division and it retained its headquarters in Bandung. These continuing local ties, plus the often-observed inclination of elite units to engage in acts of national salvation, seems to have impelled its participation in the Zulkifli Lubis Affair, in which, as we will remember, its officers and men played vigorous if sometimes diverging roles.[52]

If the RPKAD was not a perfect instrument of the center, it was nonetheless effective, after the purge of its members that followed the Lubis affair, in providing a show of central force in the regions. In situations where officers were eager to expand their independence but not to engage in armed conflict, the timely addition of even a small number of troops greatly added to the arguments extended by deputations from the high command. During the regional rebellion itself, RPKAD units reinforced Pakanbaru and went into Riau, established beachheads for larger forces in Bukittinggi, Menado, and Minahasa, and lent support to the local authorities in Ambon to prevent the outbreak of a rebellion brewing there. By and large, however, the RPKAD remained fairly obscure during the 1950's, carrying out the specialized smallscale operations fitted to the then still very minor capabilities of the army for mounting airborne actions.

There were other elite units attached to the principal divisional commands which passed, if less completely, under central control. These were Ranger-trained ("Green Beret") battalions which formed the top combat units in their respective regions and which came under Djakarta's jurisdiction in the early 1960's. The oldest of them were

---

51. *Berita Yudha*, May 15, 1965, provides a history of the RPKAD.

52. See "The Post-Revolutionary Transformation," Part I, pp. 168-170.

the Banteng Raiders of the Diponegoro Division, which originated as a tactical reserve of the Gerakan Banteng Nasional (GBN) command set up at the end of 1949 to combat the Darul Islam insurgents in Central Java. Efforts to form units which would be able to act swiftly and flexibly against the guerrillas were begun in 1951, but it was only when the command came under Ahmad Yani's leadership in 1953 that two companies of Raiders were actually set up.[53] They were shortly expanded into two Ranger-qualified battalions, both of them stationed in the area outside Semarang. In the Siliwangi Division, the removal of its commando unit to become the RPKAD meant the creation of other elite groups; two Raiders-type "Kudjang" battalions were formed during the 1950's, and these saw extensive service against the Darul Islam and in the North Sumatra action which constituted the main effort of the Siliwangi Division against the regional revolt.[54] Raiders units were not formed in the Brawidjaja Division until the early 1960's, and then it was evidently only to create East Java components for the emergent Army General Reserve system.[55]

The incorporation of these units by the center took place as part of a general restructuring of the army, the implementation of which was begun in 1961. Prior to that year, divisions had consisted of battalions and, above them, regiments which were identified with a particular territorial responsibility. Now, however, a distinction was made between battalions that were to be used principally for garrison duty and local defense and those which would serve as mobile units used both within and outside the divisional boundaries. The former territorial units were to be grouped under Military Area Commands (Korem) and, below them, Military District Commands (Kodim), the latter normally being the province of one territorial battalion. The units designated as field battalions were gathered into brigades, day-to-day authority over which rested with divisional headquarters. When the brigades were called on duty beyond divisional boundaries, **operational authority passed to a centrally-established command.**[56] Under normal conditions, these brigades consisted of three battalions plus auxiliary units; they had no logistical or administrative support of their own but depended for this on the territorial defense system, to which they were usually linked through a territorial battalion stationed at the same locality as brigade headquarters.

Though the brigades thus had substantial ties to the regions of their origin, they were also given strong reason to feel a qualitative difference between their own status and that of the territorial units and to value particularly their relationship with the center. They contained the better combat units; normally, field battalions and not territorial ones had the chance for Ranger qualification or absorption into the RPKAD and other elite forces. They were very conscious of this enhanced status, and the members of territorial

---

53. Pikiran Rakjat, November 13-15, 1965; and see Madjalah Angkatan Darat, No. 3 (March 1955); No. 7/8 (August 1956).

54. Waspada, April 7 and 16, 1959; Pikiran Rakjat, August 19, 1960.

55. Kedaulatan Rakjat, April 26 and December 6, 1963.

56. Kedaulatan Rakjat, October 27, 1961, explanation of the reorganization by General Sarbini.

units were jealous of it;[57] they were also quite well aware that advancement as elite forces meant greater association with the center. Accordingly, brigade officers wishing to be transferred to a more desirable post or hoping for the upgrading of their units would look to the center rather than to their divisional associations. The whole system appears to have been a step towards the realization of Nasution's vision of a defense force divided into territorial units with strong local roots and a highly mobile strike force; its net effect on center-region relationships was to diffuse the power of the panglima by introducing two hierarchies into their commands, one of which was rather ambiguously tied to their authority. At the same time, it took a small but significant step toward psychologically orienting an important part of the better infantry units toward the center.

Three of the new brigades were still more definitely associated with Djakarta. These were attached operationally to a new institution, the Army General Reserve (TJADUAD), which was created in August 1961. Their component battalions were not necessarily identified with any one division--in fact, they were deliberately formed of one battalion from each of the Java regional commands. In normal day-to-day activities these components were responsible to the division in whose territory they were based (not through any divisional brigade or Korem but directly to divisional headquarters), while the TJADUAD had prior claim on their services whenever it found it necessary to call them up. Into this new category of reserve battalions went the best-qualified units, the Raiders from Central and East Java and the Kudjang battalions from the Siliwangi Division. In addition the RPKAD was placed under the authority of the TJADUAD.

The commander of the TJADUAD was Major General Suharto, who held the position from its inception. Suharto also headed the Mandala Command, which had operational control over the Irian campaign. This provided the first combat experience for the Reserve units in their new association, and it was very important for inculcating in them a consciousness of new loyalties--to each other, to Suharto as their commander, and to Djakarta as the center of the ambitions. The high heat of the political campaign for Irian, the massive preparations for the invasion of the island, and the dropping of RPKAD and Airborne (mostly Brigade III) troops into Dutch-occupied territory--all served to create a sense of identity and common experience greater than one might expect from the lack of actual major battle. In the course of the campaign Suharto firmly established his image as a key combat commander, and he subsequently worked to preserve his stature among his men by personal attention to their welfare.[58]

---

57. Thus, when Lieutenant Colonel Witono witnessed the disbanding of a number of battalions in his command in 1963 he found it necessary to stress that those soldiers who had been reassigned to territorial units should not feel themselves thought inferior to colleagues who had been posted to field battalions. Pikiran Rakjat, February 11, 1963.

58. Suharto was head of the Trikora (Irian campaign) Orphans' Fund, and seems to have made various efforts at fundraising and visiting the units which had fought in Irian (see, for example, Nasional, May 22, 1963; Kedaulatan Rakjat, January 30, 1964; Pikiran Rakjat, September 23, 1964). If other central army leaders made similar efforts I have not seen it reported.

General Suharto also became head of the Army Air Defense Command (Kohanudad) at the time he was appointed commander of the TJADUAD,[59] and both his own enthusiasm for air activities and the importance of Indonesia's new airborne capability led him to take a particular interest in the development of an airborne central strike force. The armed forces in general and the army in particular, he argued, must become "Para-minded."[60] It was the ambition of Suharto and other air-minded army leaders to create an Airborne division for the army, but at the time the Mandala Command began military operations in January 1962 only the RPKAD and Infantry Brigade III were so qualified.[61] Soon, however, more units were added and various Airborne units were promoted into the RPKAD, which during the early 1960's expanded from a small and highly specialized group into an impotant force; some were also taken up into the Tjakrabirawa (Presidential Guard) regiment, which was formed in 1963.[62] A great deal of public fuss was made over the elite units, which were seen as a symbol of Indonesia's arrival as a world power. Their accomplishments in the Irian campaign were celebrated, and their strength and derring-do were demonstrated on public occasions. All this, together with their special training, superior equipment, and privileges, helped to create in these units a sense of separateness from the army rank and file.

In developing a powerful central strike force, the army leaders greatly reduced the territorial commanders' ability to resist them, but at the same time they created a potential source of challenge at the center. The force which in 1965-1966 served General Suharto as a vehicle to power, replacing President Sukarno in political and General Nasution in military leadership, was the Army Strategic Command (KOSTRAD), successor to the TJADUAD. The KOSTRAD, formed following the dissolution of the Mandala Command in May 1963, initially had jurisdiction over the RPKAD and the first three infantry brigades which it had inherited from the TJADUAD. However, unlike the regular army divisions, the KOSTRAD underwent no period of temporary retrenchment following the end of the Irian campaign; instead, it expanded very rapidly, adding cavalry and artillery brigades, upgrading its infantry components, and strengthening the RPKAD. In the quarrel with Malaysia, General Suharto headed the army component of the Mandala Siaga (Confrontation) Command, and this gave the KOSTRAD units

---

59. *Kedaulatan Rakjat*, October 5, 1961.

60. *Pikiran Rakjat*, September 22, 1964. Suharto learned to jump himself and was awarded paratrooper's wings by the air force. *Pikiran Rakjat*, September 28, 1964.

61. In June 1966, the KOSTRAD achieved the long-sought goal of an Airborne division (LINUD) system. *Berita Yudha*, June 18, 1966. In spite of the many difficulties budgetary deficiencies and lack of sufficient expertise caused this body, the achievement of the LINUD was important as a demonstration that Indonesia was continuing to aim at acquiring as sophisticated a strike force as it could.

62. Airborne units were trained at the Army Paracommando School (SEPARKOAD), which indoctrinated them with the ideals of the RPKAD—a sort of air-age version of the traditional bravo. They also worked closely with the air force paratroop force, PGT. After the October 1965 coup the training of all three groups of air-qualified troops—Airborne, RPKAD, and PGT—was placed under one institution, the Joint Airborne Instruction Command (KOGABDIK PARA). *Berita Yudha*, February 9, 1966.

a further opportunity for common experience and the strengthening of central ties. It also provided Suharto with new possibilties to display himself as a leading commander and to solicit the affection of his men. By the time of the October 1965 coup Suharto had headed the same key force for four years and was the only commander it had ever had. Furthermore, since 1963 he had been the most senior officer on active military duty after the Commander of the Army, and, following the practice of the Indonesian army, he therefore replaced Yani whenever the latter was absent.[63] He thus had very powerful claims to succeed Yani as army commander at the time of the coup, but his very qualifications endeared him the less to Sukarno, who needed a pliable man in the job.[64]

* * * * * * * * *

In the development of the army after 1956 we see a tendency toward greater centralization and at the same time a proliferation of function--both in the sense of greater military specialization and of expansion into the civilian sphere--that created new problems of control. The problem of containing the panglima was gradually reduced, but new rivalries appeared at the center, resulting eventually in the overthrow of the old army leadership and the establishment of one with a quite different style. But many of the same basic assumptions regarding the role of the military in society, the need for a highly sophisticated armed force, and the importance of enhancing central control remained. By the late 1960's General

---

63. *Pikiran Rakjat*, June 6, 1963 and July 10, 1964; *Kedaulatan Rakjat*, January 8, and June 23, 1964, "Speech by Major-General Suharto on October 15, 1965, to Central and Regional Leaders of the National Front," p. 161. Suharto achieved this position in April 1963, when Lieutenant General Hidajat became Minister of Communications.

64. This was probably the reason why Sukarno refused to appoint Suharto to the command of the army on the death of Yani in the October 1965 coup, arguing that Suharto was "too stubborn" and instead attempted to name the more sympathetic General Pranoto.

   Suharto, having used the KOSTRAD as his own vehicle to power, was naturally concerned to prevent its similar utilization by anyone else thereafter, and he devoted some thought to providing it with commanders dependent on his good will and to preventing them from becoming entrenched. But the KOSTRAD's developing activities also made for a weakening of its effectiveness as an instrument of power. Its very rapid post-coup expansion reduced its coherence; moreover, the great power which it enjoyed in the first flush of the New Order led both officers and men to assert themselves in the civilian sphere. The KOSTRAD as a whole, in fact, began to branch out into side activities, providing funds, licensing opportunities, protection, and so on for a considerable range of enterprises. Because the KOSTRAD possessed power, wealth sought it out; but with this came all kinds of attachments, interests, and rivalries which have probably weakened its ability for concerted military action on behalf of a commander.

Suharto was in a much better position to wield power than General
Nasution had ever been, for the army's main civilian opponents had
been destroyed and the intra-military opposition to him had been
thrown into disarray by a series of purges. At the same time, the
greatly increased role of the military in the country's affairs, and
particularly the demands on its leader, who also held the office of
President, made it urgent to make the command structure as efficient
as possible and also to limit the opportunities for rival claimants
to power to find bases within it. The result was the 1969 reorganization of the armed forces. Because the changes made at that time both
carry forward the main lines of development we have discussed with
regard to the 1956-1963 period and illustrate how different the army
has become from what it was in its early post-revolutionary days,
we might, by way of conclusion, consider briefly the reorganization.

In terms of power, the 1969 reorganization downgraded the top
echelons of the army as well as the other services and greatly enhanced the powers of the Minister for Defense and Security and the
Commander of the Armed Forces, which offices were held by Suharto.[65]
Whereas previously the commanders of the individual services had
had operational charge over them, this authority was now placed, down
to company level, in the hands of the Commander of the Armed Forces.
Hitherto the service commanders had had ministerial rank, but this
was now taken from them, and, as befitted their loss of actual command functions, they now assumed the title of service chief of staff.
The size and competence of the staffs over which they presided were
reduced, and the powers they lost were transferred to the Ministry
of Defense and the Armed Forces General Staff. Coordination of the
services was extended below the general staff level by the replacement
of the KOANDA, together with their naval and air force counterparts,
with the Regional Defense Command (KOWILHAN) system. This created
six regional commands, presided over by members of the three major
services, who were responsible to the armed forces commander and
the Ministry of Defense and not to their own service heads.[66]

Because Suharto was himself clearly too busy with affairs of
state to devote as much time to the supervision of military operations
as his new powers required, the post of Deputy Commander of the Armed
Forces was created, and day-to-day charge of operations was handed
over to him. The deputy commander at the same time headed the
Command for the Restoration of Security and Order (KOPKAMTIB) which
had been set up in the wake of the 1965 coup and was a major instrument for controlling the civilian population. Here again, transfer
of operational control occurred: day-to-day command rested with the
Deputy Commander of the KOPKAMTIB. This arrangement reflects a main
theme of the entire reorganization, the desire to achieve maximum
concentration of power and yet to provide checks and balances against
the independent use of this strength by any of Suharto's high sub-

---

65. For details of this reorganization, see "Current Data on the Indo-
    nesian Military Elite after the Reorganization of 1969-1970,"
    Indonesia, No. 10 (October 1970), pp. 195-208. Note especially
    the official motivation quoted in the introduction (p. 195),
    which makes it clear the purpose was to eliminate any likely
    source of a coup.

66. These were I, Sumatra; II, Java and Madura; III, Kalimantan;
    IV, Sulawesi; V, Lesser Sundas; VI, Maluku and West Irian.

ordinates. General Staff control was extended into the territorial defense system by composing the KOWILHAN staffs of more than one service and counterposing their members to their service headquarters above and the single-service regional commands below. There has also been a diminishing of divisional ties and even of corps affiliation for the panglima, for in some of the Outer Island territories officers from the cavalry and artillery have been appointed to regional command.

The 1969 reorganization made the position of Commander of the Armed Forces far stronger than any Indonesian military office had been before. Simatupang, as Chief of Staff of the Armed Forces in the early 1950's, had been responsible to the Minister of Defense (which Suharto now embodies in himself). Furthermore, Simatupang's formal function had been to preside over the Joint Chiefs of Staff (GKS), who were supposed to provide the major military decision-making center, even if the army had dominated in fact. Nasution had combined the functions of Defense Minister and Armed Forces Chief of Staff, but his authority was limited by Sukarno as Supreme Commander of the Armed Forces, who used this role to promote the fortunes of Nasution's rivals both within the army and among the other services. Under the 1969 reform, the chiefs of staff of the individual armed forces appear to have been given no joint role in theory or practice, and their individual powers were much diminished with the withdrawal of operational command over their services.

Most notably, the 1969 reorganization greatly diminished the preeminence of the army, for at the higher levels of command it now appeared as only one of three major services. That Suharto, an army man, chose to diminish that service's stature once his position as national leader was secure seems to flow from the fact that he is no longer in a position to control it closely, and he must therefore prevent its being too potent a weapon in the hands of another. This was not a path to domination which Nasution could have followed as Armed Forces Chief of Staff, for he had found himself between Sukarno and the services; his strength had rested on his continuing influence within the army, and if he had not acted as its spokesman he would soon have lost the backing he needed to maintain himself against Sukarno. Because of this, and because of Nasution's generally much weaker position, supra-military organization had remained at a minimum during his tenure, consisting of little more than the general staff offices and a series of commands and agencies linking the services for special projects and functions. Under Suharto, however, there has been a proliferation of inter-service bodies and a vast extension of the authority of the armed forces staff.

The 1969 reorganization followed the general trend of post-revolutionary military consolidation in its search for centralization and the elimination of particularistic ties. Much has been accomplished, especially in the matter of reducing the power of territorial commanders, the achievement of technical sophistication, and the general acceptance of central authority and bureaucratic procedure. At the same time, the complexity and expanded role of the military have created new problems of control for the army leadership. The military bureaucracy has proliferated to take care of the diversity of the services' activities, the increasing specialization of their forces, and the desire of leaders to ensure dominance by creating countervailing forces and layers of command. Whereas once local commanders could act independently because the lines tying them to the center were few and weak, now they find a certain degree of autonomy because the lines of communication and command are complex and tangled. At the same time, however, the expansion of the military role in Indonesian society which began with Guided Democracy and reached undisputed dominance in the New Order has given army members a strong sense of their corporate elite status, and with the fading of revolutionary memories and the reduction of Sukarnoist ideological ties, this has become a central source of army solidarity. Whether unity can be maintained in the long run in the face of the pressures and temptations of the army's social role and whether the army can both govern and be an effective military machine are questions that the future must answer. The role of Leviathan is not an easy one, but the army has come very far from the weakness and confusion that marked it only some fifteen years ago.

DIVISIONS AND POWER IN THE INDONESIAN
NATIONAL PARTY, 1965-1966*

Angus McIntyre

The principal division which split the PNI into two sharply opposed factions in 1965-1966 had its origins as far back as 1957, when the PKI made spectacular advances in large part at PNI expense in the 1957 regional elections in Java and South Sumatra. In Central Java, where the PKI supplanted the PNI as the region's strongest party (based on the 1955 general elections results), the PNI reaction at the time was most outspoken. Hadisubeno, the regional party chairman, blamed the party's poor showing on its past association with the PKI[1] and accordingly urged the party's central executive council to review this relationship. He suggested that the party consider forming an alliance with the Masjumi (the modernist Islamic party) and the Nahdatul Ulama (NU, the traditional Islamic party).[2] A conference of the Central Java PNI passed a resolution forbidding cooperation with the PKI.[3]

These acts were interpreted by many as a slap at President Sukarno,[4] who had made it increasingly clear in the preceding months that to oppose the PKI was to oppose him as well; however, the party's central leadership, no less hostile to the PKI, was unwilling to risk such an interpretation and thereby further impair its relations with Sukarno. Indeed, only a few months before, Sukarno had indicated strong displeasure with the PNI in his address to the party on the occasion of its thirtieth anniversary celebrations. He implied that PNI members had lost their commitment to the goal of a socialist or marhaenist[5] society, the realization of which had been his very reason

---

* The writer would like to express his gratitude to the Jajasan Siswa Lokantara Indonesia for providing him with the opportunity to conduct research in Indonesia in 1966 and 1967 and to the Myer Foundation for giving him financial assistance in 1967. I would also like to thank Benedict Anderson, Donald Hindley, Michael Leigh, and Rex Mortimer for their helpful suggestions.

1. See Daniel Lev, The Transition to Guided Democracy: Indonesian Politics, 1957-1959 (Ithaca: Cornell Modern Indonesia Project, 1966), pp. 105-106.

2. Ibid., p. 106.

3. Ibid., p. 108.

4. Ibid., p. 109.

5. For Sukarno, a socialist or marhaenist society was one which advanced the social and economic well being of small farmers, farm laborers, and others who had been impoverished by imperialism--people for whom he had coined the phrase "Marhaen." Soekarno, Marhaen and Proletarian (Ithaca: Cornell Modern Indonesia Project, 1960), pp. 3 and 5.

for establishing the PNI in the first place in 1927:[6] "Look at your face today. Is it the same, or not, as the portrait of 1927? If it is the same, thanks to God who be praised, I say. If it is not the same, then--self-correction."[7] Accordingly, the central leadership issued no public rejection of the PKI.[8]

As it turned out, however, improvement of relations with the President involved far more than merely forfeiting the opportunity to oppose the PKI openly. It also involved a commitment to a Marhaenist society and to whatever means Sukarno chose to adopt for its realization. Between 1957 and 1959, a commitment to the President's concept of Guided Democracy had been required, and on this matter party leaders such as general chairman Suwirjo and central leadership council member Hardi, dedicated as they were to the preservation of the parliamentary system, were unable to satisfy Sukarno. They thereby left themselves open to challenge from the younger leaders of the PNI mass organizations who were attracted to Sukarno's brand of radical nationalism and supported his concept of Guided Democracy.

Immediately prior to the 1960 party congress the younger leaders distributed a brochure to the delegates entitled *Appeal Djuli 1960* (July 1960 Appeal).[9] Invoking the authority of *Mentjapai Indonesia Merdeka* (To Achieve an Independent Indonesia), a pamphlet written by Sukarno in 1933, and its Leninist prescriptions for party composition and organization,[10] the appeal deplored the "embourgeoisement" and "liberalization" of the PNI and its leaders since 1946.[11] In order to remedy this situation and to restore the PNI to its proper role as vanguard party of a marhaen mass movement, it called on the

---

6. In fact, the Indonesian National Party, founded in January-February 1946, is organizationally distinct from the party of the same name founded by Sukarno in July 1927 and was dissolved by party members in April 1931. The post-independence party, however, has not recognized such a distinction and therefore dates its founding from July 1927.

7. Soekarno, Marhaen and Proletarian, p. 26.

8. Daniel Lev, The Transition to Guided Democracy, p. 110.

9. Appeal Djuli 1960 Organisasi-Organisasi Karya Front Marhaenis kepada Kongres PNI ke-IX (1960) was compiled and signed by the leaders of the following PNI mass organizations: Pemuda Demokrat Indonesia (Democratic Youth of Indonesia), Gerakan Mahasiswa Nasional Indonesia (Indonesian National Student Movement), Kesatuan Buruh Kerakjatan Indonesia (Indonesian People's Labor Front), and Persatuan Tani Indonesia (Indonesian Peasants' Front).

10. In this document Sukarno had written that the vanguard party of the marhaen mass movement must have a highly centralized organization of radical orientation whose leadership would have far reaching power and authority. Mentjapai Indonesia Merdeka (1933), p. 61. Borrowing the term as well as the idea from Lenin, Sukarno referred to this arrangement of power within the party as democratic centralism. Ibid., p. 62.

11. Appeal Djuli, passim.

congress to elect men of true revolutionary spirit to the party leadership.[12] It blamed the PNI's estrangement from Sukarno on those party leaders, such as Hardi, who had opposed the President's plan "to do away with the liberal form of parliament."[13] This proposal called for the introduction of functional group representation into Indonesia's next parliament and the inclusion of such groups as peasants, students, and youth. As prospective beneficiaries of this plan, the PNI mass organizations had given it their full support.[14]

The leaders of the mass organizations argued that the restoration of the party to its vanguard role could only be achieved within the context of Guided Democracy and that the preservation of the parliamentary system was associated with the malaise of liberalization which had afflicted the party since 1946.[15]

In light of these statements, the mass organization leaders must have regarded the party election results of the 1960 Congress with mixed feelings. Ali Sastroamidjojo, who had been complimented in the *Appeal Djuli* for his organization of the Bandung Conference,[16] replaced Suwirjo as general chairman, but the latter was elected first chairman and Hardi was elected secretary general.[17]

The growing prominence of these young leaders in the affairs of the party greatly enhanced the President's influence over the central leadership, for now there was an emerging group with leadership aspirations and an ideological persuasion similar to Sukarno's whom he could threaten to support, should the central party leadership fail to accede to his various demands. Indeed, he offered a clear challenge along these lines to the incumbent party leadership in his address to the PNI Congress in Purwokerto in 1963:

> Without being personal, I say that Pak Ali [Sastroamidjojo] is already old. This morning I said to Pak Abikusno: "Bung Abi, why, you're looking old." Bung Hardi is old, Pak Sartono is old. They are all old. Don't tell me there are no young people, brothers and sisters, whose spirit is like Hatta's was when he was still

---

12. *Ibid*.

13. *Appeal Djuli*, p. 12; see also p. 13.

14. For elaboration of this point, see J. Eliseo Rocamora, "The Partai Nasional Indonesia, 1963-1965," *Indonesia*, No. 10 (October 1970), p. 150 f.

15. *Appeal Djuli*, *passim*.

16. There were other reasons why these leaders supported Ali at the 1960 party Congress. Firstly, he enjoyed considerable prestige within the party as a former prime minister. Secondly, as ambassador to the United States between 1957 and 1960, he was immune to the charges of vacillation, "embourgeoisement," and the like which they levelled at the Suwirjo leadership.

17. The other offices were filled by Dr. Moh. Isa (second chairman) and S. Hadikusumo (treasurer). *Antara*, July 30, 1960 (morning edition).

young, whose spirit is like Tjokroaminoto's was when he
was still young, like Muljadi Djojomartono's was when
he was still young and working as a postal clerk, brothers
and sisters. Rejuvenate, rejuvenate, rejuvenate, rejuvenate![18]

Although Ali was able to survive this challenge and was elected general chairman, he was nonetheless aware of his vulnerability to the "politicking" of Sukarno on the one hand and to a challenge from the young leaders of the mass organizations to whom Sukarno had given the nod in his address, on the other. Indeed, one of these leaders, Ir. Surachman, the secretary general of *Persatuan Tani Indonesia* (Petani) and one of the signatories of the July 1960 Appeal, was elected party secretary general.[19]

Accordingly, Ali cast off such associates as Hardi, who had been elected first chairman at Purwokerto, and second chairman Osa Maliki and began to work more closely with Surachman and like-minded radicals in following the course which Sukarno was mapping out for the party. Clearly, Ali had given priority to improving relations with the President in order to secure his own position as party leader. Thus, the following year, Sukarno was successful in having his conception of Marhaenism, as Marxism adapted to Indonesian conditions, enshrined by the Congress Working Committee (Badan Pekerdja Kongres) of the PNI in its *Deklarasi Marhaenis* or Marhaenist Declaration.[20] Sukarno first formulated this notion in 1958[21] and had been urging it on the party ever since.

Some participants at the meeting of this organization, such as Hardi, viewed the outcome with alarm. Believing that the distinction between Marhaenism and the ideology of the PKI had been all but obliterated, they assumed that this definition could only work to the PKI's advantage. Consequently, they began to entertain deep suspicions regarding Sukarno's intentions towards the PNI.

Why did Ali Sastroamidjojo not share these suspicions? Unlike most other members of the central leadership council he cherished a

---

18. *Amanat PJM Presiden Sukarno Pada Resepsi Pembukaan Kongres Ke-X PNI Di Purwokerto Pada Tanggal 28 Agustus 1963* (Mimeographed), p. 8. Sukarno's hostility towards Hardi is particularly apparent from the fact that he included him along with Ali and Sartono as targets for party rejuventation despite the fact that he was fifteen years younger than the former and eighteen years younger than the latter.

19. J. Eliseo Rocamora, "Political Participation and the Party System: The PNI Example" (Paper delivered to the Association of Asian Studies Conference, April, 1971), p. 46. The remaining offices were filled at the Congress by Dr. Moh, Isa (third chairman), Dr. Roeslan Abdulgani (fourth chairman), Subamia (fifth chairman), Mh. Isnaeni (deputy secretary general), and S. Hadikusumo (treasurer). *Antara*, September 2, 1963 (evening edition).

20. See *Deklarasi Marhaenis* (Deppenprop DPP-PNI, January 1, 1965), p. 5.

21. Daniel Lev, *The Transition to Guided Democracy*, p. 163.

long political relationship with the President. This relationship dated back to the time Sukarno had been leader and Ali a prominent member of the first Indonesian National Party founded in 1927. Born of this long association was a belief on Ali's part that Sukarno would never sacrifice his former party, and his longtime political associates within it, to the interests of another political party. It was this historical factor peculiar to Ali which facilitated his adoption of Sukarno-inspired radical policies for the PNI.

After the Congress Working Committee session of November, Ali's former friends in the central leadership began to establish more systematic contact with like-minded regional party leaders such as Hadisubeno in Central Java. In this province the party and its front organizations, particularly Petani, which was made up of both landlords and landless peasants,[22] had been engaged in a number of physical clashes with the PKI's peasant union, BTI (*Barisan Tani Indonesia* or Indonesian Peasant Front), which consisted largely of landless peasants.[23] These clashes had occurred after BTI had taken the law, namely the Basic Agrarian and Sharecropping Acts of 1960,[24] into its own hands in March 1964[25] and attempted to implement it in a number of so-called "unilateral" actions against landlords who were in many cases PNI members or supporters.

Despite the class-based appeals of the PKI, there were few, if any, defections by landless peasant members of Petani. This loyalty was largely a consequence of the skillful appeal by provincial and local PNI leaders to traditional patron-client relations between richer and poorer villagers.[26] Thus, the PNI was able to maintain its peasant support and Hadisubeno was able to mobilize Petani in vigorous support of these landlords.

It was not only Hadisubeno who was concerned about these actions; so, too, was Ali Sastroamidjojo. Yet, under the constraints he had imposed upon himself by the choice to maintain close relations with the President, he confined his criticism of the PKI to saying that the PNI "cannot agree to those unilateral actions."[27] He attempted to wield the President's most favored symbols of political unity to the PNI's advantage by calling on those involved in the land disputes "to overcome the problem together by consultation [*musjawarah*], and cooperation [*gotong-rojong*] based on NASAKOM [i.e., the unity of

---

22. E. Utrecht, "Land Reform in Indonesia," Bulletin of Indonesian Economic Studies, 5, No. 3 (November 1969), p. 81.

23. Ibid.

24. For an account of these acts see ibid., passim and Selo Soemardjan, "Land Reform in Indonesia," Asian Survey, 1, No. 12 (February 1962).

25. Merdeka, July 2, 3, 1964, quoted in Polemik, p. 151.

26. Rex Mortimer, "The Ideology of the Communist Party of Indonesia under Guided Democracy 1959-1965" (Ph.D. Thesis, Monash University, 1970), pp. 7:48-49.

27. Ali Sastroamidjojo, Dengan Apinja Marhaenisme Kita Laksanakan Dwikora (Djakarta, July 4, 1964), pp. 6-7.

nationalist (NAS), religious (A) and communist (KOM) political forces]."[28]

Eventually, on December 12, 1964, following joint consultations at the Bogor palace presided over by President Sukarno,[29] Indonesia's ten political parties produced a statement calling for the peaceful resolution of land disputes.

On March 7, 1965, Hadisubeno convened a "Lightning Conference" of the Central Java branch of the PNI which, at his instigation, condemned the party's secretary general, Ir. Surachman, for implying that the police had been at fault in the handling of a land clash in the *kabupaten* of Bojolali.[30] This clash had occurred on November 18, 1964 in the village of Ketaon where three peasants, presumably BTI members or supporters, were shot dead by the local police during a dispute with a landlord, presumably a PNI supporter.[31] According to one source, Ir. Surachman actually paid a special visit to the graves of the dead peasants, much to the amazement and confusion of local PNI members.[32]

In a commentary attached to the announcement of the conference decisions, both of which were published under the same cover as *Buku Putih Adjakan PNI-Front Marhaenis Djawa-Tengah* (The White Book: An Invitation of the Central Java PNI-Front Marhaenis), it was strongly suggested that some members of the PNI's central leadership council were being manipulated by the PKI.[33]

Just as Surachman's enthusiastic brand of NASAKOM-style politics appeared incongruous, to say the least, to the more conservative PNI members in Central Java, so Hadisubeno's insinuation that some members of the central leadership council were PKI instruments appeared very heavy-handed even to such like-minded men as Hardi and Osa Maliki, who had felt it necessary to phrase their opposition to the PKI in pro-Sukarno terms in the hope of avoiding a head-on clash with him. No such constraint, however, acted on the outspoken Hadisubeno. Accordingly, he became the frankest proponent of the anti-PKI side of the issue in the party, even to the extent of occasionally embarrassing his political allies.

On March 24, 1965, President Sukarno joined the fray in a speech to the "Marhaenist Vanguard Cadres": "I say to the Marhaenists that

---

28. Ibid.

29. The text of the statement, commonly referred to as the Bogor Declaration, may be found in Amankan dan Amalkan Deklarasi Bogor (DPP-PNI, pamphlet), pp. 5-6.

30. DPD-PNI Djawa Tengah, Buku Putih Adjakan PNI-Front Marhaenis Djawa Tengah, pp. 4-5.

31. Rex Mortimer, "The Ideology of the Communist Party," p. 7:61.

32. Interview, Semarang, December 18, 1966.

33. Buku Putih, p. 11.

if there are false Marhaenists among them, expel them from the
Marhaenist group. Why do they hang on to people who are like that?
Yes, if they are false, expel them, expel them from your circle."[34]
Later in the speech, the President gave some indication as to what he
meant by the phrase "false Marhaenist": "I say that if there is a
person who calls himself a Marhaenist and he is anti-NASAKOM, or if
he balks at the policy of Nasakomization, he is a false Marhaenist who
ought to be expelled from the Marhaen group."[35] Hedging his bets in
public at least, Sukarno mentioned no names.[36] Yet, his association
in this speech, which he delivered only two weeks after the "Lightning
Conference" of the Central Java PNI, of "false Marhaenists" with those
opposed to his NASAKOM policy, strongly suggests that it was Hadisubeno,
for one, whom the President had in mind.

Whatever the case, a plenary session of the central party leadership, held on May 12-13, 1965, ordered Hadisubeno to retire from his
position as first chairman of the Central Java party council and
suspended Oemar Said (third chairman, Central Java), Soetopo
Koesoemodirdjo (first chairman, Kudus branch), and Soegeng
Tirtosiswojo (first chairman, Tjilatjap branch) from party membership
on the grounds that their compilation and propagation of the *Buku
Putih* had damaged party unity.[37] By all accounts, this meeting was
conducted in an extremely tense and acrimonious atmosphere.[38]

President Sukarno, apparently unsatisfied with the May 14 decision, returned to the fray in another address to the party on the
occasion of its thirty-eighth anniversary in July:

> Once again I say, quickly kick these false Marhaenists
> out of our ranks! The Sundanese say, *iraha deui* [when
> again]. *Ngadagoan naon deui*. It means what else
> are you waiting for? It is already obvious that they
> are false Marhaenists. Kick them out, don't let them
> remain in our ranks![39]

The President's use of Sundanese in this speech perhaps suggests that
he believed that many of the "false Marhaenists" were in the West Java

---

34. Amanat Gemblengan PJM Presiden Sukarno Pada Kader Pelopor Marhaenis Di Gedung Basketball, Senajan, 24 Maret 1965 (Mimeographed, Sekretariat Negara Kabinet Presiden Republik Indonesia), p. 2.

35. Ibid., p. 4.

36. It has been suggested that he did mention privately whom he considered to be "false Marhaenists."

37. Surat Keputusan Tentang Brosur dan Pamplet DPD-PNI Djawa Tengah (Mimeographed), pp. 1-2.

38. See Kepada Kawanku I (August 8, 1965), p. 9 and Kebenaran Menggugat 2 (Kata Pengantar, August 20, 1965), p. 8; Cf. Tendang keluar Marhaenis 2 Gadungan!! Pendjelasan Latar Belakang Ideologis Politis Tentang Pemetjatan Hardi SH DKK (Deppenprop DPP-PNI, August 11, 1965), p. 25.

39. Amanat PJM Presiden Sukarno Pada Peringatan Hari Ulang Tahun PNI Ke-38 di Stadion Utama Gelora Bung Karno Senajan, Djakarta, 25 Djuli 1965 (Mimeographed, Sekretariat Negara Kabinet Presiden Republik Indonesia), p. 6.

(Sundanese) branch of the party. At the very least, it must have been apparent to Ali that he had not yet gone far enough to satisfy the President.

At the Kesatuan Buruh Marhaenis (Marhaenist Labor Front) Congress convened from July 25 to August 1, 1965, Bachtiar Salim Haloho, who was reelected general chairman, put forward a resolution which he claimed had the full approval of the President. Essentially, it stated that if the PNI central leadership did not expel the "false Marhaenists" then KBM would refuse to recognize them either as members or leaders of the party.[40] This resolution was followed in the next few days by a number of similar ones issued by the leadership councils of other PNI front organizations such as GMNI (Indonesian National Student Movement), GPM (Marhaenist Youth Movement), and Petani. Whether the front organizations, in collaboration with the President, were endeavoring to force Ali's hand on this matter or whether Ali himself had mobilized them to clear the way for a final showdown with the "false Marhaenists" in a further attempt to appease the President is unclear. It is clear, however, that it was Sukarno who was calling the tune.

On August 3, Hardi, Mh. Isnaeni, Osa Maliki, Karim M. Duriat, Sabilal Rasjad, and Moh. Achmad sent a letter to members of the PNI leadership stating that they saw no use in attending the plenary meeting of the central party leadership on August 4 on the grounds that they believed it, like the preceding plenary session of May 12-13, would not provide a forum for free discussion.[41] They wrote, however, that they would attend a session of the central leadership which would specifically discuss the matter of holding an extraordinary congress "where it is hoped the Father of Marhaenism, Bung Karno, will agree to issue an order for the restoration of unity in the PNI Front Marhaenis."[42]

It was this event which proved the occasion of their suspension from the party. The following day the central leadership, in a letter of decision signed by general chairman Ali Sastroamidjojo and secretary general Ir. Surachman, suspended the above six as well as Hadisubeno from party membership.[43] This action was greeted favorably

---

40. *Suluh Indonesia*, August 2, 1965.

41. *Kepada Kawanku I*, p. 9.

42. *Ibid.*

43. *Surat Keputusan Tentang Pemetjatan Sementara Sdr. Hardi Cs*. (Mimeographed, DPP-PNI), pp. 1-2. It is of course true that changes in the party leadership at all levels were foreshadowed in the *Deklarasi Marhaenis* of 1964. See J. Eliseo Rocamora, "The Partai Nasional Indonesia," pp. 174-175. Whether these particular suspensions and the ones that followed were also foreshadowed in the declaration cannot, in the writer's view, be established on the available evidence. Cf. *ibid.*, p. 176.

by Partindo[44] and the PKI[45] and with alarm by the NU.[46] The "false Marhaenists," as their opponents characterized them, or the "Ten Friends,"[47] as they initially styled themselves, did not drop their demand for an extraordinary congress. Indeed, they immediately tried to enlist sufficient branch support to call such a congress.[48]

A dispute among the party's leaders over whether to support the President or oppose the PKI had thereby been transformed by the Osa Maliki faction into a contest for the party leadership as the best means of most forcefully presenting their side of the argument without at the same time relegating themselves to the ineffectual status of a splinter group. And, having flouted the authority of the central leadership council, this would almost certainly have been the consequence of failing to appeal to the highest policy-making body within the party, namely, congress, to vindicate their actions. Although the prospects for such vindication may have appeared dim at that time, there was, in fact, no other course open to them.

The position of the Osa Maliki faction was most precarious. All they could point to in terms of tangible support was a radiogram dated August 21 from Brigadier General Sutjipto, the chairman of the fifth (political) section of the Supreme Operations Command (KOTI), to all the military commanders of Indonesia, instructing them not to interfere in the internal affairs of the PNI/Front Marhaenis.[49] This instruction did not deter the minister/commander of the police force, Sutjipto Judodihardjo, from issuing an order on September 6 to all local police commanders to prohibit the activities of the "false Marhaenists."[50] The police force, in addition to the President, PKI, and Partindo, had to be counted among their enemies.

The situation within the PNI changed dramatically and suddenly after the central leadership council severely compromised itself in the eyes of the army and other anticommunist political groups as a result of its statements of apparent support for the short-lived

---

44. *Bintang Timur*, August 7, 1965.

45. *Harian Rakjat*, August 7, 1965.

46. *Duta Masjarakat*, August 7, 1965.

47. This term refers to the seven members suspended on August 4 in addition to Oemar Said and Sugeng Tirtosiswojo suspended on May 14, and Drs. F. Sutrisno. See *Kepada Kawanku I*, pp. 7-8.

48. *Ibid.*, pp. 6-7.

49. *Sinar Harapan*, October 21, 1965. In terms of intangible support, a prominent member of the Osa Maliki faction informed the writer that they received "moral support" from General Nasution. Interview, June 26, 1967.

50. J. Eliseo Rocamora, "The Partai Nasional Indonesia," p. 180. A copy of the Supreme Operations Command radiogram of August 21 was attached to a letter, dated September 8, which Osa Maliki and Isnaeni sent to Sutjipto Judodihardjo to protest his order. *Ibid.*, p. 180, n. 97. However, this was to no avail as the commanders of the Djakarta and West Java police districts issued similar instructions to those of the minister/commander for their areas of jurisdiction on September 20 and 24. *Warta Bhakti*, September 21, 25, 1965.

Gerakan Tiga Puluh September (September 30th Movement), or Gestapu, as it became known. In fact, two PNI statements were published in the ensuing days--one in *Suluh Indonesia* on October 2, which reappeared in *Patriot* (Medan) on October 6, and one in *Antara* on October 2.[51] While both may be interpreted as statements of support for the September 30th Movement, the *Antara* one lends itself more easily to such an interpretation.

In a subsequent "clarification" issued by the central leadership of the events surrounding the emergence of the PNI statement[52] of October 1, 1965, a list of fifteen men allegedly responsible for its formulation was provided.[53] Strikingly, the vast majority--twelve of the fifteen--were current or ex-leaders of the party's mass organizations including such people as Bachtier Salim Haloho of KBM, former GMNI leader John Lumingkewas, and Ir. Surachman.[54] Karna Radjasa (first chairman, Djakarta branch), Satyagraha (managing editor of *Suluh Indonesia*), and Selamat Ginting (acting chairman of the organization department since Hardi's suspension)[55] were the three who had not been leaders of the mass organizations.[56]

As for the other party leaders, general chairman Ali Sastroamidjojo was in Peking, third chairman Dr. Moh. Isa was outside Djakarta, fifth chairman Subamia was overseas, and Dr. Ruslan Abdulgani "had duties

---

51. Cf. "Continuity and Change," Indonesia, No. 2 (April 1966), pp. 198-201 which points out that the Antara version is different from the Patriot version but fails to mention that the Patriot version is identical to the statement which appeared in Suluh Indonesia on October 2.

52. The "clarification" does not account for the fact that two different statements of the PNI central leadership appeared in the press in the days following the abortive September 30th Movement. It also leaves the question open as to whether the statement which the "clarification" asserts was completed at about 11:30 a.m. on October 1 (i.e., when the Gerakan was still in control of Djakarta) was the same as either one of the two which was subsequently published. It does, however, state that the PNI statement was handed over to the Antara press agency at 8:00 p.m. or three-quarters of an hour before the first army broadcast announcing the suppression of the September 30th Movement in Djakarta. It is feasible, therefore, that the statement formulated by the leadership council on the morning of October 1 was the same as the one delivered to the Antara office before the city had changed hands again and published in Antara's morning edition of October 2. On the other hand, the version published in Suluh Indonesia (and Patriot) probably did not go to press until after 8:45 leaving time for its modification in an attempt to take account of the dramatic new power shift which took place in the capital after 8:00 p.m.

53. For the text of the "clarification" see Harian Nasional (Jogjakarta), November 5, 1965.

54. Warta Bhakti, August 11, 1965.

55. Ibid.

56. The complete list may be found in Harian Nasional, November 5, 1965.

elsewhere."[57] Unrestrained by the elder and more experienced party members, who presumably would have cautioned restraint in such a fluid situation, the leaders of the mass organizations overreached themselves on that day.

On October 2, Brigadier General Sutjipto called a meeting of representatives of political parties at KOTI headquarters. The PNI leadership did not attend, although the Osa Maliki faction was present.[58] *Suluh Indonesia* was promptly banned on the grounds that it had sided with the September 30th Movement[59] which was now being generally interpreted as inspired and controlled by the PKI. A few days later, the first of the army-sponsored demonstrations against the PKI was held in Djakarta.

Encouraged by these events, the Osa Maliki faction publicly set its sights on the party leadership in a somewhat cavalier declaration which it made on October 6. It "banned the PNI central leadership council led by Ali-Surachman"[60] on the grounds of "the involvement of several members of the DPP-PNI in the counter-revolutionary September 30th Movement . . ."[61] and established a new leadership under the general chairmanship of Osa Maliki. The remaining leadership positions were filled by Hardi (first chairman), Sabilal Rasjad (second chairman), Isnaeni (third chairman), Moh. Achmad (fourth chairman), Usep Ranawidjaja (secretary general), Abadi (first deputy secretary general, I.G.N.), Gde Djaksa (second deputy secretary general), and Karim M. Doeriat (treasurer).[62]

The Osa Maliki faction, by forming themselves into a rival central leadership council on October 6, had clearly violated party conventions. There was no precedent, let alone provision in the party constitution, for such a step. Moreover, Osa Maliki supporters subsequently conceded this fact by attributing de jure status to the leadership council of Ali Sastromidjojo and only de facto status to their own faction: "There were those who hesitated faced with the 'legality' of the DPP-PNI Ali-Surachman' on the one hand and the 'reality' and purity of the 'DPP-PNI Osa-Usep' on the other."[63] Thus, if a divided party may be defined as one in which at least one group

---

57. Ibid.

58. O. G. Roeder, The Smiling General (Djakarta: Gunung Agung, 1969), p. 24.

59. Angkatan Bersendjata, October 7, 1965 quoted in U. S. Embassy Translation Unit Press Review (October 7, 1965).

60. Deklarasi Pembentukan D.P.P.-P.N.I. Osa-Usep (Deppenprop DPP-PNI, October 7, 1965), p. 4.

61. Ibid., p. 3.

62. Ibid.

63. Laporan Umum Dewan Pimpinan Pusat Partai Nasional Indonesia pada: Sidang ke-I Madjelis Permusjawaratan Partai P.N.I./Front Marhaenis Tgl. 28 s/d 30 Nopember 1966 Di Djakarta (Mimeographed), p. 4.

by-passes or exceeds the limits imposed by party convention for the resolution of differences of opinion or rival ambitions for party office, then by early October the PNI fit such a definition.

The Contestants

A closer examination of the Ali and Osa Maliki factions and their supporters reveals that ethnic and regional differences underlay the conflict between the two factions. If the 140 members who were suspended from the PNI between August 4 and October 1 for lending support to the Osa Maliki faction[64] may be regarded as representative of the faction as a whole, then, as the following table makes clear, it consisted largely of non-Javanese, among whom the Sundanese (West Java) were predominant.

Table 1. Ethnic and Regional Composition of Members Suspended from the PNI and its Mass Organizations between May 12 and October 1, 1965, for supporting the Osa Maliki faction.

Region	Number	Percentage of Total
Atjeh	7	5.0
North Sumatra	2	1.42
West Sumatra	3	2.14
Banten/West Java	3	2.14
Djakarta	34	24.28
West Java	43	30.71
Central Java	15	10.71
East Java	26	18.60
Sulawesi/Makasar	7	5.0
Total	140	100.00

Source: Fungsionaris PNI/GMM Jang Ditindak Oleh Ali-Surachman (Mimeographed).

In the 1955 general elections the PNI gained only 37.5 percent of its vote in non-Javanese areas.[65] If this distribution of the PNI vote in 1955 can be taken as a rough guide to the proportion of Javanese and non-Javanese members in the party in 1965, then, clearly,

---

64. For details of the suspension of these members from the party, see Warta Bhakti, August 28, September 1, 3, 1965 and Suluh Indonesia, August 20, 28, 1965; see also J. Eliseo Rocamora, "The Partai Nasional Indonesia," p. 179.

65. This percentage was calculated from figures to be found in Herbert Feith, The Indonesian Elections of 1955 (Ithaca: Cornell Modern Indonesia Project, 1957), pp. 58, 85.

the non-Javanese, or more precisely, people resident in non-Javanese areas, were overrepresented in the ranks of the Osa Maliki faction.

The other side of this coin, of course, is that non-Javanese must have been underrepresented among the supporters of the Ali leadership. Indeed, according to its own assessment, this appeared to be the case. Immediately prior to the Extraordinary Congress, the Ali leadership calculated that it would command a majority of congress votes in Central Java (including the Special Region of Jogjakarta), East Java, and North Sumatra, whereas it estimated that the Osa Maliki faction would command a majority in West Java, Atjeh, and South Sulawesi.[66]

If this characterization of the ethnic bases of the two groupings is correct, the question arises: What factor did the non-Javanese PNI members hold in common which set them sufficiently apart from the Javanese members to be able to explain, in part at least, the division which occurred in the party in September? Nominally Islamic non-Javanese PNI members do not share the antipathy of their Javanese counterparts[67] for devout Moslems.[68] Relatively tolerant of Islam, they are much more inclined to perceive a threat in communism or, more precisely, the PKI. Javanese PNI members, on the other hand, have been more susceptible to the appeals of communism[69] and highly distrustful of Islam, especially in its modernist political form, as represented by such organizations as Masjumi and the Islamic Student Association (*Himpunan Mahasiswa Islam* or HMI). They feared that such organizations wished to turn the Indonesian state into an Islamic theocracy.

Thus the Ali leadership chose to support Sukarno, rather than oppose the PKI, not only because of Sukarno's considerable influence within the PNI and his standing as the trusted founder of the Indonesian National Party, but also because he had, since 1945, stood clearly and unequivocally for a secular, that is non-Islamic, Indonesian

---

66. <u>Daftar Rekap PNI</u> (Mimeographed), p. 1.

67. The statement that PNI members are nominally Islamic is based on the assumption that devout Moslems join the specifically Islamic parties, such as Masjumi (until its banning in 1960), <u>Partai Sarekat Islam Indonesia</u> (PSII), and NU.

68. Daniel Lev (<u>The Transition to Guided Democracy</u>, p. 95) has stated that "West Javanese PNI leaders did not perceive in Islam the threat feared by PNI supporters in the ethnic Javanese areas of the island." In a similar vein, Feith (<u>The Indonesian Elections</u>, p. 82) has pointed out that outside the islands of Java and Bali "a self-conscious group of anti-Moslem Moslems, the equivalent of the Javanese abangan" do not exist. The fact that these two writers disagree on the religious orientation of the Sundanese should be borne in mind in assessing the worth of the argument. For a discussion of the Javanese abangan, see C. Geertz, <u>The Religion of Java</u> (New York: The Free Press, 1969), pp. 11-112.

69. For example, in the 1957 regional elections the PKI captured a large segment of the former PNI electoral support. Donald Hindley, <u>The Communist Party of Indonesia 1951-1963</u> (Berkeley and Los Angeles: University of California Press, 1964), p. 224.

state.[70] Although the Islamic state issue lost most of its urgency when Masjumi was banned in 1960, it regained it, as shall be seen, after October 1, 1965.

Members of the Osa Maliki faction attached less importance to Sukarno's role as guardian of the non-Islamic state, as they were less inclined to attribute such political designs to the Islamic organizations in the first place. They were far more concerned about the Ali leadership's seemingly uncritical acceptance of Sukarno's policies at a time when he appeared to them to be falling increasingly under the influence of the PKI. Thus they chose to oppose the PKI, rather than support Sukarno, by building up anti-communist opinion in the party.

Obviously, the difference between the two groups should not be cast solely in cultural terms. The antipathy of the Osa Maliki faction for the PKI was bound to attract the more politically conservative members of the party--at least so long as they regarded communism as a greater threat to their positions than the political aspirations of Indonesian Islam, and, indeed, it is in these terms that the support of the Javanese Hadisubeno for the Osa Maliki faction is to be explained. Likewise, the Ali leadership's close identification with and support of the President attracted those younger party members for whom Sukarno's radical nationalism had appeal, and it is for this reason that the predominately non-Javanese leaders of the mass organizations supported the Ali group. Just as the different political orientations of the Javanese and non-Javanese members of the PNI contribute to an explanation of the division within the party, they also help explain why the rival groupings sought the outside allies they did in the struggle for control of the party.

The Alliances

The preparedness of various political forces to intervene actively in the PNI leadership struggle suggests that the PNI was too important a political factor to ignore in the struggle that was taking shape between army and Sukarno-led forces. The reasons for its importance lay principally in its large mass base, the influence it enjoyed in the state bureaucracy, and the fact that it had the largest parliamentary representation of any political party.[71]

Army support for the Osa Maliki faction, which was forthcoming as early as August 21, assumed a more concrete form in mid-October when Brigadier General Sutjipto of KOTI instructed all the regional military commanders of Indonesia to allow the Osa faction a free hand

---

70. "Belief in the One Deity," and not an Islamic confession of faith, was one of the five principles which Sukarno advocated in June 1945 as a basis for an independent Indonesia. Subsequently, these five principles, or Pantja Sila, were adopted as the official ideology of the Republic.

71. See Herbert Feith, "The Dynamics of Guided Democracy," in Ruth T. McVey, ed., _Indonesia_ (New Haven: HRAF, 1967), p. 345.

in ridding the PNI of Gestapu elements.[72] Moreover, General Sutjipto informed the PNI of this move in a letter addressed to "The Chairman of the Central Leadership Council of the Indonesian National Party."[73] Clearly, KOTI had extended recognition to the Osa Maliki faction as the leaders of the PNI.

In line with the political orientation of its predominately non-Javanese members, the Osa Maliki faction was quick to cooperate with Islamic organizations such as PSII, NU, and Muhammadijah, in addition to the two Christian parties and various functional groups. These organizations subsequently joined to form the Kesatuan Aksi Pengganjangan Gestapu (Crush Gestapu Action Front) or KAP/Gestapu, which demanded the dissolution of the PKI.[74] The Ali leadership continued to offer its undivided support to Sukarno. It even committed itself in advance to support whatever decision the President might reach regarding the PKI.[75] The fact remains, however, that the physical elimination of the PKI by the army and its civilian supporters proceeded apace from mid-October until January 1966. Under such circumstances, who else could the President turn to apart from the PNI? Did not this change of circumstances provide the PNI with an opportunity to reestablish a close relationship with Bung Karno--to approximate that ideal (and idealized) state of affairs that had existed in 1927 when Sukarno had been chairman and people such as Ali active members of the Indonesian National Party. Such a relationship, however, would obviously be of little consequence if the President were to lose out in his power struggle with the army, and the task the Ali leadership set itself was to lend such support as it could to the President. The inevitable price of such a policy was that it incurred the further anger of the army high command.

The Ali leadership's fears concerning the designs of the Islamic political groups assumed renewed urgency after October 1 and provided it with additional incentive to rally to the President. Pointing suspiciously to the prominence of such Islamic organizations as PSII, Muhammadijah, and NU in KAP/Gestapu, it argued that their aim was not merely the dissolution of the PKI but also the overthrow of Sukarno and the PNI in order to facilitate the establishment of an Islamic state. An epigramatic statement of this point of view was published in bold type in the pro-Sukarno newspaper *Genta*: "ANTI BUNG KARNO = ANTI PANTJASILA = PENGCHIANAT [TRAITOR]."[76]

---

72. *Angkatan Bersendjata*, October 20, 1965.

73. Letter, Sutjipto SH Brigdjen TNI Komando Operasi Tertinggi Ketua Gabungan V to Jth. Ketua Dewan Pimpinan Pusat Partai Nasional Indonesia di Djakarta, October 15, 1965, (Mimeographed).

74. See *Api Pantjasila*, October 22, 1965.

75. *Sokoguru Revolusi*, November 5, 1965.

76. *Genta*, February 4, 1966. A similar although considerably more subtle statement of this point of view is to be found in an editorial in the Catholic newspaper, *Kompas*, as early as October 22, 1965. In the same month Major General Ibrahim Adjie declared in a speech to members of West Java branches of the PNI that the counter-revolutionaries will not cease in their efforts to replace the state ideology (Pantja Sila) and to seize power. The full text of his speech may be found in *Angkatan Bersendjata*, October 25, 26, 27, 28, 29, 1965.

The Ali leadership's choice of allies among the various student organizations was also largely determined by its concern both to support the President and to stem any resurgence of Islamic political aspirations. Thus, it instructed GMNI not to join KAMI.[77] It obviously believed that GMNI's participation in an overtly anti-PKI organization would jeopardize its relations with the President. The prominence in KAMI of modernist Islamic political organizations such as HMI, which had enjoyed a close association with Masjumi prior to its banning in 1960, and Ikatan Mahasiswa Muhammadijah, the student association of Muhammadijah, a former constituent organization of Masjumi, not to mention Persatuan Mahasiswa Islam Indonesia (PMII) and Serikat Mahasiswa Muslimin Indonesia (SEMMI), the ancillary student organizations of NU and PSII respectively, aroused the Ali leadership's suspicions of its intentions as had the presence of Muhammadijah, NU and PSII in KAP/Gestapu. For example, GMNI attempted to clarify its position with respect to KAMI in a statement of early November in which it warned of the need "to oppose the efforts of the right wing reactionaries [i.e., members of the banned Masjumi party] who wish to rehabilitate themselves in the wave of destruction of the September 30th Movement and divert our left wing Pantjasila revolution to the right. . . ."[78] The Osa Maliki faction, as noted above, did not perceive such a threat from the Islamic organizations, and so the recently established GMNI (Osa Maliki faction) joined KAMI.[79]

The Iskaq Committee

On May 29, 1965, Iskaq Tjokrohadisurjo, a prominent and long standing member of the PNI, wrote a letter to the central leadership council requesting that a meeting of the consultative body of the party be called to examine the council's decision to remove Hadisubeno from the Central Java branch leadership and suspend Oemar Said, Soetopo Koesoemodirdjo, and Soegeng Tirtosiswojo from the party membership.[80] The meeting did not eventuate.

After the leadership council suspended Osa Maliki, Hardi, and their associates from the party on August 4, Iskaq, Sumaneng, and a number of other like-minded party men, at a meeting in Djakarta on August 13, called on the party leadership to convene an emergency congress in order to resolve the dispute within the party.[81] This

---

77. Hasil2 Pertemuan Tanggal 25 Oktober 1966 [sic] Hasil Risalah/Notulen Tertemuan [sic] Tsbt. (Mimeographed), passim. For a full list of the member organizations of KAMI, see Angkatan Bersendjata, October 29, 1965. For a general account of the activities of this organization, see Harsja W. Bachtiar, "Indonesia" in Donald K. Emmerson, ed., Students and Politics in Developing Countries (London: Pall Mall Press, 1968).

78. Sokoguru Revolusi, November 13, 1965.

79. Letter, Kartomo to Kombes Sumirat, n.d.

80. Letter, Iskaq Tjokrohadisurjo S.H. to Jth. Sdr. Dewan Pimpinan Pusat Partai Nasional Indonesia, Djalan Tegalan No. 1, Djakarta, May 29, 1965 (Mimeographed).

81. Surat Keputusan Tentang Saran2 Djalan Keluar Guna Mengatasi Segala Akibat Dari Peristiwa 4 Agustus 1965 (Mimeographed, Djakarta, August 13, 1965).

appeal was almost identical to the one contained in the letter sent by Osa Maliki and his associates to members of the central leadership on August 3.

After the open establishment of the DPP-PNI (Osa Maliki faction) on October 6 and its recognition by KOTI on October 15, Iskaq argued that such a congress, if it was not to prejudice the aspirations of one faction in advance, could now only be convened by a "third party."[82] In an attempt to assume this role, Iskaq and his colleagues formed themselves into the Panitia Penegak Persatuan dan Kesatuan PNI-FM (Committee for the Maintenance of the Unity of the PNI-FM).[83]

Not only had Iskaq and his committee pleaded the cases of the suspended party members and echoed their call for a congress, but they had also elevated the Osa Maliki faction, following the KOTI letter, to the position of one of two equal disputants within the PNI. As this directly contradicted the position of the Ali leadership, which did not even recognize the existence of a split within the party, doubt was cast on the veracity of Iskaq's claim to impartiality by Ali's son, Karna Radjasa, amongst others. He alleged that the Iskaq committee was not a "third party" but a front organization of the "Hardi-Isnaeni clique."[84] It is hardly surprising, therefore, that the Ali leadership declared in a letter distributed to the party's branches that it neither supported nor had any contact with Iskaq's committee.[85] Moreover, it announced its intention of holding a session of the Congress Working Committee in Lembang, West Java, between December 18 and 20.[86]

The Osa Maliki faction immediately declared that it would not attend such a session at that time.[87] This move was apparently inspired by the belief that the committee offered even fewer opportunities than a congress to press its leadership claims upon the party,

---

82. Letters, Iskaq Tjokrohadisurjo to Jth. Saudara Ali Sastroamidjojo SH Ketua Umum Partai Nasional Indonesia di Djakarta and Jth. Saudara Osa Maliki Ketua Umum Partai Nasional Indonesia di Djakarta, October 18, 1965.

83. The committee consisted of the following members: chairman, Iskaq Tjokrohadisurjo S.H.; vice-chairman, Dr. Soeharto; secretary, I. A. Muis; treasurer, Achmad Suladji; head of information section, Soebagio Reksodipuro S.H.; assistants, Nj. Supeni, Nj. Jusupandi, Soemaneng S.H., Djaswadi Suprapto, M. Tabrani, Noor Sutan Iskandar, and B. J. Rambitan. Berta Republik, November 25, 1965.

84. This charge is recounted in Teks Pidato Lengkap Sdr. Iskaq Tjokrohadisurjo, Anggota Badan Pekerdja Kongres P.I.N. [sic] jang sedianja diutjapkan dalam sidang Badan Pekerdja Kongres ke 11 jang berlangsung di Jogjakarta pada tg. 22 dan 23 Desember 1965 (Mimeographed), p. 7.

85. Duta Masjarakat, December 18, 1965.

86. Undangan Sidang Badan Pekerdja Kongres ke II D.P.P.-P.N.I. kepada Jth. Sdr. Iskaq Tjokrohadisurjo Anggota BPK PNI Djakarta, 30 Nopember 1965 (Mimeographed).

87. Berita Republik, December 3, 1965.

and that it would therefore be better to hold out in hope of the latter rather than accepting the former. After all, Osa Maliki's supporters could expect little from a party organization made up of plenary members of the central leadership council that had suspended them and their regional and mass organization appointees from party membership.[88] The prospects for a party congress convened under favorable circumstances would be greatly enhanced if their allies should prove victorious in the national power struggle. But as its outcome was still uncertain in December 1965, it was clearly in the interests of the Osa Maliki faction to play for time by refusing to attend the conference of the Congress Working Committee.

Immediately prior to the Committee session, Iskaq gained additional support for his proposal for party unity. On December 17, 24 out of a total of 43 PNI members of parliament[89] called for the convening of an extraordinary congress in the shortest possible time to be administered by a body or committee acceptable to both sides.[90] The national leadership of the Djamiatul Muslimin Indonesia issued a statement signed by Hadji Moh. Djambek, who had replaced Osa Maliki as chairman after the latter was suspended from party membership, and eight other members calling for an extraordinary congress to be organized by "a *Body/Committee* acceptable to all *sides* which truly desire to maintain the PNI/Front Marhaenis *intact*."[91]

The Congress Working Committee meeting which was finally held on December 22 in Jogjakarta[92] met these demands half-way. It decided to hold a congress, but not an extraordinary one. Instead, it agreed to call together the eleventh Congress ahead of schedule in March 1966. This decision meant, of course, that it would be held under the auspices of the incumbent leadership and not a group or committee acceptable to both sides.[93] The Osa Maliki faction promptly declared that if the Iskaq committee proved unable to hold a party congress,

---

88. For details of the composition of the Badan Pekerdja Kongres, see Berita Republik, December 10, 1965.

89. This number is based on the number of PNI members listed in Daftar Alamat Anggota Dewan Perwakilan Rakjat Gotong Rojong (Sekretariat DPR-GR, Djakarta, August 15, 1965); cf. the figure of 44 given by Feith, "Dynamics of Guided Democracy," p. 345.

90. Pernjataan (Mimeographed, Djakarta, December 17, 1965). For a press account (which erroneously attributes the statement to 28 members), see Kompas, December 24, 1965. Of the 24, at least 3 (Rh. Koesnan, B. J. Rambitan, and Soebagio Reksodipoero) were closely associated with Iskaq's Committee.

91. Sokoguru Revolusi, December 21, 1965. Italics in the original.

92. Berita Republik, December 16, 1965. The fact that the meeting was not held in Lembang as originally intended has been attributed to the action of the West Java Military Commander, Major General Ibrahim Adjie, who allegedly refused permission for it to be held in his area of jurisdiction. Ibid.

93. Sinar Harapan, December 29, 1965.

then it would call one of its own.[94] Thus, by year's end, these various attempts to resolve the division in the PNI by means of a conventional congress had come to nothing. The party remained divided.

Political Change, 1965-1966

It has been pointed out that the Osa Maliki faction had gained the active support of the army high command, KAP/Gestapu, and KAMI. In the other camp, there had been some signs of rapprochment with President Sukarno who, without the PKI to lean on, had become more susceptible to the blandishments of the Ali leadership. This group also enjoyed considerable support in the bureaucracy and sections of the armed forces. Indeed, as we have seen, in the case of the police force this support extended, at least for a period, to its commander-in-chief. The point about these alliances and associations was that they had been made with the rival contenders for national power. Therefore, the national conflict, provided it was resolved first, would obviously have considerable bearing on the outcome of the PNI leadership struggle. Just how much bearing it would have would depend on the extent to which the victor, or victors, chose to become involved in PNI affairs. Given this partial interdependence at least between the national power struggle and the PNI leadership struggle, we shall now pay attention to the former in the hope of subsequently clarifying the latter.

Only days after General Suharto had defeated the September 30th Movement in Djakarta, the city was engulfed by anti-PKI demonstrations organized by student organizations and political parties, which subsequently formed the constituent bodies of KAMI and KAP/Gestapu, with the support of the army. The government gave these demonstrations an inadvertent boost with its harsh anti-inflationary measures of November and December. In late November it raised the official price of petrol from Rp. 4 per litre to Rp. 250 per litre.[95] The following month it raised the price again to Rp. 1,000 per litre.[96] A commensurate price increase was also ordered for, among other things, bus fares.[97]

These measures provided KAMI with a genuinely popular issue--the demand that these price increases should be revoked[98]--and a scapegoat, namely, the minister responsible for the increases, Dr. Chairul Saleh.[99] And to this goal the students attached their long standing demand for

---

94. Ibid., December 31, 1965.

95. D. H. Penny, "Survey of Recent Developments," *Bulletin of Indonesian Economic Studies*, No. 3 (February 1966), pp. 1-2.

96. Ibid.; *Sinar Harapan*, December 30, 1965.

97. Penny, "Survey of Recent Developments," p. 2.

98. *Kompas*, January 15, 1966.

99. Cf. Harsja Bachtiar's more sympathetic portrayal of KAMI's motives, "Indonesia," p. 194.

the banning of the PKI and a more recent one calling for a "retooling" of the cabinet.[100]

It was with this last demand that Sukarno took issue in a speech before his cabinet, students, and journalists on January 15, 1966. The real target of those who demanded a "retooling" of the cabinet, he asserted, was not the cabinet ministers themselves, but the President: ". . . it is not you, Chairel Saleh. . . . In effect everything points at Sukarno."[101] By choosing to interpret a criticism of his ministers as criticism of himself, Sukarno forfeited considerable area for maneuver. He could not now allow his ministers to bear the brunt of criticism, let alone sacrifice them, in the name of political expediency. Yet, such actions would have been quite consistent with the view of many members of KAMI and KAP/Gestapu that it was not President Sukarno but his ministers who were at fault. Sukarno's "January 9, 1905"[102] had not yet come, but by taking such a stand he had only hastened its arrival.

One can only assume that he still placed very considerable store by his own political resources. And such an assumption appears to be borne out by the remarkable contents of the remainder of the speech. Declaring himself responsible to the nation, Almighty God, and the Prophet Muhammad and likening his stance to that of Martin Luther in the Würtemberg Cathedral,[103] he continued:

> Come on, whoever like Sukarno, agrees with Sukarno,
> as Great Leader of the Revolution, join forces,
> form your ranks, maintain Sukarno! Because I see that
> other people wish to overthrow Sukarno. Only I say
> to my followers, don't take wild steps! Wait for
> my command![104]

Cognizant of the President's still widespread support, most political groupings moved hastily to declare their loyalty for Sukarno. General Suharto issued a statement which declared that the army "stands behind the President/Great Leader of the Revolution waiting for his command."[105] In an apparent attempt to establish military control over the Sukarno Front, Suharto, in a KOTI announcement, ordered all mass organizations, political parties, and persons who were willing to carry out the President's command

---

100. *Kompas*, January 15, 1966.

101. *Amanat PJM Presiden Sukarno Di Sidang Paripurna Kabinet Dwikora Dengan Dihadiri Djuga Oleh Wakil-Wakil Dari Mahasiswa-- Mahasiswa Dan Wartawan, Bogor, 15 Djanuari 1966* (Mimeographed, Sekretariat Negara Kabinet Presiden Republik Indonesia), p. 16.

102. This was the date when the Petersburg workers ceased to believe "in the good kind Tsar who was fooled by his wicked ministers." Eugenia S. Ginzburg, *Into the Whirlwind* (Melbourne: Penguin, 1968), p. 225.

103. *Amanat PJM Presiden Sukarno Di Sidang*, p. 16.

104. *Ibid.*, pp. 16-17.

105. *Berita Yudha*, January 17, 1966.

to submit their names either to the KOTI office in Djakarta or to the office of the Regional Military Commanders.[106]

Of course, the Ali leadership needed no prompting. Delighted by Sukarno's fighting speech, it declared ". . . that it stands fully and without reserve behind Bung Karno and is prepared to implement the command of the President/Commander-in-Chief of the Armed Forces/Great Leader of the Revolution/Father of Marhaenism."[107] The enthusiasm of the party leadership was more than matched by GMNI and other PNI mass organization members who gathered in front of the Presidential palace on January 20 to listen to an address by the President. They carried signs, one of which stated: "The People—ABRI [Armed Forces of the Republic of Indonesia] love Bung Karno."[108] Another declared that its bearer was "prepared to die for Bung Karno."[109] After the rally was over, they became involved in a fight with KAMI members. An armed forces unit moved in amidst a hail of stones to separate the warring sides.[110]

Then, on February 21, President Sukarno announced that he had, as he put it, "perfected" the composition of the cabinet. He did not, however, demote Chairul Saleh or Dr. Subandrio as KAMI and KAP/Gestapu had demanded, but instead he demoted three people who had been closely associated with the anti-PKI movement and who enjoyed high prestige in military, KAP/Gestapu, and KAMI circles, namely General Nasution, Arudji Kartawinata, and Vice-Admiral Martadinata.[111] Furthermore, he promoted Sumardjo and Asmara Hadi, regarded by many as crypto-communists, to ministerial rank. The former was given the important and, in light of student unrest, sensitive portfolio of Basic Education and Culture. Piling insult upon injury, he even appointed the well-known Djakarta gang leader, Lieutenant Colonel Imam Sjafe'i, to the position of minister seconded to the President for Special Security Affairs.[112]

What had prompted the President to take such a provocative step? Above all, it appears he believed that the time had come to make a stand in order to stop the various efforts to "divert the Indonesian revolution to the right."[113] Sukarno was desperately anxious to con-

---

106. Dwikora, January 21, 1966.

107. Genta, January 17, 1966.

108. Pelopor, January 21, 1966.

109. Ibid.

110. Berita Yudha, January 21, 1966.

111. For President Sukarno's announcement and a list of members of the perfected cabinet, see Pengumuman PJM Presiden Sukarno Mengenai Susunan Kabinet Dwikora Jang Disempurnakan, Istana Merdeka Djakarta, 21 Pebruari 1966 (Mimeographed, Sekretariat Negara Kabinet Presiden Republik Indonesia). Further details about the cabinet may be found in Indonesia, No. 2 (October 1966), p. 185 f.

112. Ibid.

113. Amanat PJM Presiden Sukarno Pada Peringatan Sapta Warsa GSNI (Gerakan Siswa Nasional Indonesia) Di Istora Senajan, Djakarta, 28 Pebruari 1966 (Mimeographed, Sekretariat Negara Kabinet Presiden Republik Indonesia), p. 1.

tinue ruling, and if he could not rule, then he did not want to reign either.

Outraged by the President's action, KAMI blocked all access roads to the Presidential palace on the morning of February 24 in a determined bid to prevent the swearing in of the new cabinet ministers. Although they managed to delay the ceremony for three hours, they were unsuccessful in preventing it from taking place as most of the ministers were eventually able to reach the palace either in the President's helicopter, or in the case of the less fortunate ones, on foot. Consequently, the students gathered in front of the palace to show their disapproval of the new cabinet's composition. The Presidential guard tried to disperse the demonstrators first by firing into the air and then into the crowd itself. One student, Arief Rachman Hakim, a member of GMNI (Osa Maliki faction), was shot dead.[114] Eighteen others were wounded.[115] At Hakim's funeral, attended by thousands of students, wreaths from Lieutenant General Suharto, General Nasution, Major General Ibrahim Adjie, and many others were laid.[116] There could be little doubt that this last act of Sukarno's had exhausted the patience of Suharto.

Suharto continued, however, to move cautiously. He was willing to mouth support for the President, thereby depriving military commanders of a choice between the President and himself. He also worked quietly to prevent Sukarno from developing any organized support of his own by coopting any initiative he took in this area. An example of this was his order, mentioned above, that all Sukarno Front supporters must register with KOTI or their regional military commanders.

In addition to containing the President's influence in this way, Suharto was also intent upon whittling it away. Thus he did nothing to prevent KAMI with the support and protection of Colonel Sarwo Edhie, the energetic and single-minded commander of the Resimen Para Komando Angkatan Darat (Army Commando Regiment or RPKAD), from constantly agitating for the dissolution of the PKI and a further retooling of the cabinet. Indeed, he was quite prepared to let Sarwo Edhie and the students "ride shotgun" in this way for him even though from Suharto's point of view it was premature to take decisive action against the President. It was they who incurred the hostility of the pro-Sukarno forces for the chaos which they wrought, involving as it did an open flouting of the President's will, whereas Suharto was the ultimate beneficiary of their actions insofar as they brought about a decline in Sukarno's authority.

---

114. Kompas, February 26, 1966. If he really were a member of the GMNI (Osa Maliki faction) it is difficult to explain why it did not claim him as one of its own in a message of condolence published two days later in the same paper. See Kompas, February 28, 1966. It is possible that he was a member of another KAMI affiliated organization who joined GMNI (Osa Maliki faction) to help swell its ranks and thereby give the impression that it commanded greater support than was the case.

115. "Menengok Sebentar Rangkaian Peristiwa Indonesia ditahun silam," Kompas, December 31, 1966.

116. Kompas, February 26, 1966.

In early February, President Sukarno accepted an invitation from the Ali leadership to address a rally of the Gerakan Siswa Nasional Indonesia (Indonesian National Pupils' Movement or GSNI), the PNI high school student front, on February 28 in Djakarta.[117] This was the day after Iskaq's congress was scheduled to begin in Bandung. This acceptance provided further evidence, if any was needed, of Sukarno's preference for the Ali leadership in the PNI leadership struggle. On February 28, Sukarno delivered a low-key speech stating that he interpreted the rally as a demonstration of GSNI's loyalty to Bung Karno as Great Leader of the Revolution,[118] however, the presence at the rally of his two top aides, Chairul Saleh and Dr. Subandrio, as well as Sumardjo suggests that Sukarno attached great importance to it. Dr. Subandrio, in a sensational speech which he had presumably cleared with the President beforehand, called on GSNI to confront the terror of those who wish to divert the revolution to the right with "counter-terror."[119] Presumably, he looked to GSNI support in particular and PNI mass support in general to counter the militant anti-government activities of the student organizations affiliated with KAMI, which had been officially banned by the President two days earlier.[120]

No sooner had the rally ended than Ali leadership supporters attacked KAMI students at the University of Indonesia, inflicting one casualty[121] before being driven off by a unit of the armed forces. And on March 4, Djakarta citizens were treated to the spectacle of thousands of high school students organized less than a month before into the Kesatuan Aksi Pemuda Peladjar Indonesia (Indonesian Youth and Student Action Front or KAPPI) over-running and occupying the Department of Basic Education and Culture to protest Sumardjo's appointment.[122]

On March 8, PNI (Ali leadership) mass organization members demonstrated in front of the United States Embassy shouting: "Green is anti-Bung Karno."[123] Many succeeded in gaining access to the embassy grounds where they set fire to a number of diplomatic cars. Eventually, they were driven away by a small detachment of soldiers.[124] A little earlier, KAPPI students invaded the Department of Foreign Affairs, situated only half a mile from the US Embassy, upturning furniture, tearing up documents, and painting anti-Subandrio slogans on the walls. Finally, they withdrew from the building[125] only to run into

---

117. Sinar Revolusi, February 10, 1966.

118. Amanat PJM Presiden Sukarno Pada Peringatan, p. 1.

119. Kompas, March 1, 1966.

120. Dwikora, February 26, 1966.

121. Kompas, December 31, 1966.

122. Kompas, March 5, 1966.

123. Marshall Green was the US Ambassador to Indonesia at that time. Dwikora, March 9, 1966.

124. Ibid.

125. Kompas, March 9, 1966.

the PNI demonstrators.[126] A sharp clash ensued which armed forces units were only able to break up after firing warning shots above the heads of the feuding students.[127]

On March 11, President Sukarno hurriedly left a cabinet session in Djakarta for Bogor on the basis of a report from the Presidential guard that armed forces without insignia had surrounded the palace.[128] On March 12 it was announced over the radio that President Sukarno had entrusted General Suharto "to take all necessary steps to guarantee peace, calm, and stability as well as the personal safety and authority of the President . . . for the sake of the integrity of the Nation and the State of the Republic of Indonesia."[129] From this new position of authority, Suharto was able to pursue more effectively his skillful policy of whittling away the power of the President while maintaining a credible public posture of loyalty to him. For example, on March 12, he banned the PKI "in the name of his Excellency [President Sukarno],"[130] a step which Sukarno had refused to take because he had desired to maintain this base of his own power as well as his concept of a NASAKOM state. He did not reshuffle the President's "perfected" cabinet announced on February 21; rather, he "perfected it again."

Most people were surprised by the announcement of March 12. The member organizations of KAP/Gestapu, including the Osa Maliki faction of the PNI, were, of course, happily surprised. The Ali leadership was surprised too, bitterly surprised. Just as a new period of close PNI-Presidential cooperation appeared to be emerging out of the political upheaval of the last six months, Sukarno had abandoned them.[131] The outcome of the national leadership struggle had clearly worked to the advantage of the Osa Maliki faction. Just how much advantage it would reap, however, would depend on the degree to which the victor, General Suharto, chose to involve himself in the PNI leadership struggle.

The PNI Extraordinary Congress

Little progress had been made since December 1965 in attempts to resolve this struggle by means of a congress. Despite vigorous

---

126. *Dwikora*, March 9, 1966.

127. *Ibid*.

128. For Brigadier General Sutjipto's account of these events, see *Kompas*, April 9 and 11, 1966. According to all interview accounts, the unmarked forces were army commandos (RPKAD) acting under the orders of Colonel Sarwo Edhie. It is not known to this writer whether he had gained General Suharto's approval for this action or not.

129. *Kompas*, March 14, 1966.

130. *Ibid*.

131. Several prominent members of the Ali faction expressed this view to the writer. In fairness to Sukarno it ought to be stated that during those critical days he was quite literally fighting for his political life and, therefore, in no position to come to the assistance of the PNI.

action by Iskaq on behalf of the committee's planned congress, to be held in Bandung, his efforts in this direction ultimately came to nought. After postponing the congress till February 27,[132] it was again postponed to a date to be decided, despite the arrival of some branch delegates in Bandung. These were made up exclusively, or so it would appear from their statements, of supporters of the Osa Maliki faction.[133] Presumably, the number of these delegates was insufficient to be able to convene a congress.[134] In addition, the military commander of Central Java, Brigadier General Surjosumpeno, denied the Ali leadership permission to convene the eleventh PNI congress in Jogjakarta.[135]

General Suharto rapidly put an end to this stalemate. Only five days after receiving the President's order, he succeeded where Iskaq had failed, by bringing the Ali leadership and the Osa Maliki faction together at a meeting.[136] At the third such meeting, on March 24, he extracted a joint statement from the two sides.[137] It declared that both groups agreed to hold an extraordinary congress, something which both the Iskaq committee and the Osa Maliki faction had been demanding for several months. The Ali leadership, however, had refused to countenance such demands while declaring its intention to hold the eleventh party congress ahead of schedule in March. The statement also laid down the composition of the committee to run the congress. Osa Maliki supporters, if we include Iskaq, as the Ali leadership certainly would, were placed in three out of the five positions, including the chairmanship. They were Iskaq Tjokrohadisurjo (chairman), Sunawar Sukowati, and S. Rifa'i. The Ali supporters appointed to the committee were Bachtiar Salim Haloho and Soediro.[138] Obviously, the statement favored the Osa Maliki faction.

In view of the very cordial relationship existing between the army high command and the Osa Maliki faction, based on a similar political viewpoint, past cooperation, and, in the case of Hadisubeno, a long standing friendship with Suharto, it was only to be expected that once General Suharto decided to intervene in the PNI leadership

---

132. Kompas, February 28, 1966.

133. Duta Masjarakat, March 7, 1966.

134. A party congress is considered valid if it is attended by delegates from at least half the number of branches provided they have together gained the votes of two-thirds or more of those eligible to vote for congress delegates. Anggaran Rumah Tangga Partai Nasional Indonesia (1963), p. 33.

135. Letter, Iskaq Tjokrohadisurjo to Jth. Paduka Brig. Djen. Surjosumpeno, Panglima Kodam VII Diponegoro di Semarang, February 17, 1966 (Mimeographed).

136. An attempt by Iskaq to bring together the leaders of both sides on January 12 failed because Ali Sastroamidjojo and Sartono refused to attend. Kompas, January 15, 1966.

137. Sinar Harapan, March 25, 1966.

138. Pengumuman-Bersama DPP-PNI (Djakarta, March 24, 1966). For a press report on the Joint Statement, see ibid.

struggle, he would do so on the side of the Osa Maliki faction. But why did he decide to intervene in the first place? If he could succeed in imposing the leaders of the Osa Maliki faction upon the party, then clearly he would gain considerable control over the PNI which would reduce his dependence on those political organizations with large Islamic components such as KAMI and KAP/Gestapu, which had helped elevate him to power.

He would also be able to restore the balance between the Islamic and non-Islamic parties which had tipped drastically in favor of the former as a result of the internecine conflict in the PNI and the physical elimination and formal dissolution of the PKI. It is important to note that not all the leaders of the Osa Maliki faction supported General Suharto's initiative. Osa Maliki, Usep Ranawidjaja, and Sabilal Rasjad were among those opposed. When they had been only able to indicate a preference between an extraordinary congress and a session of the Ali leadership-dominated Congress Working Committee, they naturally opted for the former. But now that their hand had been strengthened within the party by the favorable outcome of the national leadership struggle, they looked forward to a continuation of the struggle with the Ali leadership for the allegiance of the branches in the belief that they would eventually prevail.[139]

On the other hand, Hadisubeno supported Suharto on this matter. As a result of his association with the Osa Maliki faction, he found himself isolated in the Central Java branch of the PNI, which had remained overwhelmingly loyal to the Ali leadership. Moreover, the Ali leadership in Central Java enjoyed the almost unanimous support of the region's district military commanders. By means of a unitary congress, Hadisubeno hoped to shed this politically invidious association and to rebuild his basis of support within the Central Java branch of the party.[140]

Despite this difference of opinion, General Suharto pushed ahead with his plans to ensure the victory of the Osa Maliki faction at the party congress. For example, local military commanders were empowered to deny delegates authority to attend the congress if they regarded them as being in any way associated with or sympathetic to "Gestapu/PKI."[141] This order represented another victory for the Osa Maliki faction, as it had pressed for the exclusion of such people from a unitary congress since October 1965. It realized that such an order could only reduce the representation of the Ali leadership at such a congress, for it was this group which had compromised itself with its statement of apparent support for Colonel Untung on October 1, 1965.

A large number of Ali faction delegates who had actually gained the requisite authority to attend the congress experienced difficulty in gaining access to the congress hall, and in some cases they were

---

139. Interview, April 28, 1967.

140. Ibid.

141. Tata Tertib Kongres Persatuan & Kesatuan PNI/Front Marhaenis (Panitya Kongres Persatuan & Kesatuan PNI/Front Marhaenis, Djakarta, April 6, 1966).

turned away at the door.[142] Indeed, Ali delegates from branches in Djakarta and West Java were only permitted to attend the opening ceremony on April 24 and the first plenary session.[143] Others, such as Lucien Pahala Hutagaol and Kartjono, were actually arrested by the West Java military authorities upon their arrival in Bandung.[144]

The Ali faction delegates who were able to attend the congress were subjected to a constant stream of heckling and abuse from KAMI members who were allowed to occupy the balcony of the congress hall.[145] Certainly, Iskaq, in his own account of the congress proceedings admitted that he, as chairman, "very nearly lost control of the situation"[146] when Ali was addressing the congress.[147] On the other hand, "speeches from delegates of branches under the leadership of the DPP-PNI Osa-Usep received," he states, "an extraordinary and tumultuous response as a sign of agreement."[148]

Between plenary sessions, private negotiations were held between the leaders of the two sides. The Osa Maliki faction demanded that Ali surrender the PNI leadership to the DPP-PNI Osa-Usep.[149] Ali responded with the proposal that members elected to the PNI leadership council at the Purwokerto Congress should be ineligible to stand again for leadership positions.[150] Although this proposal would have excluded Ali himself from the running, it would also have excluded Osa Maliki, Hardi, and Isnaeni. It is not surprising that the Osa Maliki faction flatly rejected it.

Eventually, both groups agreed to the appointment of Osa Maliki as General Chairman with full authority to choose a new central leadership council,[151] with the assistance of S. Hadikusumo, an Ali leadership suporter. This agreement, which was approved by a plenary session, reflected the dominant position the Osa Maliki faction enjoyed at the congress. So too did the composition of the new

---

142. Massa Marhaen Menuntut Hardi Risalah Kongres Luar Biasa P.N.I./F.M. Di Bandung Jang Berlangsung Dari Tanggal 24 s/d 28 April, 1966 (Mimeographed), p. 2.

143. Ibid.

144. Pelopor Baru, April 27, 1966 and Suluh Indonesia Merdeka, April 28, 1966 in U. S. Embassy Translation Unit Press Review (April 28, 1966), p. 78.

145. Massa Marhaen Menuntut Hardi, p. 2.

146. Laporan Mangenai Djalannja Kongres Persatuan & Kesatuan PNI/ Front Marhaenis Jang Diselenggarakan Di Bandung Dari Tg. 24 s/d Tg. 27 April 1966 (Mimeographed, Djakarta, May 5, 1966), p. 1.

147. Ibid.

148. Ibid.

149. Ibid., p. 2.

150. Ibid.

151. Ibid., p. 4.

Central Leadership Council.[152] Only the sixth chairman, Abdul Madjid, and the second and third treasurers, Hardjantho S. and Notosukardjo, were supporters of the former Ali leadership. The others were all either members of the DPP-PNI Osa-Usep as constituted on October 6, 1965 or close supporters of it.

The Osa Maliki faction's close alliance with General Suharto, who had won out in the national power struggle, was an important factor in explaining its capture of the PNI leadership. The decisive factor in this regard was General Suharto's preparedness to promote actively the cause of this faction within the party. The fact that Ali probably had the support of the majority of PNI members was of no immediate account, for it was the Osa Maliki faction which had the backing of the new national leader. Thus, for the period of this study at least, the source of power within the PNI was related to the influence possessed by non-party elite figures with whom a person or group in the party were associated, and whether they were prepared to wield that influence to the advantage of that person or group in the internal affairs of the organization. This situation was likely to continue so long as the party remained divided.

---

152. The members of the Council were: general chairman, Osa Maliki; first chairman, Hardi S.H.; second chairman, Sabilal Rasjad; third chairman, Mh. Isnaeni; fourth chairman, Hadisubeno; fifth chairman, Dr. Sunawar Sukowati; sixth chairman, Abdul Madjid; first secretary general, Usep Ranawidjaja; second secretary general, I.G.N. Gde Djaksa; third secretary general, Abadi; first treasurer, Budi Dipojuwono; second treasurer, Hardjantho S.; and third treasurer, Notosukardjo. <u>Sinar Harapan</u>, April 28, 1966.

IN MEMORIAM: HARRY J. BENDA

George McT. Kahin

Harry J. Benda died on October 26, 1971, just short of 52 years of age. His relatively brief career as a Southeast Asia specialist was enormously productive, and our understanding of the social and political history of Southeast Asia, and of Indonesia in particular, would today be much the poorer without him. With his death we have lost one of the preeminent scholars in the field.

I first came to know Harry Benda from a letter he wrote from New Zealand seeking a fellowship from Cornell's recently launched Southeast Asia Program. At that time our Program's fellowships were restricted to Americans and Southeast Asians. But his letter was superb, and in it his intellectual qualities came through with great force as he explained at length his reasons for wanting to become a specialist in modern Indonesian political history. That letter and his unusual background--seven years of residence in Indonesia (two as an internee of the Japanese), and a junior lectureship in political theory in New Zealand's Victoria University while completing his M.A. there--indicated a man of unusual promise. His clearly outstanding qualifications persuaded the Program that we should make an exception and offer him a fellowship, even though this meant establishing a new precedent which opened up our fellowships to residents of any country.

Certainly Harry Benda gave us no reason to regret that decision. He came to Cornell in 1952 and within three years completed his Ph.D. in Government, a record which I believe was not subsequently equalled. Those were the days when outside funds for overseas research were scarce, especially for non-Americans studying in the United States. Thus, it was primarily on the basis of Cornell Unversity's library holdings that he wrote his dissertation on the role of Indonesian Islam during the Japanese occupation, an excellent study which later was published as *The Crescent and the Rising Sun*.

In that book and in his subsequent articles and monographs on Indonesian and Southeast Asian history he reappraised and analyzed with a fresh eye processes of history whose previous accounts had usually been strongly stamped by a heavily parochial, Western-centered point of view. He helped shake up some of the long settled, but shallow and rigid perceptions of Indonesian and modern Southeast Asian history, and did much to raise the standards of historical research on the area. In these fields he was one of the first of the revisionists, and his perceptions and trenchant criticisms of past work encouraged a new generation of scholars. These qualities marked his lectures as well as his writing, and in his speaking he brought to bear with particular effectiveness the wry and ironic sense of humor that was one of his special characteristics.

Through his writings he also made a major contribution to the teaching of Southeast Asian history. In addition to his sharply focused and deeply penetrating monographs was his coauthorship of *The History of Modern Southeast Asia: Colonialism, Nationalism, and Decolonization* (with John Bastin) and *The World of Southeast Asia: Selected Historical Writings* (with John A. Larkin). In editing Yale's Southeast Asia Studies monograph series he broadened considerably the possibility for other, particularly young, specialists on the area to publish significant research, and thereby made available a larger body of materials useful in teaching.

He also played an important role in stimulating research among scholars from the countries of Southeast Asia, helping several of them to pursue their studies and research at Yale, and also enlarging the opportunities for others to carry out research in Southeast Asia itself. The outstanding example of this effort was in Singapore, where the successful launching of its Institute of Southeast Asian Studies owed much to Harry Benda's efforts. He devoted enormous energy, time, and resourcefulness to helping get the Institute firmly established and then served for fifteen months as its first director. Without him I think it highly doubtful that the Institute would have developed the momentum necessary to sustain viability and growth. Moreover, along with his two successors, he did much to ensure that, once established, the Institute's research would be marked by breadth and objectivity.

Harry Benda's interest in Southeast Asia was not limited to its modern history. The fate of his parents at the hands of the Nazis in his native Czechoslovakia and his own experiences during the Japanese occupation in Indonesia must have stimulated his inherently humanitarian outlook. Whatever the case, he maintained a continuing concern with contemporary events in Southeast Asia and a keen sensitivity to the suffering which he perceived. Thus, he was deeply disturbed by the 1965 mass killings and subsequent jailings in Indonesia, and he acted to arouse the consciousness and consciences of other scholars with respect to that tragedy. And beginning as early as 1965 he was vocal in his sense of outrage at the American intervention in Vietnam. This led him to join a small group of Asian scholars supporting Eugene McCarthy in the 1968 elections and to write a policy paper on Vietnam for use by McCarthy's supporters.

Harry Benda's contribution to developing Southeast Asian studies was evidenced especially in the time and energy which he devoted over the course of many years to strengthening this field at Yale. He took a justifiable pride in his central role in establishing a strong graduate program there. The Yale administration's lack of recognition of the importance of this effort and its arbitrariness in 1970 when it withdrew its support from the University's program of Southeast Asia studies were understandably deeply dispiriting to him. I last spoke to him shortly after that decision, and his outlook was then heavily clouded by his disappointment at the University's abandonment of a program he had done so much to build and sustain.

Harry Benda has made Yale known throughout the world for the quality of the young scholars whom he trained. If that University's administration should belatedly appreciate the contribution which he made to its reputation in Southeast Asian studies, it is unlikely to find a scholar who can fill the void left by his death.

List of Publications

Books

The Crescent and the Rising Sun: Indonesian Islam under the Japanese Occupation, 1942-1945. Bandung and The Hague: W. van Hoeve, 1958.

The Communist Uprisings of 1926-1927 in Indonesia: Key Documents, trans., ed., and with an introduction by Harry J. Benda and Ruth T. McVey. Ithaca: Modern Indonesia Project, 1960.

Japanese Military Administration in Indonesia: Selected Documents by Harry J. Benda, James K. Irikura and Koichi Kishi. New Haven: Southeast Asia Studies, 1965.

The World of Southeast Asia: Selected Historical Readings by Harry J. Benda and John A. Larkin. New York: Harper & Row, 1967.

A History of Modern Southeast Asia: Colonialism, Nationalism, and Decolonization by John Bastin and Harry J. Benda. Englewood Cliffs: Prentice-Hall, 1968.

Research in Southeast Asian Studies in Singapore. Singapore: Institute of Southeast Asian Studies, 1970.

Contributions to Books

"China: Confucius and the Commissars" and "Southeast Asia: Non-Western Pluralism in Transition," in Vera M. Dean and others, The Nature of the Non-Western World. New York: American Library, 1957, pp. 92-112 and 131-153, resp.

Translated selections from Hamka's "My Father," and "Vanished Childhood" by Pramoedya Ananta Toer, in John M. Echols, ed. and comp., Indonesian Writing in Translation. Ithaca: Modern Indonesia Project, 1956, pp. 38-51 and 153-171, resp.

"Revolution and Nationalism in the Non-Western World," in Warren S. Hunsberger, ed., New Era in the Non-Western World. Ithaca: Cornell University Press, 1957, pp. 17-52.

"The Japanese Interregnum in Southeast Asia," in Grant K. Goodman, comp., Imperial Japan and Asia: A Reassessment. New York: East Asian Institute, 1967, pp. 65-79.

"Hukūma" pt. vi - Indonesia," in Encyclopedia of Islam, new ed. Leiden: E. J. Brill, 1967, III, pp. 566-568.

"Snouck Hurgronje, Christian," in International Encyclopedia of the Social Sciences. New York: MacMillan, 1968, XIV, pp. 340-342.

"Southeast Asian Islam in the 20th Century," in P. M. Holt, A. K. S. Lambton and Bernard Lewis, eds. The Cambridge History of Islam. Cambridge and New York: Cambridge University Press, 1971, II, Chapt. 8.

"Mainland Southeast Asia in the 19th and 20th Centuries," in Mario A. Levi, ed., *Storia universale dei popoli e delle civiltà*. In press.

Articles

"Indonesia," *The Australian Outlook*, IV (1950), pp. 41-59 and 86-97.

"The End of Bicameralism in New Zealand," *Parliamentary Affairs*, IV (1950), pp. 57-72.

"Man, Society and the State in the Early Discourses of J. J. Rousseau," *Political Science*, V (1953) and VI (1954), pp. 13-20 and 17-28, resp.

"The Communist Rebellions of 1926-1927 in Indonesia," *The Pacific Historical Review*, XXIV (1955), pp. 139-152.

"Indonesian Islam under the Japanese Occupation, 1942-1945," *Pacific Affairs*, XXVIII (1955), pp. 350-362.

"Communism in Southeast Asia," *The Yale Review*, XLV (1956), pp. 417-429.

"The Beginnings of the Japanese Occupation of Java," *The Far Eastern Quarterly*, XV (1956), pp. 541-560.

"Christiaan Snouck Hurgronje and the Foundations of the Dutch Islamic Policy in Indonesia," *The Journal of Modern History*, XXX (1958), pp. 338-347.

"Non-Western Intelligentsias as Political Elites," *Australian Journal of Politics and History*, VI (1960), pp. 205-218.

"Intellectuals and Politics in Western History," *Bucknell Review*, X (1961), pp. 1-14.

"The Structure of Southeast Asian History: Some Preliminary Observations," *Journal Southeast Asian History*, III (1962), pp. 106-138.

"Tradition und Wandel in Indonesien," *Geschichte in Wissenschaft und Unterricht*, XIV (1963), pp. 46-53.

"Democracy in Indonesia," (Review Article), *The Journal of Asian Studies*, XXIII (1964), pp. 449-456.

"Continuity and Change in Indonesian Islam," *Asian and African Studies: Annual of the Israel Oriental Society*, I (1965), pp. 123-138.

"Political Elites in Colonial Southeast Asia: An Historical Analysis," *Comparative Studies in Society and History*, VII (1965), pp. 233-251.

"Decolonization in Indonesia: The Problem of Continuity and Change," *American Historical Review*, LXX (1965), pp. 1058-1073.

"Peasant Movements in Colonial Southeast Asia," Asian Studies, III (1965), pp. 420-434.

"The Pattern of Administrative Reforms in the Closing Years of Dutch Rule in Indonesia," The Journal of Asian Studies, XXV (1966), pp. 589-605.

"Reflections on Asian Communism," The Yale Review, LVI (1966), pp. 1-16.

"The Samin Movement" (with Lance Castles), Bijdragen tot de Taal-, Land- en Volkenkunde, 125, No. 2 (1969), pp. 207-240.

LIST OF CONTRIBUTORS

Christine Dobbin is a Research Fellow in Pacific History at the Australian National University, Canberra.

George McT. Kahin is Professor of Government and Director of the Modern Indonesia Project at Cornell University.

Ann Kumar is a Lecturer in Asian Civilizations at the Australian National University, Canberra.

Virginia Matheson is a Ph.D. candidate in the Department of Indonesian and Malay at Monash University, Melbourne.

Angus McIntyre is a Teaching Fellow in the Department of Government at the University of Sydney.

Ruth McVey is Senior Lecturer in the Faculty of Economics and Politics at the School for Oriental and African Studies, London.

J. Noorduyn is General Secretary of the Koninklijk Instituut voor Taal-, Land- en Volkenkunde, Leiden.

Anthony Reid is a Fellow in Pacific History at the Australian National University, Canberra.

www.ingramcontent.com/pod-product-compliance
Lightning Source LLC
Chambersburg PA
CBHW080635230426
43663CB00016B/2875